D0147546

INTRODUCING PERSONS

INTRODUCING PERSONS

THEORIES AND ARGUMENTS
IN THE PHILOSOPHY OF MIND

Peter Carruthers

ROUTLEDGE
London

© Peter Carruthers 1986
First published in 1986 by Croom Helm

Reprinted 1989 by
Routledge
11 New Fetter Lane
London, EC4P 4EE

British Library Cataloguing in Publication Data

Carruthers, Peter
   Introducing persons: theories and
   arguments in the philosophy of mind.
   1. Mind and body.   2. Intellect
   I. Title
   128'.2   BF 161

ISBN 0−7099−3431−9
ISBN 0−415−04512−6

Typeset by Pat and Anne Murphy
Walkford, Christchurch, Dorset

Printed and bound in Great Britain
by Billing & Sons Limited, Worcester.

CONTENTS

To the memory of my father,
who died fighting to remain a person.
And for my mother,
who helped him succeed.

PREFACE

The best way to teach philosophy is to do it, and to be seen to be doing it. Accordingly this book is neither a survey nor a history of the subject, but a genuine attempt to think through to the truth on the matters in hand. It is however an introduction, in that I take nothing for granted, explain ideas and arguments as clearly and fully as I can, and omit some of the more technical complications. What I have tried to do is present the strongest arguments that I am capable of for and against the various main positions within my chosen subject area, arguing also for what seems to me to be the truth on each topic. The topics have been selected, from the much wider range available within the philosophy of mind, with an eye to those which have the most immediate appeal to the beginner. Students working through this book will I hope achieve an overall understanding of the different theories, as well as learning by example how to start thinking rigorously and systematically for themselves. I hope it may be useful as a seminar text for students who already have some experience of philosophy, or as a text-to-be-lectured-to for beginners.

This book is almost wholly self-contained. Aside from the occasional reference to Descartes, Locke and Hume, no other philosophers are mentioned in the text. Students new to philosophy are distracted by a work which is full of names and references. For they naturally assume that this is an important part of what they have to learn. Whereas in truth, knowledge of the 'who-said-what' variety has only a minimal place in the study of our subject. What is important is that they should come to understand the various main theories in the field (and understanding, here, involves seeing what arguments can be deployed in support of them); and that they should begin to think critically on their own behalf, developing objections and arguments of their own.

I have tried to make my written style as simple and unobtrusive as possible. As philosophers, we should express our views and present our arguments clearly and plainly, lest our readers become convinced for the wrong reasons. For our concern is the truth, not propaganda. (No doubt many have become Christians as a result of the fine language of the Authorised Translation of the Bible; and no doubt many others have become Marxists because of the ringing phrases of the Communist Manifesto.) Our business is to rely purely on the strength of our arguments to secure conviction. However, this is not to say that philosophical writing cannot be elegant. On the contrary, at its best it can have the same kind of stark beauty as a good snooker break: combining simplicity and clarity at the level of the individual moves with an overall complexity of structure, and the element of surprise with a retrospective sense of inevitability.

One feature of my grammatical style does require some comment. This is my use of 'they' and 'their' as singular impersonal pronouns, in place of the more usual 'he' and 'his'. I regard the use of the masculine pronoun in impersonal contexts as pernicious. But I find the use of 'he/she' (or even worse 's/he') stylistically barbaric, and the continuous use of 'he or she' unwieldy. I did experiment with the use of the feminine pronoun alone to do the job, but readers of all political persuasions found this distracting. Accordingly I have opted to use the plural pronoun throughout, even where strict grammar requires a singular. This is already common in colloquial speech, and I believe it can read quite naturally.

I should like to thank the following for their comments on earlier drafts of this book: David Archard, Laura Arthurs, Susan Levi, Christopher McKnight, Stephen Mills and Max Wright; with especial thanks to Tim Williamson. I am also grateful to successive generations of students, both at the University of St Andrews and The Queen's University of Belfast, who suffered under earlier drafts, and whose questions, objections and puzzlement helped to make the book very much better.

Peter Carruthers
University of Essex

INTRODUCTION

What is philosophy? This is by no means an easy question to answer, as the nature of the subject is itself a matter of philosophical dispute. But perhaps it can be said that philosophers have two primary sorts of concern. Firstly, they are concerned with matters of justification: demanding reasons for what others take for granted, and investigating the basis of even our most obvious beliefs. One characteristic philosophical question is thus 'How do I know?' Secondly, they are concerned to achieve an understanding of the essential nature of things, their other characteristic question taking the form 'What kind of thing is such-and-such?' In fact the two concerns are intimately related, as we shall see. Often the best way to understand the nature of a thing is to inquire how we know of it. And often the demand for justification can only be met by closer investigation of the things about which we hold our beliefs.

This book will be concerned both with matters of justification and understanding. But our most basic task will be to try and understand the nature of ourselves. Our most basic question will be 'What am I?' Now I shall use the term 'person' to mean whatever I (or we) am (are). In short: persons are selves. So put another way, our most basic question will be 'What kind of thing is a person?' Here we shall ask whether a person is just a special kind of animal (a living organism which can think and reason), or whether a member of the species *Homo sapiens* consists of two distinct parts, a physical body and a non-physical mind or soul (the person, or self, being the non-physical part).

We shall also be concerned to understand the nature of the various characteristic qualities of persons, such as thoughts and experiences. Are these themselves physical states, for example states of the brain? Or are they somehow non-physical and intangible? We shall, however, begin with a question of justification. Namely: what reason have I for believing that the human beings around me have mental states of their own (are in the strict sense persons) since all I ever observe is their overt physical behaviour? Various attempts at answering this apparently simple question will be interwoven through much of our later discussion.

Philosophers, especially when they become professionals, tend

1

not to be overly concerned with the possible bearing of their work on matters of everyday practical importance. Doing detailed work on a particular philosophical issue will often feel a bit like trying to solve a chess problem: one will be thinking hard, trying to find a solution to a complicated abstract problem, without being concerned with possible practical consequences or applications. Yet even the most rarefied philosophical dispute can turn out to have practical implications, as we shall see. (There is perhaps a general moral here, drawn from science as well as philosophy: that discoveries of the greatest practical importance are generally made by those whose concerns are purely abstract and theoretical.) Although it is the detailed work which chiefly interests us, and which ought to interest students of philosophy, it is certainly worth reminding ourselves occasionally of the practical importance of our work.

Throughout this book a concern with possible practical significance will never be very far away. Thus one aspect of our attempt to understand the nature of ourselves will require us to investigate the nature of personal survival. And this has a very obvious bearing on the question whether it might be possible to hope for some form of life after death. We shall also raise the question whether anything other than a human being can be a person — for example dolphins or chimps, or perhaps even computers — and this may have important implications for our treatment of animals, and for our understanding of morality generally.

If the basic philosophical concerns are with justification and understanding, the basic tool of philosophical method is argument. Someone doing philosophy will spend most of their time trying to understand arguments, trying to assess arguments, and trying to develop arguments of their own. Indeed, as the reader will soon discover, this book is full of arguments, both for and against the various doctrines considered. For this reason I suggest that those unfamiliar with the concepts of validity and invalidity of arguments, as well as the related concepts of logical possibility and necessity, should study carefully the glossary provided at the end of the book. They may also find it useful to glance at the opening chapters of any standard textbook on elementary logic.

One further piece of advice for the beginner: try not just to read, but to work at this book while you read it. Often I will present a theory and the arguments for it at an earlier stage, only later presenting my criticisms. A useful exercise would be to pause after each section and try to develop for yourself criticisms of the arguments and theories contained therein. Try to work out (preferably on paper) any ideas or objections which may have occurred to you while reading. Then read on to discover whether or not your criticisms in any way match my own. The main point of studying the subject is that you should start to think about these issues for yourself.

Note also that although this book is an introduction, that does not mean it is uncontroversial. On the contrary, almost everything that I say has been controverted by some philosopher or other, and in the readings listed after each chapter you will find references to some of them. You are certainly not required to believe me. In philosophy no one can tell you what to believe. It is in the nature of the subject that the amount of wholly uncontroversial material is extremely small, at least by comparison with other subjects. You should therefore take no particular interest in what I (or your teachers) believe as such, since you have no reason to trust my (or their) authority rather than that of other philosophers who believe something different. What matters is the quality of the arguments which we can present for our views, and these you must ultimately assess for yourself. So if you believe something different you should not be afraid to try and construct arguments of your own. This is partly what makes philosophy so difficult to do, since good arguments are hard to come by. But it is also what makes it rewarding.

PART ONE:
MYSELF AND OTHERS

1 THE PROBLEM OF OTHER MINDS

i. The Problem

The problem of other minds consists in an argument purporting to show that we can have no knowledge of any other conscious states besides our own. Our task in this section will be to build up this argument in a number of different stages.

If the conclusion of the argument were correct, then I could not be said to know that the human beings around me are, in the strict sense, persons. Although I should see them walking and talking, laughing and crying, I should not be able to know that they have thoughts, have feelings, are amused or upset, and so on. All I should be able to know is that there are certain living organisms which physically resemble myself, which move around and behave in characteristic ways, and which are the source of complicated patterns of sound which I call 'speech'.

(A) The Reality of the Problem

Many will be inclined to dismiss the problem out of hand. Since they are completely certain that other minds do exist, they will insist that there must be something wrong with an argument which makes our knowledge of them seem problematic. Either one of the premises must be false, or the argument itself must be invalid. But notice that there have been many periods throughout history when people would have been equally dismissive of any argument suggesting that we cannot have knowledge of the existence of God. They too would have insisted that since they were completely certain of God's existence ('Everybody knows it!') there must be something wrong with the argument somewhere. Yet many of us would now think that they were wrong.

The general point is that it is possible to be subjectively certain of a belief without actually having any adequate reason for holding it. One's certainty may have causes but no justification. For example, there may have been causal explanations of people's certainty about the existence of God, either of a sociological sort ('People believe what others believe') or of a psycho-analytical sort ('People need to believe in a father-figure'). Similarly, our certainty about

7

the existence of other minds may serve some biological or evolutionary function, without any of us really having adequate reason for believing in any conscious states besides our own. It is no good anyone beating the table shouting 'But of course I know!' If they think they know, then they should take up the challenge presented by the problem of other minds, and show us how they know.

It is no good complaining, either, that the whole attempt to raise a problem about the existence of other minds must be self-defeating, because of the use made of the terms 'our' and 'we'. It is true that the use of these terms does strictly presuppose the existence of other minds besides my own. But then it is not really necessary that I should make use of them. The whole argument giving rise to the problem of other minds can be expressed in the first-person singular throughout. I can present this argument to myself, and you (if there really are any of you) can present it to yourselves. At no point does it need to be presupposed that there really are a plurality of us.

(B) A Preliminary Statement of the Problem

As a way into the problem of other minds, ask yourself the question 'How do I know that what I see when I look at a red object is the same as what anyone else sees when they look at a red object?' That is: how do I know that our experiences are the same? Perhaps what I see when I look at a red object is what you see when you look at a green object, and vice versa. The point is: we naturally assume that we call objects by the same names ('red', 'green', etc.) in virtue of having the same experiences when we look at those objects; but it could equally well be the case that we have different experiences, but the difference never emerges because we call those experiences by different names.

So how do you know that the situation is not as follows: what I see when I look at a red object (e.g. a tomato) is what you see when you look at a green one (e.g. a leaf) and vice versa; but because the experience I call 'red' is the experience you call 'green', and vice versa, we always describe the colours of the objects in the same way. Diagrammatically:

Me: { tomato → experience of red → called 'red'
      leaf → experience of green → called 'green'

You: $\begin{cases} \text{tomato} & \rightarrow \quad \text{experience of green} \quad \rightarrow \quad \text{called 'red'} \\ \\ \text{leaf} & \rightarrow \quad \text{experience of red} \quad \rightarrow \quad \text{called 'green'} \end{cases}$

Thus when I look at a red object I have an experience of red which I refer to as 'red'; but when you look at a red object you have an experience of green, which you refer to as 'red'. So we both say that the object is red.

In order to get yourself into the feel of what is going on here, stare intently at a brightly coloured object, immersing yourself in its colour, and ask: 'How do I know that any other person has *this*?', referring not to the colour of the object itself, but to your immediate experience of the colour. Does it not seem that it would only be possible for you to know that another person has this sort of experience if you could look into their minds, thus in some sense having, or being aware of, their experience? But this is logically impossible. I cannot be aware of your experiences, because anything which I am immediately aware of is, by definition, my own experience. Even if two Siamese twins feel pain in exactly the same place (the place where they join) they do not feel one another's pain. On the contrary, each feels their own. So it appears impossible that I should ever know whether or not anyone else has the sort of experience which I have when I look at a red object.

(A remark here about telepathy, or 'mind-reading'. If such a thing can occur, then there would be a sense in which it is possible to have awareness of the thoughts, if not the experiences, of another person. For I might then be able to know what you are thinking, while you are thinking it, without having to ask you, or otherwise infer it from your behaviour. All the same I should not be able to have the sort of immediate awareness of your act of thinking which you have yourself. What would happen might be this: I suddenly think 'That person is thinking such-and-such', and find that I generally get it right. Or perhaps a thought pops into my mind unbidden, accompanied by the belief that my act of thinking this thought is somehow caused by your act of thinking an exactly similar thought; and again I generally get it right. But either way, telepathy can only provide me with knowledge of other people's thoughts if I have some independent way of checking my inituitive, telepathically induced, beliefs. So telepathy, even if it occurs, cannot provide a solution to the problem of other minds. For it is only if I have some other way of discovering what other people are thinking, that I could ever discover that my telepathic beliefs about their thoughts are generally correct.)

It begins to seem that I cannot know exactly what sorts of experiences other people have. But now: how do I know that they have any experiences at all? How do I know, when they utter the word 'red' on being confronted with a red object, that there is really any intervening experience? And how do I know, when other people cry and scream when they are injured, that there is any intervening pain? For why cannot the light entering their eyes, or the injury, just bring about those sorts of behaviour directly? The point is: all that I ever see, or have direct knowledge of, are other people's circumstances and behaviour. I can observe the input (injury), and observe the output (crying). But what entitles me to infer that there exists any intervening conscious experience? It would seem that the inference cannot be a valid one. For as everyone admits, there is always the possibility of pretence. Since it is possible to writhe and scream (and even have a genuine injury) without actually feeling any pain, the inference from the former to the latter cannot be valid.

As expounded thus far, the argument giving rise to the problem of other minds might be summarised as follows:

(1) It is impossible to have direct awareness of the mental states of another human being.
(C1) So our knowledge of such states (if it exists) must be based upon inference from observable physical states.
(2) Because of the ever-present possibility of pretence, no such inference can ever be valid.
(C2) So (from (C1) and (2)) it cannot be reasonable to believe in the mental states of other human beings.

Premiss (1) appears to be obviously true. I surely cannot experience another person's experiences. I cannot, as it were, 'look into' their minds. I can only, in that sense, 'look into' my own, by introspection. Premiss (2) also appears true. No matter what behaviour a human being exhibits, there are possible worlds in which they exhibit such behaviour without possessing any conscious experiences. So everything appears to turn on the validity of the two steps, to (C1) and to (C2).

(C) Perceptual Knowledge

The validity of the move to (C1) might certainly be challenged. For it depends upon the suppressed premiss that there are only two modes of knowledge, namely immediate awareness and inference. But this is false. There is a third mode of knowledge, namely observation (or perception). Thus when there is a tomato on the plate in front of me, I obviously do not have the kind of immediate awareness of it which I have of my pains, when I have them; for the tomato is not itself an experience of mine. But then neither do I have to infer that the tomato is there on the basis of anything else. Rather I observe that it is there: I see it. Now we do in fact very often say such things as 'I saw that she was in pain, so I called the doctor.' So perhaps our knowledge of the existence of other minds is not knowledge by inference, nor knowledge by immediate awareness, but knowledge by perception.

Now I think it might be acceptable to say that we sometimes know of other people's mental states by observation, if there were no problem of other minds, or if we had somehow solved that problem. It will be possible to perceive that someone is in pain if, but only if, one already knows on other grounds the sorts of behaviour which generally have pains as their cause. For although we do not, in ordinary life, normally infer — deduce, reason out — that someone is in pain on the basis of their behaviour, our claim to observe that they are suffering will only be justified given a particular background of empirical assumptions, amongst which will be the claim that behaviour of that sort is regularly correlated with pain.

The general point is that what you perceive is partly a function of what you have reason to believe. As it is sometimes said: perception is theory-laden. Thus if you know yourself to be on a Hollywood film-set then you will perceive, not buildings, but artificial frontages of buildings; even though your experiences may be indistinguishable from the experiences you would be having if you were standing in front of real buildings. Similarly an engineer might truly say 'I saw that the bridge was in danger of collapsing', where an ordinary person could only say 'I saw that the bridge was sagging in the middle'.

Consider this example: two people are standing in front of a building. The one reasonably (but falsely) believes themself to be on a Hollywood set. The other knows this to be a genuine building, with a back as well as a front. Now although there may be a sense in which both undergo the same experiences, it is surely clear that only one of them perceives a building. The other merely perceives the front of a building. Similarly then: consider two people observing a third who is obviously injured, and is writhing and screaming. Only one of them knows that this sort of behaviour is regularly correlated with pain. Then only one of them will perceive that the person is in pain. The other will merely perceive the behaviour.

Thus it will only be possible to perceive the mental states of other persons if we already possess a certain amount of background knowledge: for example that injury followed by screaming is regularly correlated with pain. But now, how are we supposed to have discovered that these correlations exist? We discovered that a falling barometer is regularly correlated with rain, by observing that when the barometer falls it often rains soon afterwards. But this required us to have independent access to the states of the two kinds: one can observe the rain independently of observing the falling barometer. But as we noted above we do not, and cannot, have any direct access to the mental states of other persons, independently of our access to their behaviour.

I conclude that we can only perceive the mental states of other persons if we can know such general truths as that writhing and screaming are regularly correlated with pain. But since these general truths cannot themselves be known on the basis of perception, it cannot be perception of the mental states of others which provides the solution to the problem of other minds. The argument as far as (C1) has thus been sustained: if we have knowledge of the mental states of others, it must ultimately be based upon inference from observable physical states.

(D) Knowledge by Analogy

The move from (C1) and (2) to (C2) is also invalid as it stands. From the fact that no description of someone's behaviour can ever validly entail a description of their mental state, it does not follow that the one cannot provide good reason to believe the other. There are two possibilities here. Firstly, such arguments may contain a suppressed premiss. For instance if we put together a description of someone's behaviour with the claim that behaviour of that sort is regularly correlated with pain, then these do now entail that the person in question is (very likely) in pain. But this is where we were a moment ago: how could we ever have discovered that there are general correlations between certain kinds of behaviour and certain kinds of mental state? For we never have direct access to other people's conscious states.

It might be replied that there is at least one case in which I have direct access to both behavioural and mental states, and that is my own. So can I not discover the empirical correlations in my own case first, and then reason outwards to the case of other people? This would be a form of inductive (as opposed to deductive) argument. This now gives us our second possibility: although an argument from descriptions of behaviour to descriptions of mental states may not be deductively valid, it may nevertheless be a reasonable *in*ductive step, founded upon my knowledge of the correlations which exist in my own case.

So the proposal before us is this: I first of all discover in my own case that when I am physically injured this often causes me pain, which in turn causes me to cry out. I then reason inductively that since other people, too, can be injured, and since when they are they generally display similar behaviour to myself, that there is very likely a similar intervening cause. Namely: a pain. But the trouble with this is that it attempts to argue inductively to a general conclusion on the basis of one case only (namely my own). It is rather as if the first person ever to discover an oyster had opened it up and found a pearl inside, and had then reasoned that all other oysters will similarly contain pearls. On the basis of this one case they were surely entitled to reach no conclusions whatever about oysters in general.

It is important to note at this point, that the problem of other minds does not arise out of any especially strong constraints being placed on the concept of knowledge. For the conclusion of the above argument is not merely that I cannot be absolutely certain of the mental states of any other human being besides myself. It is rather that I have only the very slightest reason to believe in them. For my knowledge of other minds would have to be based upon an inductive argument from one case only. So I appear to have just as little reason to believe in other minds as I would have for believing in the redness of all the balls in a sack, having selected just one of them and found it to be red.

Summary

We may now summarise the full argument giving rise to the problem of other minds as follows:

(1) There are three modes of knowledge: (a) immediate awareness, (b) perception, (c) inference from either (a) or (b).

(2) It is impossible to have immediate awareness of the mental states of another person.

(3) I can only have perceptual knowledge of the mental states of another, if I already know of general correlations between mental and physical states.

(C1) So (from (1), (2) and (3)) if I have knowledge of the mental states of others, it must ultimately be based upon inference from observable physical states.

(4) Such an inference must either be deductive or inductive.

(5) Because of the ever-present possibility of pretence, the inference cannot be deductively valid.

(6) Because based upon one case only (my own), the inference cannot be a reasonable inductive step.

(C2) So (from (4), (5) and (6)) the observed physical states of others fails to provide me with knowledge of their mental states.

(C3) So (from (C1) and (C2) I cannot have knowledge of the mental states of any other human being besides myself.

This argument gives every appearance of being a proof. I shall take it that premises (1)−(4) are true, and that the argument itself is valid. It would appear that if there is a weakness anywhere, it must lie either with premiss (5) or premiss (6). Premiss (6) will be challenged, and defended, in the next section. Then in section iii I shall argue for the conception of conscious states which makes it seem plausible. Finally in section iv I shall explain and argue for the conception of the meaning of terms referring to conscious states which makes premiss (5) seem plausible.

ii. Attempted Solutions to the Problem

I shall discuss two different ways in which it might be argued that we can reason inductively to the existence of other conscious states besides our own. I shall claim that neither is successful.

(A) Scientific Theory

Our first attempted solution takes issue with the problem of independent access, raised by the barometer/rain example in the last section. It was claimed, you will recall, that we cannot establish correlations between two different kinds of thing, unless we can have independent access to both of them. (We can observe the rain independently of the falling barometer.) It was then claimed that since we can never have direct access to the mental states of other persons, we could never have discovered that behaviour of a certain sort is a sign, e.g., of pain. We attempted to reply to this difficulty by pointing out that there is at least one case in which we have independent access to both behavioural and mental states, namely our own; and this then launched us into the argument from analogy. We could, however, have replied in a quite different way.

Notice that there is at least one sort of case where we can reasonably believe in a general correlation between two different kinds of thing, without having independent access to instances of the two kinds. Namely, where one of the kinds is a theoretical entity, postulated to explain occurrences of the other kind. Thus we postulate the existence of electrons and neutrinos in order to explain such phenomena as tracks across a photographic plate in certain laboratory conditions. And of course it is reasonable to believe in electrons, depite the fact that we have no access to them independently of their supposed effects. Similarly then, might it not be reasonable to believe in the conscious states of other persons if postulating the existence of such states provides us with the best available explanation of their observed behaviour?

What is being proposed is that our belief in other people's conscious states has the status of a scientific theory. Observing the behaviour of other human beings, we naturally seek some systematic way of explaining it. We then postulate an elaborate complex structure of conscious states, which are related causally in various ways to one another and to the behaviour we observe. Then in the absence of any competing theory to explain that behaviour, the inference to the existence of other minds will be an inference to the best available explanation of the observed phenomena. (Just as, in the absence of any suitable competition for explaining the tracks on the photographic plate, the inference to the existence of electrons is an inference to the best available explanation.)

Obviously crucial to what we might call 'the mentalistic scheme of explanation' will be attributions of suitable beliefs and desires to other persons, in terms of which one may rationalise, and to some extent predict, their behaviour. Such a scheme can often meet with a fair degree of success. Not only can we make sense of much of the behaviour of the people around us in terms of what we take to be their beliefs and desires, we can also predict on that basis much of what they will do. For instance, by attributing to you the desire to survive, and the belief that the ice on a particular pond is thin, I can predict that you will not go skating. Indeed it is not merely the behaviour of other human beings which is susceptible of explanation and prediction in terms of the mentalistic scheme. We also meet with a fair degree of success in connection with non-human animals. We postulate desires suitably related to the creature's known biological needs, and beliefs suitably related to its sensory apparatus and present and past environment, and in those terms we find that we can make sense of, and predict, much of its behaviour.

However, it is doubtful whether this proposal can really provide us with adequate reason for believing in other minds. For notice that any scientific theory is liable to be replaced by a better one. And we can, in particular, often know that our theory is only partially successful. This will then give us reason to believe that there must be a better theory, if only we could think of it. We will perhaps go on using the current theory for want of a better one, but in the belief that it will very likely turn out to be false. Now our mentalistic scheme, construed as a scientific theory, is in exactly such a position. Since it enjoys, I shall argue, only partial success, we would be well advised to look around for an alternative theory if we can find one. And we should also believe that the scheme, although useful for present purposes, will very likely turn out to be false.

It is notoriously difficult, to begin with, to make accurate predictions of people's behaviour on the basis of what one knows (or believes) about their mental states. No matter how much you (think you) know about someone, you may be constantly surprised by what they do. Moreover there will always be alternative mentalistic explanations available for any given action: someone may go out without their umbrella because they believe the weather will remain dry, or because they want to get wet, or because they would rather get wet than carry an umbrella, and so on. So it is always going to be a shaky business trying to work back from a person's behaviour to any particular explanatory scheme of beliefs and desires.

These facts might encourage us to hope that one day a better kind of explanatory theory of human behaviour will be found, perhaps premised upon suitable advances in the science of neurophysiology. Then if we regard the mental states of other persons as theoretical entities, on a par with electrons and neutrinos, we should view them as crude and tentative theoretical postulates, to be replaced eventually by others through the advancement of science.

Even if it were true that the mentalistic scheme provided a wholly satisfactory theory of human behaviour, we should still not have solved the problem of other minds. For I take it that having a mind entails possession of conscious mental states. Nothing could count as having a mind — as being a person or self — that did not have conscious beliefs and desires, and perhaps also conscious thoughts and experiences. (This claim will be properly defended in Chapter 8.) Yet it is quite unclear what in the behaviour of other human beings requires us to attribute conscious beliefs and desires to them. For would our mentalistic explanations be any less successful if we supposed the beliefs and desires in question to be merely unconscious behaviour-determining states? If it is true that an adequate mentalistic scheme of explanation need only attribute unconscious mental states, then even the total success of such a scheme would provide us with no reason for believing in the conscious states of others.

The kind of thing I have in mind can best be brought out by means of an example. Often when engaged in some routine activity — for instance driving the car — the following sort of phenomenon occurs. I have been thinking about some topic unrelated to my current activity. Perhaps I have been reviewing the day's events, or trying to compose a recipe for the evening meal. I then suddenly 'come to', and realise that I have not the faintest idea what I have been doing or seeing for the last five or ten minutes. But this is not simply a lapse of memory, since I can remember quite well what I have been thinking and feeling during that time. The truth is that I have undergone no conscious experiences and held no conscious beliefs or desires related to my current environment during the period in question. Yet I also know that in another sense I must have had experiences, beliefs and desires, or I should certainly have crashed the car. I must have *seen* that lorry parked beside the road, *believed* that unless I turned the car wheel I should crash into it, and *desired* not to crash. Someone else, providing a mentalistic explanation of my behaviour, would presumably attribute to me just such beliefs and desires.

The natural way of describing phenomena of the above sort, is to say that there occurs in me a state occupying a similar causal role to the conscious perception of a lorry — namely a state caused by patterned light striking the retina, and causing movements of my arms — but an unconscious one. Then if it is possible for unconscious states to occupy similar causal roles to conscious ones, it is left quite unclear why the mentalistic scheme need deal with anything other than unconscious states. In my own case I know that I often undergo conscious experiences, entertain conscious thoughts, and consciously hold beliefs and desires. But when it comes to explaining the behaviour of others it is unclear that I need advert to anything other than unconscious analogues of such states. Then even if the mentalistic scheme were entirely successful as a scientific theory, it would fail to provide me with reason to believe in any other minds besides my own.

It might be objected that not all human behaviour is as simple as driving a car. Think, in particular, of speech behaviour. I can hold complicated conversations with other people. How could this be possible unless they consciously understand what I say, and unless their own words are expressive of conscious thoughts and ideas? Surely — it might be said — the explanation and proper interpretation of the speech-behaviour of other people requires me to attribute to them, not merely unconscious behaviour-determining beliefs and desires, but conscious mental states like my own.

Yet it is false that the only possible explanation of speech-behaviour lies in the possession of conscious mental states. One can, for instance, hold a limited conversation with a parrot. Yet one does not have to believe that the parrot is thinking conscious thoughts to itself. Rather it has been trained to react verbally to a given verbal stimulus. So what shows that the verbal behaviour of other human beings differs from that of the parrot in anything more than degree of complexity? Moreover it is already possible to hold a relatively sophisticated conversation with a computer (e.g. relating to airline timetables) and no doubt a great deal more progress will be made in this direction. Yet it is not obvious — to say the least — that we should attribute conscious thoughts and conscious desires to computers. When scientists finally manage to create a computer with which one can hold a normal conversation, then its behaviour could be described, fairly neutrally, as 'intelligent'. (So was my avoidance of the parked lorry 'intelligent'.) But it is not obvious that we should be forced to attribute conscious thoughts to it. (Nor is it true that even the possession of unconscious thoughts would provide the best available explanation of its behaviour. On the contrary, we should have already to hand an alternative explanation, superior in both explanatory and predictive power, in the details of the computer-programme.)

I conclude that if our belief in the conscious states of other persons has the status of a scientific theory, then an equally good theory would be that they merely possess unconscious behaviour-determining states, and a much better theory would be that they are merely complex biological computers, programmed to respond to ordered patterns of sound. (In Chapter 5, I shall consider the possibility that a conscious thought might actually *be* an event in a biological computer; and in section 8.iv I shall consider the suggestion that artificial computers, of suitable sophistication, should be counted as fully-fledged persons or selves. For the moment I leave these possibilities to one side.) So our first attempted solution to the problem of other minds appears to have been a failure. If our belief in other minds has the status of a scientific theory, then it should very likely be rejected as a false and inadequate theory.

(B) Causal Analogies

We may do rather better if we look once again at the argument by analogy with my own case. Our objection was that this was like someone arguing by analogy from the existence of a pearl in their first oyster to the existence of pearls in all other oysters. But notice that one very important difference between my knowledge of my own conscious states and the case of the pearl in the oyster, is that I know of many causal connections between my conscious states and overt physical events; whereas the pearl on the other hand just sits there in the oyster, apparently inert. For instance I know that I speak in order to express my thoughts, that my decision to pick up my drink will normally cause my arm to move, that a pin driven into my flesh will normally cause me to feel a sensation of pain, and so on.

In fact it appears that I may be able to argue by analogy to the existence of other minds as follows:

(1) I observe in the world physical bodies which appear, in many respects, to be like my own.
(2) These bodies go in for the sort of behaviour which I have found, in my own case, to be causally connected with various conscious mental states.
(C) So these bodies, too, possess conscious mental states.

Of course this argument neither is, nor purports to be, strictly valid. It is rather a species of inductive argument. But it is being proposed that the argument is rationally convincing — despite the fact that the induction is based upon one case only — in virtue of the myriad causal connections mentioned in premiss (2).

It can often be reasonable to allow oneself to be convinced by an argument by analogy from one case only. Imagine that you are walking on the sea-shore one day, and discover a great many black boxes washed up on the beach by the tide. They all have an array of coloured buttons and lights, and you discover that they all behave in a similar manner: pressing a red button causes a red light to flash, and so on. Now you open up one of the boxes and discover its internal mechanism of wires and levers. Surely you are entitled to conclude that all the other boxes will have the same internal mechanism (even if, for some reason, you are unable to get them open).

Yet reflect for a moment upon what justifies you in drawing such a conclusion. It is not merely your knowledge, in this one case, of the causal connections between the internal mechansim and the external appearance and behaviour of the box: this by itself is insufficient. You must also be taking for granted (surely reasonably, in our era of mass production) that the boxes will all have been constructed according to a common pattern. For it is easy to think of some different assumptions, which would not warrant the conclusion drawn, which just happen in this case to be rather unlikely: for instance that all of the boxes have been made by different people as part of a competition to see who can produce a machine fulfilling a given function with the greatest economy of materials.

The important point is that an argument by analogy from one case can only be rationally convincing, given a certain amount of background knowledge in addition to knowledge of the causal connections involved in the one case investigated. And then the question is whether we do have the appropriate sort of background knowledge to warrant an argument to the existence of other minds.

I shall argue in the next section that our own states of consciousness appear to be radically different from anything else which we find in the natural world. If that is the case, then we shall certainly lack sufficient knowledge to warrant an argument by analogy. Our situation would be essentially similar to the following. We arrive on Mars to discover a rich natural life. Among other plants and animals, we discover a species of carnivors rather like our tigers. They seem to be made of flesh and blood: they bleed when you cut them, and they need to eat other animals in order to survive. But when we do our first post mortem on one of them, we discover that instead of a brain of living tissue it has what appears to be a silicon-chip computer inside its head. What are we to say? Can we conclude that all the other Martian tigers will be similarly constructed? I suggest not: for the case is so unlike anything we have ever come across before that any one of a thousand hypotheses is possible. There may be some intelligent being which has given this one beast (or some, or all, of the others) an artificial brain as some sort of experiment. Or there may be some natural way in which a living being (or species of being) can come to have a brain of metal and silicon. Or it may even have sprung into existence by some sort of miracle.

The case of a mind in a body is, I shall suggest, even more extraordinary than the case of the computer-brained tiger. For conscious states appear to be quite unlike physical states, having unique attributes amongst the other elements of the natural world. But the observable similarities between other human beings and myself, on the other hand, all relate to our existence as physical systems. Indeed the more I learn about other human beings the more likely it seems that their behaviour will ultimately be explicable in purely physical terms. Yet in my own case I am aware of possessing conscious states which are, I shall argue, non-physical states. Then my situation with respect to the existence of other minds will after all be like the person who first opened an oyster and found a pearl. For here was something so extraordinary — a hard smooth translucent object existing inside a living organism — that they were entitled to come to no conclusion whatever concerning the existence of pearls in other oysters.

iii. The Uniqueness of Consciousness

In this section I shall present three different arguments in support of the doctrine I shall call 'weak dualism', which asserts that conscious states are non-physical states. This doctrine deserves the title 'dualist' because it involves a duality of kinds of state: on the one hand physical states, and on the other hand non-physical (conscious) states; the two kinds being radically different from one another. But it is only 'weak' dualism, because nothing is as yet said about the kinds of thing which possess those states. The weak dualist (about states) may be a monist about things, believing that the only kinds of thing which exist in the natural world are physical things. For they may believe that conscious states are non-physical states of a physical thing, namely the living human organism. (The strong dualist, on the other hand, believes that the subject of conscious states is itself a non-physical thing, or soul. Arguments for strong dualism will be presented in the next chapter.) Note that if weak dualism is true, then there can be no question of an argument by analogy to the existence of other minds being successful.

(A) Phenomenal Qualities

Consider what takes place when you perceive a brightly coloured object, say a red post-box or a red tulip. Light of a certain wavelength enters your eye, being focused on the retina. There, receptors are stimulated by the impact of the light, and fire off electro-chemical impulses along the optic nerve. These impulses are in turn received in the visual centre at the back of the brain, where they cause a complicated pattern of electro-chemical activity. At this point you are caused to experience a sensation of red. Now here, suddenly, is something quite unlike the other elements in the causal chain. With the advent of a conscious sensation, something radically new has entered the story.

Consider the nature of the events leading up to the sensation of red. They consist in changes in the states of certain living cells in your body, the states in question having to do with the electrical and chemical properties of those cells. Now consider the nature of your experience itself. It is perhaps of a particularly bright, warm shade of red. It has, indeed, a distinctive phenomenal quality: a qualitative 'feel' all of its own. This is surely something quite different from any possible state of your brain; surely nothing electrical or chemical can have a qualitative feel. It would seem that no brain cell, or interaction of brain cells, can be either 'bright' or 'warm'. Yet this is an accurate description of your experience.

What is being argued here is that physical states and events, and conscious states and events, possess quite a different range of attributes or properties. Physical states consist of arrangements of matter possessing electrical or chemical properties. They do not themselves have any qualitative 'feel'. No physical state is 'bright' or 'warm' or 'piercing' in the senses in which a conscious state can be these things. (The piercingness of a piercing pain is not literally the same as the piercingness of a knife piercing the flesh, though described by analogy with it.) Conscious states, on the other hand, do not possess electrical or chemical properties. It seems straightforwardly nonsensical to say of your sensation of red that it has such-and-such an electrical potential. (As if someone had said 'Your green ideas sleep furiously'. Although this is a grammatical sentence — it has a subject, a verb and an object — it clearly has no literal meaning.) What they do have are characteristic qualitative 'feels'.

If physical states and conscious states possess quite different kinds of properties, then they must themselves be different kinds of states. For if they did belong to the same kind — if, in particular, each conscious state were a physical state of the brain — then they would have to have the same attributes. Identical things have identical attributes; different things have different attributes. (This point will become clearer in section 3.i; for the moment take it on trust.) So the conclusion of this argument is that conscious states are not physical states.

(B) Intentionality

Most conscious states — for instance beliefs, desires and perceptions — are intentional: they represent things. More importantly, they represent things in one way rather than another. To make use of a famous fictional example: when the police believe that Mr Hyde is the murderer, their belief contains a representation of a particular man, who is in fact Dr Jekyll. But it does not represent him *as* Dr Jekyll, but only as Mr Hyde. For they do not yet know that 'Jekyll' and 'Hyde' are associated with representations of one and the same man. Similarly, Oedipus' desire for marriage involves a representation of a particular woman, who is in fact his mother. But it does not represent her as being his mother, but rather as 'Jocasta', or perhaps as 'the woman I have recently come to love'. Hence his surprise when he discovers that Jocasta — the woman he loves — is in fact his mother.

Conscious states not only represent things in one way rather than another; they can also represent things which do not really exist. Someone looking for the lost city of Atlantis has a desire which represents something which (probably) neither does, nor ever has existed. An ancient Greek believing that Zeus has just thrown a thunderbolt possesses a conscious state containing a representation of a non-existent God.

The intentionality of consciousness provides us with a powerful argument for saying that conscious states cannot be physical states. For how is it possible for any merely physical state (e.g. a state of the brain) to represent anything? How could a particular pattern of cellular activity possess the property of intentionality? It seems unintelligible how any physical arrangement could represent something that exists outside itself, and represent it in one way rather than another. It is even less intelligible how it could represent something which does not exist at all.

Of course we know that some physical arrangements can represent things. Think for example of a portrait-painting, or of a sentence on the printed page. But it is arguable that such representation is itself derivative from the representative properties of the mental. It is only the intentions of the artist, or the beliefs of the viewer, which make a portrait-painting represent one particular person rather than another. Otherwise it is merely an arrangement of colours on canvas with an appearance similar to that of the subject, but similar also to many other people who physically resemble the subject. Equally, it is only the intentions of speakers of English to use words in particular ways which makes the sequence of marks in 'It is raining' represent anything.

If conscious states like intentions and beliefs were themselves physical states, then it would have to be possible for a physical state or arrangement to represent something without doing so via the intentionality of some other state. A physical arrangement would have to be capable of representing something in its own right. But this appears impossible. No pattern of cellular activity can represent, by itself, the fact that it is raining. So the conclusion of this argument too, is that conscious states are non-physical states.

(C) Spatial Position

Unlike all physical objects and states, many (perhaps all) conscious states appear to possess no spatial positions. Certainly it seems that some mental states possess no spatial positions. For instance the question 'Is your mental image of your mother to the right or left of your thought about the weather?' appears utterly nonsensical. (Just as if you had been asked 'Does your thought of your mother weigh less than two kilograms?') Equally nonsensical would be the question 'What is the spatial relation between your anger at the betrayal and your fear of reprisals?' So it seems that neither conscious acts like thinking and imagining, nor emotions like anger and fear, occupy positions in space.

Compare thoughts with numbers. There are many things which it makes no sense to say about a number. For instance you cannot attribute colours to them, nor spatial locations. The sentences 'The number 7 is green' and 'The number 7 is in London' are both equally nonsensical. But also nonsensical are 'The number 7 is not green' and 'The number 7 is not in London', since these suggest that 7 might have some other colour, or be somewhere else. The truth is, the number 7 is not the kind of thing which can either have a colour (or be colourless), nor have a spatial position. It therefore follows that numbers (if there really are such things) cannot be physical. For it belongs to the very essence (the logical nature) of any physical object or state that it should occupy some position in space. How could there exist a rusty bicycle for instance, unless both the bicycle and its rust occupy some particular region in space, standing in determinate spatial relations to all other physical objects? So any thing (like a number or a thought) which is not the sort of thing to have a spatial position, must be non-physical.

It might be conceded that thoughts and emotions lack spatial positions, and are therefore non-physical. But is the same true of all conscious states? What of experiences for example? Surely visual experiences, at least, occur in space. For can I not say 'My blue after-image is slightly above and to the left of my red one'? (An after-image is what you experience when you stare intently at a brightly coloured light and then look away at a blank wall.)

Now certainly I can attribute to my visual experiences spatial positions within my visual field; that is to say: in relation to one another. Yet it is doubtful whether this is to attribute to them genuine (literal) spatial positions; that is to say: positions relative to all physical objects and states. For although you can describe the position of your blue after-image in relation to that of your red one, it appears nonsensical to ask 'Where exactly is your blue after-image in relation to the mole on your left cheek?' It would be equally nonsensical to ask 'Is your blue after-image two inches behind your right eye?'

I suggest that construed literally, 'This after-image is to the left of that one' should be understood as saying something like this: this after-image is related to that one in the way in which visual experiences are related to one another, when one is an experience of something which is (in the physical world) positioned to the left of the thing of which the other is an experience. That is to say: they are related spatially to one another within the visual field (within 'visual space'), but not literally (not within physical space).

But what of bodily sensations such as pains and tickles? Surely they, at least, occupy genuine spatial positions. For do I not say for instance that I have a pain 'in my left foot'? Yet in fact we could treat these cases rather in the way that we treated visual experiences: as non-literal ascriptions of position within my 'tactile field'. And perhaps we should treat them like this. For consider the phenomenon of phantom-limb pain. For some time after the amputation of a limb it is common for the patient to continue to feel pains and itches 'in' the amputated limb. So if we insist that pains have spatial positions, while allowing that no one can be mistaken about the nature of their own experiences (see section 1.iv below), we shall have to say that the pain occurs in empty space, or perhaps in the pillow on which the stump is resting.

Since this is absurd, it seems better to say that what one is immediately aware of is a pain 'felt as emanating from' a foot. That is to say: a pain which feels as a pain normally feels when it is caused by damage to a foot. It would then be nonsensical to ask 'Where — literally — in physical space is your awareness of the pain-felt-as-emanating-from-a-foot?'

So even in the case of pains and tickles it seems coherent, and indeed plausible, to claim that they are not the kind of thing which can have genuine spatial position. It will then be plausible to claim that no conscious states occupy positions in physical space, and it will follow that no conscious states are themselves physical states. So the conclusion of this argument, as of the other two, is that conscious states are non-physical.

iv. Certainty and Meaning

Recall from section 1.i, that the main aspect of the problem of other minds may be presented as a dilemma: every argument must be either deductive or inductive, and yet neither deduction nor induction can give us knowledge of other minds. Over the last two sections we have been concerned to bolster up the second horn of this dilemma. In section 1.ii we argued that neither scientific hypothesis nor an argument by analogy can give us knowledge of the conscious states of others. Then in section 1.iii we defended a conception of the nature of conscious states — namely weak dualism — which explains why no argument by analogy with my own case can ever be rationally convincing.

In this section we return to the first horn of the dilemma: that no deductive argument can give us knowledge of the conscious states of another. I shall explain and argue for a particular conception of the meaning of terms referring to conscious states, which makes this claim seem plausible. I shall call this 'the cartesian conception of the meaning of consciousness-terms', after the French philosopher René Descartes; or 'the cartesian conception' for short. The cartesian conception is this: that the meanings of terms like 'pain' and 'experience of red' are wholly a matter of the subjective 'feel' of the corresponding states.

Although historically weak dualism and the cartesian conception have tended to go together, they are in fact logically independent of one another, as we shall later have occasion to see. The cartesian conception will come under critical scrutiny in Chapters 4 and 6, as will weak dualism in Chapter 5.

(A) An Argument from Logical Independence

In section 1.i we claimed that there can be no deductively valid arguments from descriptions of physical states to descriptions of conscious states. In fact it would be equally plausible to hold the stronger thesis that there can be no deductively valid arguments in either direction. For not only is it possible to display pain-behaviour (even after genuine injury) without actually feeling any pain; it is also possible to be in pain without this in any way revealing itself in your behaviour. It would thus appear that the appropriate sorts of physical states are neither necessary nor sufficient for the experience of pain to occur. They are not logically necessary, because you can have pain without pain-behaviour or injury. And they are not logically sufficient, because you can have the injury and the behaviour without the sensation.

The notion of 'necessary and sufficient conditions' is an extremely important one in philosophy. For most philosophers believe that the meaning of an expression is constituted by the conditions necessary and sufficient for its correct application. At any rate this is the way in which I propose to understand the term 'meaning' throughout this book. (This assumption is controversial, but I believe I can make it without begging too many important questions in the philosophy of mind.)

Consider the term 'bachelor' (to take a hackneyed example). It is clearly necessary to being a bachelor that you be a man, since neither infants nor women can be bachelors. But this is of course not sufficient, since a married man is not a bachelor either. A sufficient condition for being a bachelor is that you are a man who has never been married. And what more natural than to think that the word 'bachelor' *means* 'man who has never been married', thus equating meaning with necessary and sufficient conditions for truth? (Note that meaning cannot be equated with sufficient conditions alone. It is a sufficient condition for someone being my uncle that they be my father's brother. But 'uncle' does not mean the same as 'father's brother', since although this condition is sufficient, it is not necessary. Someone can be my uncle by being my mother's brother.)

It thus appears that descriptions of physical states can form no part of the meaning of consciousness-terms. Since the behaviour and physical injury which are characteristic of pain are neither logically necessary nor logically sufficient for the occurrence of pain, they cannot form any part of our concept of that state. Then the cartesian conception is the only remaining alternative: the meanings of such terms must be wholly concerned with the subjective qualitative feel of the states they describe. The condition necessary and sufficient for the occurrence of pain is that there should occur a sensation with the characteristic feel of pain.

(B) An Argument from Certainty

Another argument for the cartesian conception is based on the premiss that I can be absolutely certain of my own conscious states. (As it is sometimes said: my knowledge of them is 'incorrigible'.) By the phrase 'absolutely certain' here, I mean that it is logically impossible that I might turn out to be mistaken: if I sincerely believe myself to be in pain, then is it inconceivable that I might turn out to be not really having that experience at all. If this were correct, then the cartesian conception would appear to provide the only plausible explanation of it. The explanation being that I am, in my own case, immediately presented with the conditions necessary and sufficient for the correct application of the terms I am using, namely a particular qualitative feel. I cannot be mistaken about being in pain because there is no 'gap' between what I mean when I judge that I am in pain — the state of affairs I am describing — and the awareness on whose basis I judge. On the contrary, what I am judging about (the conditions necessary and sufficient for truth) is itself a particular state of awareness: a feeling.

In connection with any belief about the external physical world it is always at least logically possible that I might turn out to be wrong. This is because in such cases there always *is* a 'gap' between what is represented by my belief (a state of affairs in the physical world) and the awareness on which my belief is based (my experience of that world). For example while delivering a lecture I believe myself to be faced with a room full of people. But of course I could be hallucinating (someone might have slipped something into my coffee without my knowing). Or they could all be cleverly designed robots. And so on. So it would seem that, in possible contrast with beliefs about my own experiences, 'Are you sure?'-questions will always make sense (be intelligible) in connection with any belief about the physical world (even beliefs about my own body).

Suppose then that the cartesian conception of the meaning of consciousness-terms were wrong. For instance, suppose that some physical state were logically necessary to the state of being in pain. Then it would seem to be possible for me to be mistaken in thinking that I am in pain, e.g. by hallucinating the presence of that necessary physical state. So if my awareness of my pain is incorrigible, as suggested above, then the cartesian conception must apparently represent the true picture of the meaning of the corresponding term. It is therefore a matter of some importance to establish whether or not I really can be absolutely certain about my own states of consciousness.

(C) The Certainty-Thesis

It needs to be conceded straight away that there are some kinds of mistake which it is possible to make about one's own experiences. Firstly, it is possible to be mistaken about the true cause of an experience, as with the phenomenon of 'referred pain'. Thus I might go to my doctor complaining of a pain in my back, but after examining me she might say 'It is not your back which hurts, it is your stomach'. This is a loose way of saying that the pain I feel in my back is in fact caused by a disturbance in my stomach. Secondly, one can be mistaken about the relations which obtain between a current experience and one's past or future experiences. Thus I might be mistaken in claiming that my current headache is more intense than the one which I had yesterday. Thirdly, it is possible to be mistaken about anything which involves some sort of intellectual operation upon a current experience. As when I claim to have an eight-sided after-image but then later, after a recount, realise that in fact it has nine sides. And then finally, there will of course be the usual sorts of mistakes due to such things as slips of the tongue, or to linguistic ignorance. As when I misdescribe a tickle as 'a pain' because I am under the mistaken impression that that is what 'pain' means.

In the light of the above, our thesis ('the certainty-thesis') will have to be this: that it is impossible to be mistaken in simple judgements of recognition of one's own experiences; where the terms of those judgements do not bring in anything extraneous to current experience, such as causes, earlier times, or numbers; and where the judging subject adequately understands the terms involved in the judgement, and uses the terms which they intend to use.

For example, although I cannot be absolutely certain that I see (really see) a room full of people, I can surely be certain that I at least *seem* to see a room full of people. It appears inconceivable that I should turn out to be not really having that experience. Suppose someone were to ask me 'Are you sure that you haven't mistaken the nature of your experience? Are you sure that it is a room full of people that you seem to see, and not a pink elephant climbing the wall?' These questions appear to be nonsensical. Equally unintelligible would be the question 'Are you sure that it is a headache that you have, and not an itchy foot?' To this I should want to expostulate 'Surely I know what I feel!'

Someone might concede that it is impossible to make mistakes of this order of magnitude, but claim that in other more subtle cases it is possible to be in error (or at least uncertain). For example, could I not have occasion to say 'I am not sure whether what I am feeling is a pain or an intense tickle'? But in reality this is just like the case where I say I am uncertain whether a particular object is coloured yellow or green. And this is merely a loose way of saying something of which I can be perfectly certain, namely that the object is yellowish-green. Similarly, can I not be absolutely certain of this: that what I feel is an experience midway between a pain and a tickle?

There are other more interesting cases in which I can apparently misclassify an experience. For example, suppose that I am being played a tape of various bird-calls, and am asked to describe my experiences. Might I not say 'At first I thought I was experiencing the call of an Oystercatcher, but now I realise it is the call of a Redshank'? Here I have changed my classification of an experience, yet it does not appear very plausible to claim that the experience itself changed in the interim; for I am being played exactly the same bit of tape. So was not my first judgement a mistake?

In fact I think we *ought* to say that my experience has changed, for a reason which is both interesting and important. Namely: experiences are themselves partly interpretative. To change the interpretation (the classification) is to change the experience itself. Thus consider the famous duck-rabbit, which you can see either as a picture of a duck or of a rabbit (see Fig. 1.1). When you see it one way or the other, what happens is not simply that you have a particular ('neutral') experience accompanied by the belief 'This is a picture of a duck', or 'This is a picture of a rabbit'. You actually *see* the picture differently. So the correct response to make to the example above is that to hear a sound as the call of an Oystercatcher, and hear the same sound as the call of a Redshank, are in fact two different experiences. So neither judgement was false. The only mistake was over the kind of bird which would normally cause such a sound.

It would seem that our thesis has been sustained. The mistakes which it is possible to make about one's own experiences are not of

Figure 1.1

a kind to threaten the cartesian conception. Since I cannot be mistaken in simple recognition judgements, the content of those judgements (the meanings of the terms employed) must apparently be wholly confined to the immediate contents of consciousness: to the subjective qualitative feel of the states described.

(D) The Scope of the Certainty-Thesis

It is by no means easy to see exactly how the scope of our thesis should be formulated. For it is obviously not the case that I may be absolutely certain about the application of literally any mental term. Of course I may be wrong in thinking that I am intelligent, in believing that I understand the French word 'ouvert', or in thinking that I am generous. These terms refer to mental capacities or dispositions. That I am capable, on the whole, of solving problems more easily than most (intelligence), that I am able to use a word correctly (understanding), and that I am sufficiently disposed to help those in need (generosity), are not things which I can be immediately conscious of. What I suggest is that I at least cannot be mistaken about the (first-person, present tense) application of any mental term which refers to a sensation or experience ('seem to see', 'seem to hear', 'am in pain', etc.), nor any term which refers to a mental action ('think', 'imagine', 'wonder whether', etc.).

But what of emotions, like anger and fear, as well as beliefs and desires? Do they fall within the scope of the certainty-thesis? Should the cartesian conception be extended to them? Now what is distinctive about such states as opposed to states of thinking and feeling, is that someone can possess them without being currently aware of them. For instance it may truly be said of someone who is asleep 'She believes she has been betrayed, is angry at it, and wants revenge.' In contrast, it could not be said of the sleeper that she is in pain, or thinking about the weather. If someone is not aware of any pain, then they are not in pain. As it is sometimes said: pains and thoughts are 'self-intimating' (to have them is to be aware of them), whereas beliefs and desires are not.

The fact that they are not self-intimating need not prevent us from bringing emotions, beliefs and desires within the scope of the certainty-thesis. Although they can continue to exist while the subject is not currently aware of them, it might be said that they are nevertheless always infallibly *available* to consciousness. Then if someone thinks that they have a particular emotion, or belief, or desire, then so they do. And if they think that they do not, then they do not. All that is possible, is that they may have emotions, beliefs or desires which they are not currently thinking about.

(E) Unconscious Mental States

So far we have provided two distinct arguments for the cartesian conception of meaning, one of which has involved us in explaining and defending the certainty-thesis. Now it is important to note that all conscious states will admit of unconscious analogues — that is to say: states occupying causal roles similar to those of conscious states, but which are unavailable to consciousness — which may sometimes be described (confusingly) by the same names. This is entirely consistent with both the certainty-thesis and the cartesian conception.

Thus, as we noted in section 1.ii, I might sometimes be said to have seen things which I was not at the time conscious of having seen. Here the idea is that there occurs in me a state with the same causes and effects as a conscious visual experience. There will also be cases in which someone might be said to believe something, or desire something, which they sincerely declare themselves not to believe or desire. There might even be cases in which someone could be said to be in pain without being aware of it; e.g. a soldier in battle who jerks their hand off a red-hot object, although too busy concentrating on the fighting to be conscious of any pain.

All we need to say, in order to preserve the cartesian conception intact in the face of such usage, is that the above uses of the terms 'see', 'believe' and 'be in pain' involve an ambiguity (a difference of meaning). We can say that unconscious experiences, beliefs and thoughts are not really (literally) experiences, beliefs or thoughts. (Compare: a trainee doctor is not really a doctor, and a forged banknote is not really a banknote.)

The two kinds of meaning will reflect quite distinct interests and purposes. We will be indifferent whether the states are conscious or unconscious when we adopt an impersonal scientific standpoint, regarding human beings (including ourselves) as complex systems whose behaviour we are trying to explain or predict. From this perspective it will generally be irrelevant whether or not the agent is conscious of feeling angry, or is aware of the beliefs and desires determining their behaviour. But more usually when we use terms such as 'anger' or 'belief' we are trying to see things from the first-person perspective of the subjects themselves, trying to represent how things feel or seem from their point of view. And when we use the terms in this way the cartesian conception will provide the correct account of their meaning.

Conclusion

This now completes our preliminary discussion of the problem of other minds. In this chapter we have outlined the problem, and have explained and argued for the views — weak dualism, and the cartesian conception — which apparently underlie it. We shall be returning to various aspects of the problem at different points throughout the remainder of the book. But for the moment we shall be leaving the problem of other minds to one side. We turn from the question how we know of other minds, to consider the question what minds themselves really are.

Questions and Readings

In order to help you get to grips with the material covered in Chapter 1, you may like to discuss/think about/write about some of the following questions:

(1) What do you consider to form the basis of our knowledge of other minds: (a) immediate awareness, (b) perception, (c) some sort of inference?

(2) Is our belief in other minds the best available scientific explanation of other people's behaviour?

(3) Are there sufficiently many similarities between myself and other human beings to warrant an argument by analogy to the existence of other minds?

(4) How convincing do you find the arguments for saying that conscious states are non-physical? Can you think of any arguments for the opposite conclusion?

(5) Is it possible to be mistaken about one's own conscious states? How is this question related to the problem of other minds?

In thinking about the above questions, you might like to consult a selection of the following readings (names in capital type refer to collections of papers, details of which may be found in the Bibliography):

A. J. Ayer, 'One's Knowledge of Other Minds', *Theoria*, vol. XIX (1953). Reprinted in AYER [1], and GUSTAFSON.

————, 'Privacy', *Proceedings of the British Academy* (Oxford: Oxford University Press, 1959). Reprinted in AYER [2].

Charles Chihara and Jerry Fodor, 'Operationalism and Ordinary Language', *American Philosophical Quarterly* vol. II (1965). Reprinted in PITCHER.

R. Chisholm, 'Intentionality'. Entry in *The Encyclopaedia of Philosophy*, Paul Edwards (ed.) (London Collier-Macmillan, 1967).

Paul Churchland, *Scientific Realism and the Plasticity of Mind* (Cambridge: Cambridge University Press, 1979), Ch. 4.

————, *Matter and Consciousness* (Mass.: MIT Press, 1984), Ch. 4.

René Descartes, 'Meditations on First Philosophy', 1 & 2, in *Descartes: Philosophical Writings*, E. Anscombe and P. Geach (eds.), (London: Thomas Nelson & Son, 1954).

Keith Lehrer, *Knowledge* (Oxford: Oxford University Press, 1974), Ch. 4.

Norman Malcolm, 'Knowledge of Other Minds', *Journal of Philosophy* vol. LV (1958). Reprinted in GUSTAFSON, CHAPPELL and PITCHER.

Jerome Shaffer, 'Could Mental States be Brain Processes?', *The Journal of Philosophy*, vol. LVIII (1961). Reprinted in BORST.

J. M. Shorter, 'Other Minds'. Entry in *The Encyclopaedia of Philosophy*, Paul Edwards (ed.) (London: Collier-Macmillan, 1967).

Jenny Teichman, *The Mind and the Soul* (London: Routledge and Kegan Paul, 1974), Chs. 3 and 7.

PART TWO:
IMMATERIAL PERSONS

2 DUALISM: BODY AND SOUL

i. An Argument for Dualism

In section 1.iii we offered a proof of weak dualism, apparently establishing that conscious states are non-physical. Our task in the present section is to see whether we can construct a proof of strong dualism (sometimes called 'cartesian dualism' after René Descartes; more often simply called 'dualism').

(A) Preliminary Points

Like the weak dualist, the strong dualist believes that there are two radically different kinds of states and events in the world. But they also believe that the world contains two radically different kinds of substance and thing. They believe that there exists matter, which goes to make up physical objects, which must always occupy some position in space. And that there exists consciousness, which goes to make up minds or souls, which are non-physical and non-spatial. On the strong dualist view it is the soul which is the bearer of conscious mental states. It is the soul, not the body or brain, which thinks, feels, imagines and undergoes experiences.

Note that weak dualism does not by itself entail strong dualism. Indeed it does not even follow that it is logically possible for strong dualism to be true. For all that has so far been shown, it may be a necessary truth that conscious states are non-physical states of a physical thing. An example of the kind of idea I have in mind might be as follows. The state of being married is not a physical state, since marriage is a conventional rather than a physical relation. Yet only a physical being can be in that state, at least if one takes the traditional view that marriage requires consummation in order to be genuine. For the sexual act is necessarily a physical act. So it may be that something similar holds true in the case of conscious states also: although they are not themselves physical states, there may nevertheless be some reason why only a physical being can possess such states.

A word about terminology before we proceed further. I shall henceforward reserve the term 'soul' for use in referring to the non-physical thing which is, according to the strong dualist, the bearer of our conscious states. So to deny the truth of strong dualism would be to deny that souls exist. However, I shall continue to use the term 'mind' neutrally, to mean the collection of conscious states, whether they be states of a physical or a non-physical thing, and whether those states themselves be physical or non-physical. So to deny the truth of either form of dualism would not be to deny that minds exist. Since we shall be concerned with strong dualism throughout the remainder of Part II, I shall for brevity speak simply of 'dualism'. We shall return to consider possible criticisms of weak dualism in Part III.

What should the dualist say about the person or self? Should they identify persons with souls? Or should they say that a person is a union, a combination, of a soul and a body? I can see no reason why they should say the latter. For after all it is the soul which is said to be the bearer of conscious thoughts and experiences. So if it were to prove possible for my soul to survive the destruction of my body, why should I regard *myself* as having been destroyed? For I should presumably still be able to go on thinking, remembering and feeling. I might even be able to go on experiencing, since it seems conceivable that experiences should be caused in some other way than the stimulation of the various bodily organs (think of hallucinations and dreams for instance). Why should my body be so important to me that I ought to regard myself as ceasing to exist without it, if my conscious mental life could continue relatively unchanged? (Similarly if it were to prove possible for my soul to become attached to a different body: surely the only reasonable way to describe this would be to say that I myself had changed bodies, in the way that a lorry-driver may change from one vehicle to another.)

The dualist holds that the person, or self, should be identified with the soul. The body should be relegated to the status of mere vehicle, providing the focus for the soul's causal intercourse with the rest of the natural world. (It is this body which I can cause to move around by making decisions, and it is things happening to this body which cause most of my experiences.) Strange as this view may seem, it does at least hold out the logical possibility of some sort of life after death. For to say that the self is logically distinct from the body is to say that it is possible that it should continue to exist even when the body no longer exists.

(B) The Argument

Let us now see how strongly we can argue for the truth of dualism. A good place to begin is with the conceivability of disembodied thought and experience. It seems I can imagine dropping dead in the middle of a train of thought, my thoughts continuing uninterrupted. Or I can imagine hearing the doctors pronounce me dead, thinking to myself 'Well this is not so bad as I feared!' I can then imagine a sequence of experiences which do not in any way involve the experience of having a body. I can imagine perceiving physical objects without there being any visible hands, feet, out-of-focus nose, etc., especially closely connected with my visual field. Indeed I can imagine my visual field shifting away from the body which I now regard as mine, so that I look back on that body from a separate point of view. (Many people have reported having such experiences.) I can then imagine the experience of moving through the physical world, but in such a way that my progress is unimpeded by any physical obstacle (e.g. I am able to move through walls and so on).

All of this seems sufficient to establish that it is logically possible for there to occur thoughts and experiences which are not the thoughts or experiences of any physical organism. There are possible worlds in which conscious states occur in the absence of any physical subject of those states. However, there is surely no possible world in which conscious states occur in the absence of any conscious subject whatever. Thoughts and experiences surely cannot occur in the absence of any thinking experiencing thing: thoughts require a thinker, experiences require an experiencer. It therefore follows that there can exist conscious things (persons) which are not physical things. (Or to put it in other ways: I — the thinker — am not an essentially physical thing; physicality is not an attribute which I necessarily have to possess.)

Note that it has not yet been established that I am not, in fact, a physical thing. From the fact that I am not essentially (necessarily) physical, it does not follow that I am not in fact physical. To see this, compare the following. Physical things are not essentially coloured things (think of a pane of glass, or an electron). But it obviously cannot follow from this that physical things are not coloured, since many of them are in fact coloured. Yet it is the stronger conclusion — that I am not a physical thing — which we need to establish if we are to establish the truth of dualism. For the dualist believes that I (the thinker) am in fact a non-physical thing.

However, it is not as if we had made no progress at all. On the contrary, if the argument above is as convincing as it appears, then we have proved that it is logically possible for dualism to be true. And this is already more than many philosophers would be prepared to admit.

What could justify the move from 'I am not an essentially physical thing' to 'I am not in fact a physical thing'? It would apparently be sufficient if we could show that any object which is in fact a physical thing is an essentially physical thing. For in that case, anything which was not essentially physical would not be physical at all. Now such a claim can be made to seem extremely plausible. For it would seem that the physicality of any physical thing must always form an essential part of our conception of that thing. (In contrast: the colouredness of any particular coloured thing — e.g. a pane of glass — need not form an essential part of our conception of that thing.)

The argument for thinking that all physical things are essentially physical is as follows. Firstly, we can make no sense of the idea that any particular physical object might not have been physical. We cannot conceive of any possible circumstances in which that object might have existed, only without being physical. Look at a particular chair, for instance, and try to think the thought 'This chair might have existed without being physical.' Can you do it? The best you can achieve is to imagine say a holograph of a chair, which would present you with a similar three-dimensional appearance of a chair without there really being anything physical there. But then of course a holograph of a chair is not a genuine chair. (In contrast, you can look at a particular piece of coloured glass and think 'This piece of glass might not have been coloured.' You just have to imagine the glass-maker forgetting to put in the dye when they made it.)

Secondly, we can make no sense of the idea that a particular physical object might cease to be physical without ceasing to exist. It cannot be intelligible that a particular chair might cease to be physical without ceasing to exist, because we have no conception of what, in that case, would make it true that there still exists that very same chair. (In contrast, a physical object can cease to have a colour without ceasing to exist. Think of a piece of coloured glass whose colour fades away. Here we have a clear conception of the conditions under which we should still be left with the very same piece of glass, rather than a substitute.)

It thus appears that the move from 'X is not essentially coloured' to 'X is not coloured' (which is, as we saw, obviously invalid) is really quite different from the move from 'X is not essentially physical' to 'X is not physical'. The latter move now appears to be justified, because the physicality of any physical thing must always form an essential part of our conception of the existence of that thing. So we have now done enough to establish dualism. We appear to have shown that I — the thinker — am not a physical thing.

Indeed I believe we may go further. For suppose we had reason to believe that everything has an essence: suppose that for every kind of thing there must be some property, or range of properties, which it possesses necessarily. Then it would be reasonable to conclude that I am an essentially thinking (or at least an essentially conscious) thing. For if I am not a physical thing, then I possess no physical attributes. In which case my essential attributes obviously cannot be physical ones. Then the only remaining candidates would be attributes of consciousness. (It is worth noting that this is what Descartes himself asserts: I am an essentially conscious thing, in exactly the sense in which a particular chair is an essentially physical — that is to say 'space-occupying' — thing. I thus could not have existed without being conscious, and I cannot wholly cease to be conscious without ceasing to exist.)

Is it true, then, that everything must have an essence? It would certainly appear so. For if there were some thing, every one of whose properties were contingent (non-necessary), then there would be possible worlds in which that thing exists without having any of those properties; and it would be logically possible that all those properties might change at once without the object ceasing to exist. But neither of these ideas is in fact intelligible.

Suppose that there were to exist an object X which possessed, contingently, just three properties: F, G and H. Now consider the possible world in which X is supposed to exist having only the properties I, J and K. What could make it true that it is X, rather than some quite different object, which exists in that world? No answer can be given. Similarly if we are told that X might instantaneously change from having the properties F, G and H to having the properties I, J and K. What could make it true that X would here have changed, rather than ceased to exist and been replaced by some quite different object? Again no answer can be given.

We shall return to some of these ideas in greater detail in

Chapter 3. But for the moment the moral of the story appears to be this: it is an essential part of our concept of an individual thing, that we should have a conception of what distinguishes one individual thing from others, and of what constitutes the continued existence of any one particular thing over time; and such conceptions would not be possible in connection with individual things which possessed no essential attributes. So it follows that all individual things must have an essence.

To summarise, the full argument for dualism runs as follows:

(1) It is logically possible that thinking (or experiencing) should occur while no physical thinker exists.

(2) It is not logically possible that thinking (or experiencing) should occur while no thinking thing exists.

(C1) So it is logically possible that thinking things are not physical things.

(3) All physical things are such that their physicality is a logically necessary attribute of them.

(C2) So (from (C1) and (3)) thinking things are not physical things.

(4) Every kind of thing must possess some essential (logically necessary) attributes.

(C3) So (from (C2) and (4)) thinking things are essentially thinking, or conscious, non-physical entities. That is to say: souls exist, and persons are souls.

Premiss (1) is established by the conceivability of disembodied thought and experience. Premiss (2) appears intuitively obvious: how could there be thoughts which are not thought by any thinker, or experiences which are not experienced by any experiencer? Premiss (3) was established by considering what is required for the existence of a particular chair. And premiss (4) is the thesis for which we have just been arguing. Then if the whole argument is valid, as it appears to be, we have constructed a proof of the existence of the soul.

(C) Immortality

If dualism is true then it is logically possible that I (my soul, my self) might survive the destruction of my body. So the above argument may be taken as a proof of the possibility of disembodied after-life. It is worth considering whether the argument can be strengthened still further. Is it possible for us to go on to prove that I shall in fact survive the destruction of my body? Can we develop the argument for dualism into a proof of the immortality of the soul? Some philosophers have thought so. They have believed that they could show the soul to be simple (not made up of parts), and that it follows from this that it must be indestructible. But in my view neither of these claims can be adequately defended.

Firstly, how are we supposed to establish that the soul is a simple (non-complex) entity? This certainly does not follow from the fact that it is a non-physical thing, and so is not (of course) made up out of physical parts. It is true that when we use the phrase 'composite object' in ordinary life, we naturally tend to think of such things as tables and chairs, which are made up out of physical parts standing in various spatial relations to one another. But 'composite' surely does not mean the same as 'made up of physical parts standing in some spatial relation to one another'. It simply means: 'made up of objects which could exist separately, but which presently stand in some sort of relation to one another'. So who knows? Perhaps a non-physical soul is made up of some arrangement of non-physical entities, in such a way that the dissolution of that arrangement would mean that the soul ceases to exist as such. There is certainly no way of ruling out such a possibility merely by reflecting on the concepts of 'soul' and of 'composite object'.

Secondly, even if souls were simple, why should it be supposed to follow from this that they must be immortal? For why should it be thought that the only possible way for an object to cease to exist is for it to be broken up into parts? The ideas of 'creation out of nothing' and 'destruction into nothing' are perfectly intelligible (not self-contradictory), even if a trifle mysterious. It is surely conceivable that I might have the magical ability to point my finger at any physical object (even a simple atom, if there are such things) pronouncing the words 'Away with you!', whereupon that object would cease to exist. And it would cease to exist not by being destroyed into its parts (for it may have no parts), but simply by disappearing out of existence. If this is conceivable, then it is logically possible for non-composite things to cease to exist. In which case even if the soul were simple it would not follow that it is immortal.

If it is true that the soul is immortal, then it will only be possible to know that it is on the basis of some sort of empirical evidence, or perhaps religious revelation. This is one area where philosophical argument cannot help us.

ii. Hume'n Bundles

In the last section we constructed what appeared to be a proof of the existence of the soul. However, some philosophers have challenged this and similar arguments at precisely the point where they appear most solid, namely the claim that thoughts require a thinker. They have argued that the sense of obviousness which attends this claim derives entirely from our commonsense beliefs about physical human beings: never to our knowledge have thoughts occurred in the absence of a human thinker. But of course this cannot show it to be logically impossible that this should happen. And in any case we had better not rely upon our beliefs about physical human beings, if we are trying to prove that the real subject of thoughts and experiences is a non-physical soul.

The foremost exponent of this line of objection to our argument was the Scottish philosopher David Hume. He made two points: firstly, all that can be immediately established on the basis of introspection is the extistence of conscious states and events themselves. When I 'look into' myself, I am aware of thoughts, experiences, feelings. I am not aware of any self which has or possesses these states. The self is not an item in consciousness. Secondly, the existence of a thinking, feeling self cannot be validly deduced from the occurrence of the thoughts and experiences of which we are aware.

The first point may be granted as obvious. It is the second claim which will occupy our attention throughout the remainder of this section. We shall consider three different arguments attempting to prove that conscious experiences necessarily require the existence of some conscious thing. Each tries to do this on the basis of the necessity of some more general principle. I shall argue that none is successful.

(A) Events

Many experiences belong to the category of event: they are happenings, changes which take place within the contents of consciousness. Then if we could show that an event must take place in (or to) some subject, we could argue thus:

(1) Experiences are conscious events.
(2) It is logically necessary that events occur in (or to) some subject or thing.

(C) So experiences require an experiencer.

Note that premiss (1) will state a necessary truth. For all propositions assigning something to its most general category (telling you what basic kind of thing it is) are necessary truths. Compare: red is a colour; tables are items of furniture; trees are plants.

Unfortunately for our purposes, premiss (2) is in fact false. Think of a flash of lightning for example. This is very definitely an event, a happening. But is there any individual thing which is the subject of the event? *Which* thing is it that flashes? The clouds? But they are rather the cause of the flash. The discharge of electricity? But an electrical discharge is itself an event (indeed plausibly the very same event as the flash of lightning). The air or region of space through which the lightning passes? But it sounds strange to speak of either of these as though it were an individual thing like a person or a house or a tree. It seems best to say that a flash of lightning is an event without a subject. In which case it does not follow, from the mere fact that a conscious mental event takes place, that there must exist some subject of that event.

(B) Attributes

Even more fundamental than the category of event, are the categories of property and attribute (I shall treat these as roughly equivalent). An event is, as we said, a change. And for a change to take place is for there to be at an earlier time one attribute, and then for there to be at some later time a different attribute. For example, think of a light going off. At one moment the light has the property of being on, and then at the next moment it is off. But for the light to be either on or off are states or properties of it. They are not themselves changes, although there may be changes underlying them (e.g. the movement of electricity through a filament).

Now we might wonder whether it is not a necessary truth that an attribute requires a subject. For what *is* an attribute, but a property *of* something? We could then argue as follows.

(1) Some states of consciousness are properties, or attributes.
(2) Any attribute must be an attribute of some subject or thing.
(C) So some states of consciousness require the existence of a conscious subject, or self.

But here again, premiss (2) is in fact false (or at least is not true in a way which enables us to derive the conclusion). Think of what is being said by a statement like 'It is cloudy'. Cloudiness seems definitely to be a property or attribute. It is not itself a change, although there may be changes underlying it (i.e. millions of water-droplets travelling across the sky). But what is the cloudiness an attribute of? The only two candidates are: a region of space (e.g. the sky above Belfast), or a period of time (e.g. this afternoon). But again it seems strange to think of either of these as if they were some sort of individual thing.

The general point is that properties appear not only to figure in genuine subject/predicate statements ('The pavement is wet', 'Mary is tall') but also in discourse which is merely 'feature-placing' ('It is raining', 'It is cloudy', etc.). So again it does not follow, from the mere fact that there occur conscious states, or conscious attributes, that there must exist some conscious subject who possesses them.

Now it is true that, on the face of it, statements attributing conscious states to oneself seem to be of genuine subject/predicate form. (Consider: 'I am in pain', 'I am thinking of mother.') But here Hume can set us a dilemma, demanding to know what the word 'I' is intended to refer to. If on the one hand it refers to my body, then the statements will indeed be of genuine subject/predicate form. But then they will be useless to figure in an argument for dualism. For the dualist believes that conscious states are not states of the body, but rather of the soul. If on the other hand the word 'I' is intended to refer to my soul, then again we shall have a statement of genuine subject/predicate form. But then I shall not be in a position to know these statements to be true, until I know that I really do have a soul. Yet that is just what we are trying to prove.

The most that we can be aware of on the basis of introspection is that pains and thoughts are taking place. So perhaps we ought properly to restrict ourselves, in the present context (that is: attempting to provide a proof of dualism) to statements of the form: 'It hurts', and 'A thought of mother is presently occurring.' Then these will be genuinely analogous to mere feature-placing discourse. (Of course I have no objection if someone wants to insist that a region of space is the subject of the property of being cloudy, or if they want to insist that because cloudiness does not have a subject it is not a genuine attribute. For then it will only follow, either that the 'subject' of thoughts and experiences may be something like a region of space (which is of course not the sort of thing which we think a conscious soul, or self, should be); or that states of consciousness may not be genuine attributes.)

On Hume's view, the most that we have reason to believe on the basis of data available to introspection, is the existence of the stream of consciousness itself. We have no reason to believe in any underlying subject or self in which, or to which, the stream occurs. On the contrary, the mind is to be compared to a thunderstorm. Here is an immensely complicated sequence of events and states: the clouds and the gathering darkness; the rain and the hail; the rolls of thunder and the flashes of lightning. These stand in many complex relations to one another: some occur simultaneously, some at different times; some are near to one another in space, some further apart; some are causes or effects of one another, others are causally independent. But there is no substantial subject, no individual thing, in which the thunderstorm occurs. A thunderstorm does not have a subject. All that exists is a particular bundle of meteorological states and events. Similarly then, the mind is simply a bundle or collection of conscious states and events. This is sometimes called 'the no-self view' of consciousness, or more simply 'the bundle theory'.

(C) Actions

It might seem that we stand a better chance of finding an argument against Hume if we confine ourselves to a particular class of mental event, namely those belonging to the category of action. Thinking, imagining and judging all appear to be conscious activities. Now how could an action occur without an actor? For what distinguishes an action (e.g. kicking a football) from a mere event (e.g. someone turning over in their sleep), if not that an action is an event which is intentionally brought about by an agent? Then it seems we may construct the following argument:

(1) Thinking (or imagining, or judging) is a conscious activity.
(2) It is impossible for a action to occur in the absence of an acting subject.
(C) So at least some conscious states require the existence of a conscious subject, or self.

Since this argument is valid, everything will turn on the truth of the premises.

Hume might challenge premiss (1), demanding how we are to

know that thinking is an activity. You may reply that this is just obvious: for what else could it be? But he might say that this sense of obviousness derives entirely from our commonsense beliefs about (physical) human beings. We are accustomed to distinguish between things which happen to a human being ('Mary is injured', 'Mary is in pain') and things which a human being does ('Mary is talking', 'Mary is kicking a football'). And of course we should normally place thinking in the latter category. Yet as before, we had better not rely upon our ordinary beliefs about human beings if our objective is to prove the existence of a non-physical soul. All we should allow ourselves to take for granted is what we can be immediately aware of: the character of our own conscious states.

But now we are in difficulty. For in order to be able to know on the basis of introspection that thinking should be classified as an activity ('a change intentionally brought about by an agent') we should have to be aware, not just of the change, but also of the agent (and perhaps also the bringing about). Yet as we saw earlier, the most that we are in fact aware of is that a certain thought takes place. We are not in addition aware of a particular self which has the thought, or which does the thinking. So perhaps the most that we are entitled to believe is that a thought, like the onset of a head-ache, is a conscious event or change.

Hume might also challenge premiss (2). He might deny that actions necessarily require actors, by denying that the concept of an action is the concept of a change intentionally brought about by an agent. He might claim instead, that what distinguishes an action from a mere event is its distinctive causal history in prior conscious states. Perhaps an action is an event which is caused by beliefs and desires. Thus what caused the kicking of the football will have been a particular desire (to win the game) combined with some particular beliefs (that this is the appropriate moment to kick). Whereas what caused the person to turn over in their sleep will not have been any conscious beliefs or desires. If this were correct, then there would be nothing in the concept of an action, as such, to imply the existence of some acting thing or subject.

In fact the proposed definition is inadequate as it stands. Firstly, not everything caused by beliefs and desires is an action. My belief that I am about to be shot, combined with my desire to stay alive, may cause me to have a heart-attack; but the heart-attack is not itself an action of mine. Secondly, not all actions are caused by beliefs and desires. Suppose that I am sitting idly twiddling my thumbs. The twiddling is an intentional activity alright, but it is not being done for any reason. I do not twiddle *for* anything — because I believe this and want that — rather I just twiddle.

All the same, it is hard to be confident that no adequate analysis of the concept of action can be provided along these lines. There is certainly no easy way of proving that the distinction between actions and mere events cannot be defined in terms of the causal connections between the event which is the action, and other mental states and events: beliefs, desires, thoughts, decisions. In which case there is no easy way of showing, against Hume, that the concept of an action has to bring with it the notion of an acting subject, or agent.

Conclusion

All our attempts to demonstrate that conscious states necessarily require the existence of a conscious self, in terms of the necessity of some more general principle ('an event requires a subject', 'an attribute requires a possessor', 'an act requires an actor'), have been a failure. So the only remaining possibility is that there is something peculiar to conscious states themselves which implies that they cannot exist in the absence of a conscious subject or self. In the next section we shall investigate this possibility, by seeing whether or not we can show the Humean bundle theory to be a necessary falsehood. If the 'no-self view' of consciousness cannot be true, then the 'some-self view' must be.

iii. Against the Bundle Theory

If we are to prove the existence of the soul, then we must show that the mind cannot merely be a bundle of conscious states and events (in the way that a thunderstorm is in fact a mere bundle of meteorological states and events). We must show that, on the contrary, there must exist some self which is their subject. And since we are trying to prove the existence of a non-physical self, we should not rely upon any of our commonsense beliefs about physical human beings. Rather we may take for granted only the data immediately available to introspection. In this section I shall present the three main traditional objections to the bundle theory. The first fails, but the second and third are conclusive.

(A) Singular Conscious States

If the mind is merely a bundle of states and events, then it must be logically possible for the various elements of the bundle to exist on their own. It is logically possible for a bolt of lightning to strike out of a clear blue sky, in the absence of any of the other events which normally go to make up a thunderstorm. It is even possible that the universe might have contained nothing except this one event. There is a possible world which consists only of a single flash of lightning. So is it similarly possible for a single pain to occur independently of any mind (i.e. for the Humean, independently of any bundle)? Is it logically possible for all organic life to be extinguished in a nuclear holocaust, and yet a single headache goes on? Is there a possible world which contains nothing whatever except this: a single pain?

We have no difficulty conceiving of a world which contains nothing except a single flash of lightning. But a world which contains nothing except a single headache seems, on the face of it, to be *in*conceivable. For how could a unitary pain 'hang around all by itself' as it were? Yet the Humean may respond that our difficulty only arises because we are trying to imagine the pain, like the lightning, from a standpoint outside it. Of course you do not know what to imagine if you are asked to conceive of someone else's pain existing in the absence of any physical body, and so in the absence of any perceptible manifestation of that pain. But it may be different in the case of one of your own pains.

Consider the following example. You are lying on the dentist's couch, having a tooth worked on without the benefit of an anaesthetic. The drill strikes a nerve, causing you intense pain, but the dentist does not stop. In a case like this the pain can come to flood your whole consciousness. Its intensity may leave no room for any other thought or idea. You may cease to be aware of your own body, perhaps even ceasing to be aware of the sound of the drill. There might simply be nothing that you are aware of except this: an intense pain. If you are asked to imagine a world which contains only a single pain, then imagine a pain like this, only without the story about the dentist and the drill. Imagine to yourself a pain which floods the whole of consciousness, unaccompanied by any other conscious states, and frame to yourself the thought 'and nothing else exists besides this'.

It seems that a single pain, like a single flash of lightning, really can be imagined to exist on its own. However, the case of many other conscious states may be different, particularly those involving the use of concepts, such as beliefs, thoughts and judgements. Could there be a world which contains nothing besides the occurrence of a particular thought, say the thought that money does not grow on trees? I suggest not. For what would make this thought be about money, or about trees? And what would give it the structure which it has? (E.g. what would make it different from the thought that trees do not grow on money?)

The point will emerge most clearly if we consider a public act of thinking: a public saying. Imagine Tarzan brought up by the apes in the jungle. He never learns a language, but on just one occasion — out of the blue — he utters an English sentence. He says 'Money does not grow on trees.' So far the story is imaginable, if unlikely. (Just as it is imaginable that an ape tapping randomly at a typewriter might produce the sentences 'To be or not to be? That is the question.') But can we also imagine that Tarzan means what he says? I claim not. For someone only means something by uttering a sequence of sounds, against a background of linguistic capacities. Only someone who is capable of using the words 'money' and 'tree' in other contexts and in other combinations, and who is capable of identifying money and trees when they see them, can mean that money does not grow on trees. (This is the reason why a parrot does not mean what it says: because it is not capable of using its words in other combinations, and in application to reality.)

What is true at the level of language is true at the level of thoughts and beliefs as well. Someone can only have the thought, or the belief, that money does not grow on trees, against a background of conceptual capacities and other beliefs. They must be capable of using those concepts in other thoughts, and must be able to tell the difference between trees and other things. They must believe that money is a conventional means of exchange, that trees are plants, that growth is part of the life-cycle of living organisms, and so on. A thought is only a thought within a conceptual system. A belief is only a belief within a network of other beliefs. Neither thoughts nor beliefs can occur singly, but only in groups.

Hume might concede these points, but deny that it follows that there must be some underlying self who possesses the network of beliefs and thoughts. Consider, by analogy, a move in a game of chess. A particular physical event — e.g. the moving of a pawn forward one space — is only a move in a game against a background of other similar events. If I simply walk up to a chess-board one day and move a pawn, leaving the board forever after untouched, then I have not made a move in a game. Moves in games, like thoughts, cannot occur singly but only in groups. For they only acquire their significance *as* moves within the wider context in which they occur. But of course it does not follow from this that there must be some individual thing ('the game') in which the moves occur. For the game itself is not a thing. It is, like a thunderstorm, merely a complex arrangement of states and events, in which things participate.

Hume could also concede that thoughts and beliefs are only possible against an enduring background of conceptual capacities, but deny that it follows from this that there must be some underlying self who possesses those capacities. He need only say that the mind is a bundle of conscious and unconscious states and events, where some of the unconscious states are enduring conceptual capacities, which are exercised in acts of thinking. For compare: a weather-system, too, may have capacities. At a particular time it may be capable of hailing. That is to say: if certain other things happen (e.g. a drop in temperature) then it will hail. But of course there is no enduring thing in which the capacities of a weather-system reside.

Our first line of objection against the bundle theory has been a failure. Many conscious states can indeed be imagined to exist on their own. And there is no obvious objection to the theory arising out of the necessary interconnectedness of many other conscious states, nor out of the dependence of many of these states upon unconscious capacities.

(B) The Unity of Consciousness

What binds together the bundle? What makes it true that a particular thought or experience is a member of one bundle rather than another? There are in fact two rather different questions here, one relating to the unity of consciousness over time (i.e. what makes my experiences today and my experiences last week part of the same stream of consciousness?) and one relating to the unity of consciousness at a time (i.e. what makes my visual experiences now and my auditory experiences now part of the same bundle or mind?). If we can solve the latter problem then I can see no particular difficulty about solving the former. If we can sort mental states into discrete bundles at any one time, then I can see no real difficulty in keeping track of those bundles over a period of time. (See section 3.ii for some ideas as to how such tracking might be done.) I shall thus concentrate upon the latter problem: what binds together the elements of consciousness at any particular time, giving it its characteristic unity?

Hume's own account is provided in terms of the notions of resemblance and causality. In his view it is the resemblance of the different conscious states to one another, and the causal relations between them, which binds them together into a single bundle. Now this might stand some chance of success as an account of the unity of consciousness over time, but is obviously hopeless as an account of the unity of consciousness at any particular time. For there will often be neither resemblance nor causal connection between the various elements in consciousness at any given time.

For example, think of someone whose ingrowing toe-nail is causing them pain at the same time as they listen to a Beethoven sonata. There is obviously not the slightest resemblance between the pain and the sound of the sonata. Nor is there any causal relationship between them. On the contrary, both are directly caused by external physical events, in the one case tissue-damage in the toe, in the other a physical stimulus to the ear-drums.

Moreover, the use of resemblance as a criterion will bundle together experiences in quite the wrong way. Imagine two people, Mary and Joan, each of whom is examining a modern painting. Mary is looking at a painting whose left half is red, and whose right half is blue. Joan is looking at a painting which is the reverse: its right half is red and its left half is blue. Now the experience making up the left side of Mary's visual field will resemble the experiences making up the right side of Joan's visual field much more closely than they resemble the right side of her own visual field. If we were to rely upon resemblance to bundle together experiences, then we should have to say that there is one consciousness here containing a uniform visual field of an experience of red, and another containing a uniform visual field of an experience of blue. And of course this would be absurd.

Hume's best response to these difficulties would be to give up any appeal to resemblance and causality, and to appeal instead to certain 'higher-order' states of consciousness. Thus when Mary looks at the painting there is not merely an awareness of red and an awareness of blue. There is also an awareness that there is a simultaneous awareness of both red and blue. Similarly with the suffering sonata-lover: there is not merely an awareness of pain in the toe and an awareness of the sound of the piano. There is also the second-order awareness: that there is an awareness of pain which is simultaneous with an awareness of sound.

So Hume should say that what binds together the bundle of states of consciousness is: other states of consciousness. For consciousness is not merely a collection of discrete thoughts and experiences. It also contains second-order states of consciousness, namely states of awareness of the simultaneous presence of the various first-order states of consciousness. Then what makes an experience X part of the same bundle (the same mind) as a simultaneous experience Y, will be the presence of a third state of consciousness Z, caused by X and Y, which takes the form of an awareness that there is a simultaneous occurrence of X and Y.

Construed in this way the bundle theory is not altogether implausible. However, there remains a decisive objection: not all states of consciousness belonging to the same mind are in fact united by higher-order states of awareness. In which case the only remaining explanation of what makes all these states belong to the same mind is that they are all states of the same person or self. What makes consciousness a unity is not any of the relations existing between the conscious states themselves, but rather the fact that they all belong to the same individual thing.

For example, suppose that I am listening to a Beethoven sonata while thinking about the nature of the self. I may be aware of the music, and aware of what I am thinking, without being aware of what I am simultaneously hearing and thinking. I may in fact hear the music reach a crescendo at the same time as I think 'There is a distinction between strong and weak dualism.' But I may not be aware that the experience of the crescendo and the thinking of that thought are simultaneous with one another. Looking back afterwards I may recall the sequence of the music, and recall the sequence of my thoughts, without in any way being able to correlate the two sequences. So what is it which makes both the experience and the thought part of the same mind, if not that they are both states possessed by the same underlying person or self? (Note that neither resemblance nor causality can be of any help here. For there is no resemblance, and there is no causal relation.)

Hume's last resort is to appeal to the mere possibility of second-order awareness. He may say that what binds together the elements of consciousness is the *capacity* for there to be an awareness that all of them are occurring simultaneously. For even if I am not at the moment aware that I currently possess both experience X and experience Y, I *can* be aware of it. And this may be sufficient to make both of those experiences part of the same bundle of consciousness.

But in fact it may not always be possible to have such a second-order awareness. For example, it may be that if I had tried to maintain a simultaneous awareness of both my train of thought and the sequence of the music, that I could not have had that train of thought. It may be that I was incapable of being aware that my experience of the crescendo was simultaneous with my thought about the distinction between strong and weak dualism, because had I tried to have such an awareness, I could not have thought that thought.

I conclude that the bundle theory must be false, because it is incapable of explaining how all of a person's conscious states come to be part of a single mind. In fact what makes them all part of the same bundle is that they are all possessed by the same individual self.

(C) The Particularity of Conscious States

On the Humean view, minds are *constructs* out of thoughts and experiences, since particular minds are merely bundles of particular conscious states. If this is so, then our notion of the particularity of any given particular conscious state (what makes that state the individual state which it is) must be logically prior to our notion of the particularity of any given particular mind. What makes an individual mind be the individual mind which it is, will be the fact that it is made up out of the individual conscious states which make it up. ('Same conscious states' implies 'same mind'; 'different conscious states' implies 'different mind'.)

I shall argue that this order of priority is in fact the wrong way round. We have a concept of persons (minds) as distinct individual things, and distinct (though exactly similar) experiences are distinguished precisely because they are the experiences of two distinct persons. We do not, and cannot, first establish that we are dealing with two distinct but exactly similar experiences, and then settle the question whether those experiences belong to two distinct minds or only one. On the contrary, the question 'Are there two exactly similar experiences here, or only one?' can only be answered in terms of whether or not the experiences belong to two different experiencing things, or only one.

For example, consider a case where two siamese twins each feel pain in the place where they join. Suppose that they are joined back-to-back, and that they both feel an exactly similar pain in the centre of their back. Now we provide the Humean with a complete list of their thoughts and experiences, demanding that they be sorted into bundles. What we want to know is whether the two twins constitute a single mind (a single bundle), or two distinct minds (bundles).

The list might go something like this: there is a pain in the back, a thought about the weather, an awareness that there is a pain in the back simultaneous with a thought of the weather, a pain in the back, a thought about Mozart, an awareness that there is a pain in the back simultaneous with a thought about Mozart, and so on. Now the Humean will need to know whether the same pain gets mentioned twice over in this list (in which case we shall be dealing with a single bundle or mind) or whether the two occurrences of the phrase 'a pain in the back' refer to two distinct pains (in which case we shall be dealing with two distinct bundles or minds). But in fact there is no way for this issue to be decided. Not only does the Humean have no way of telling whether there are two pains or only one, they can surely have no conception of what might constitute the fact of the matter, one way or the other.

Of course what we should say, is that there are two pains if there are two persons, and that there is only one pain if there is only one person. We should treat questions of identity and distinctness amongst pains as depending upon questions of identity and distinctness amongst persons. Then since we should certainly say that the two siamese twins are two distinct persons, we shall say that we are dealing with two distinct (though exactly similar) pains, rather than with only one. The particularity of persons is thus prior to the particularity of experiences, rather than (as Hume would have it) vice versa.

The conclusion of this argument is that minds cannot be mere bundles of conscious states, because we can have no conception of the particularity of conscious states prior to, and independently of, a conception of the particularity of persons. The only way in which we can distinguish and identify particular conscious states is by first distinguishing and identifying the persons (selves) who possess them.

iv. Difficulties with Dualism

In the last section we refuted the bundle theory of the mind. Conscious states, unlike meteorological states, can only exist as the states of some underlying individual thing: a person or self. So we have fought off the Humean challenge to the argument of section 2.i. That argument has survived intact, apparently providing us with a proof of the existence of the soul.

In this section I shall consider some of the traditional objections to dualism. If they were accepted, then we should be forced to look again at the argument of 2.i. (Remember it is impossible to have a proof of a false conclusion. So if dualism were false, then there would have to be something wrong with the argument: either one of the premises must be false, or the argument itself must somehow be invalid.) But in fact I shall show that these objections are less than conclusive. They may make dualism hard to believe, but they do not refute it.

(A) The Soul Asleep

One traditional objection has been this: if it is of the essence of the soul to be conscious, then what are we to say about sleep? If conscious attributes are necessary to the existence of the soul, in the way that physical and spatial attributes are necessary to the existence of the body, then what is to become of the soul during sleep? For we all believe that although sleep may contain periods of dreaming, it also contains a number of periods of unconsciousness. If I (my self) am a soul (an essentially conscious thing), then how is it possible for me to exist in a state of complete unconsciousness?

There are at least two possible lines of reply that a dualist can take. Firstly they might reject as false the claim that a person is ever really unconscious. They may insist that the soul (the person) is always in fact thinking or experiencing throughout its existence, maintaining that the appearance to the contrary merely arises from the fact that some periods of consciousness are much easier to remember than others. On this view, what we call 'sleep' or 'unconsciousness' are really periods in consciousness about which nothing can later be remembered, or which can only be remembered imperfectly (what we call 'dreams').

This view is certainly a possible one. Moreover it is exceedingly difficult to refute. If you think you know that you are sometimes unconscious, then reflect for a moment upon whether you could convince someone who believes otherwise. Certainly there are periods of your life — some of them fairly recent — about which you now remember nothing. But how do you know that this is because there really was nothing to remember (you were unconscious) rather than that you have merely forgotten it? It seems that your memory (or lack of it) is not by itself sufficient proof that you are ever unconscious. But then neither can you directly verify that you are ever unconscious. For of course if you really are unconscious, then you are in no position to verify anything.

In fact we all do believe, for whatever reason, that we are sometimes completely unconscious. But if the dualist chooses to believe otherwise, then it is hard to see how we can prove them wrong. Moreover, if it came to a straight choice between belief in dualism and belief in periodic unconsciousness, then it seems we should give up the latter, no matter how counter-intuitive this might seem at first. For in support of dualism we have an extremely convincing argument. Whereas it is not obvious that we have anything at all to support of our belief in unconscious existence.

A second line of response for the dualist would be to allow that periods of unconsciousness do occur, and to allow that during these periods no soul exists. They need only claim that the soul, like some kinds of physical object, can have intermittent existence; claiming that one and the same soul can survive across periods of non-existence.

An example will make clear what I mean. Suppose that you are the owner of an expensive motorcycle, of which you are hugely fond. Fearing for its theft, it is your practice when going on holiday to dismantle it as completely as you can, leaving the parts spread around your attic and garage wrapped in oily rags. Then when you return from holiday you reassemble it again just as it was. Now during the time you are away there exists no motorcycle. For a collection of unrelated motorcycle parts no more constitutes a motorcycle than a pile of bricks and a bag of cement constitutes a house. Yet when you reassemble the parts, you rebuild your original machine, rather than construct a new one. If you continue your practice for five years, going on holiday each year, then you have during that time owned only one motorcycle, not five.

This is what I mean by intermittent existence: one and the same motorcycle exists at the end of the five-year period as existed at the beginning, although during part of that time no motorcycle existed at all. It is thus open to the dualist to say that the soul, too, has intermittent existence, ceasing to exist during periods of uncon-sciousness. (In section 3.ii we shall develop in more detail a concep-tion of soul-identity which would make such a view possible.)

Now again this conflicts with something which we are all intuitively inclined to believe. We all tend to believe that during periods of unconsciousness we continue to exist. But how do we know? For while we are unconscious we are of course in no position to know whether or not we still exist. And after we are conscious once again, we seem to lack any positive evidence either way. So here, too, if it came to a straight choice between our belief in dualism and our belief in our own continuous existence, it seems that it is the latter which should give way.

(B) The Relation between Body and Soul

The other main traditional objections to dualism have concerned the kind of relation which is supposed to exist between body and soul. Notice to begin with that the soul cannot literally be in the body. For since the soul is non-physical it cannot literally occupy any position is space. Only physical objects (together with spatial lines and points themselves) can occupy spatial positions. Thus consider for instance the number 9. This object — if there really is such an object — is certainly not physical. And as a result it makes no sense to speak of it occupying a particular place (nor indeed all places). Sentences like 'The number 9 is in London' are obviously nonsensical.

The soul is only metaphorically 'in' a particular body. The literal truth, for the dualist, is this: I am 'in' my body in the sense that it is only via that body that I can engage in causal commerce with the rest of the physical world. As a matter of fact there is only one body (my body) which I can cause to move around the world just by thinking about it: by forming intentions and making decisions. And as a matter of fact my experience of the world only comes to me via its effects upon that very same body. So the relationship between my soul and my body is causal, not spatial.

(C) Interactions in Principle

Now this is where the difficulties start. For how is it possible for soul and body to have causal effects upon one another? How can a non-physical, non-spatial, soul interact causally with a physical, space-occupying, body? Certainly not by bumping into it. Nor can the soul affect (nor be affected by) the body magnetically, electrically or chemically. For all of these kinds of causal relation can only be entered into by physical objects and states. So how is it supposed to happen? It appears that there must be some kind of radical 'quantum leap' between the last event in the causal chain of mental events (a thought causing another thought, causing a decision) and the first event in the causal chain of physical events (one particular brain cell firing off an electro-chemical impulse to another). Many have found it unintelligible how anything could ever bridge this gap, and have concluded that the whole idea of soul/body interaction is unintelligible (i.e. impossible).

The dualist should reply that a causal connection does not have to be intelligible (in the sense of being explicable in terms of some other kind of causal connection) in order to be real. Consider the force of gravity for instance. In the manner of the above objection to dualism, we might demand to know how it is *possible* for massive bodies to attract one another with a force inversely proportional to the square of the distance between them. It seems we cannot provide a model for this form of causal interaction in terms of anything more basic. (Perhaps physicists now can, I don't know.) Certainly the bodies are not pulled towards one another by invisible elastic bands. Yet for all that, we are sure that the causal connection exists.

The general point is that at any given stage in the development of science there will always be some kinds of causal connection which have to be treated as basic, being inexplicable in other terms. So it is open to the dualist to claim that the causal connections between soul and body fall into just this category.

It seems that all that is really required, in order for there to be a causal connection between two particular events, e and f, is that those events should belong to two event-kinds, E and F, which are governed by the universal law: whenever an event of type E occurs, then so does an event of type F (so long as the law is sufficiently strong to warrant counter-factual claims: if e had not happened, then f would not have happened either). Thus if we believe that the taking of a cyanide pill caused Mary's death, then we must believe that there is some general description of the first event (the ingestion of such-and-such quantities of cyanide by a person with such-and-such bodily constitution) and some general description of the second event (death), such that events of the first kind are invariably followed by events of the second.

But now this might seem to play into the hands of the opponent of dualism. For the fact is, we just do not possess such general laws when it comes to mind/body interaction. The most plausible candidate for such a law would be this: whenever someone has decided, all things considered, that doing X right now would be the best thing to do in the circumstances, then they will do X. Yet this runs up against the familiar phenomenon of weakness of will. It is a disturbing fact of human experience that someone may after deliberation decide that the best thing to do in the circumstances would be X rather than Y, and then go ahead and do Y all the same. I may decide not to have another chocolate, and then the very next moment, without apparently changing my mind, reach out and take one.

The dualist has a reply to this too. It is that we often have reason to believe in the existence of a causal relation in a particular case, prior to the discovery of any general law. For example, this is very likely our situation in the case of a death caused by cyanide. I very much doubt whether scientists know of any precise law correlating quantities of cyanide and bodily constitution with resulting death. Yet for all that we may be certain, in the particular case, that Mary's death was caused by cyanide. So the dualist may defend the reasonableness of our belief in the causal connections between mind and body in particular cases (of course a decision will sometimes cause a bodily movement; and of course a thorn in the flesh will sometimes cause a sensation of pain), despite our ignorance of any universal causal laws connecting the two. Perhaps such laws will one day be discovered.

(D) Interactions in Fact

So far dualism has survived our attack unscathed. There is nothing unintelligible in principle in the idea of causal interaction between soul and body. And our ignorance of any strict causal laws governing such interactions need not make it unreasonable for us to believe in them in particular cases. But now the dualist faces a rather more specific difficulty, premised upon the way in which most of us expect the future of neuro-physiological science to develop. It is this: we may have to give up believing that our thoughts and decisions constitute the true causal explanations of many of our physical movements.

Imagine a scientist trying to trace the causal antecedents of a particular type of bodily movement, say a wiggling of my left big toe. They have, let us suppose, traced the immediate causes in the contraction of the muscles of the foot, and the causes of that in the activity of certain nerve-cells in the left leg and spinal cord. It is conceivable that when they trace the causal chain back up into events in the brain, there might come a point where the causation just runs out into the sand as it were. They might discover a particular type of brain-event which has no discoverable causal antecedents in earlier brain-events; yet these events happen at times when the subject would report having made a decision to wiggle their big toe. Then the best overall explanation would be that it is here, at this point, that an event in the soul causes an event in the body.

However, we surely don't really expect that things will turn out like this. Do we not expect that the causal chain of bodily events being caused by other bodily events will turn out to be unbroken? Are we not confident that every item of cellular activity will ultimately be causally explicable in terms of some prior physical stimulus? Then it seems likely that the dualist will be left in the absurd position of having to deny that our decisions — construed as non-physical events in a non-physical soul — are ever really the causes of our physical movements.

They may try to get around the difficulty by appealing to the notion of 'causal over-determination'. Very roughly, this is the idea that an event may have more causes than are necessary. For example, imagine someone being shot by a firing squad, each member of which has a loaded gun (contrary to normal practice). Suppose that every soldier's aim is true, that all fire at the same time, and that every bullet strikes the heart. Then it is true of every soldier that even if the others had not fired, their action would have caused the prisoner's death. (Each shot individually is causally sufficient.) But it is also true of every soldier that even if they themselves had not fired, the prisoner's death would still have been caused by the others. (No shot individually is causally necessary.) Similarly then: the dualist may propose that brain-events are caused both by prior brain-events (so the chain of physical causes is unbroken) and by prior mental events; where either type of event on its own is sufficient to produce the effect, but neither type of event on its own is necessary.

By deploying the thesis of causal over-determination, a dualist can hold on to one aspect of our commonsense beliefs in face of the likely discovery of unbroken causal chains of brain-events. Namely: the belief that our decisions are sometimes, in the circumstances, sufficient to bring about a bodily movement. Yet one aspect of commonsense would also have to be given up. Namely: the belief that a decision is sometimes causally necessary for a bodily movement to occur. We should no longer be able to claim that had the subject not decided in a certain way, then the bodily movement would not have taken place. On the contrary it would still have occurred, brought about by its other cause: a particular brain-event. But are we really prepared to give up this belief? Do I not believe almost as firmly as I believe anything, that if I had not decided to write this book (mental event) I should not now be typing at this keyboard (physical event)?

There is a way for the dualist to avoid this difficulty. They can claim that each mental event will be correlated with a particular brain-event as a matter of causal necessity. In that case it will be causally impossible for the mental event to occur without the corresponding brain-event occurring, the true picture looking something like this:

Mental event

↑   ↑

Brain-event 1 → Brain-event 2 → Bodily movement

Then it will be true that if I had not decided to write this book, I should not now be typing. For the only way in which I could have failed to take that decision, would have been if the corresponding brain-event had failed to occur; and if that had failed to occur, then the bodily movement would not have been caused.

Although a theory of this sort can save our belief that certain of our bodily movements would not have occurred if certain decisions had not been taken, it does so at the cost of explanatory redundancy. For the decision is no longer part of the true explanation of why the bodily movement took place. To say that our decisions are causally correlated with the events which cause our bodily movements, is not the same as saying (what we intuitively believe) that our decisions themselves constitute their true causal explanations.

It seems likely, then, that a dualist will end up having to deny some of our commonsense beliefs about the relation between mind and body. But I doubt whether this is by itself sufficient reason for declaring that dualism must be false. For once again, if the dualist challenges us to provide an argument in support of commonsense which will be equally as strong as the argument for dualism, then it is doubtful whether we shall be able to reply.

Conclusion

What has emerged in this section is that the dualist will either have to deny that we are ever really unconscious, or deny that our existence is continuous throughout our lives. And it seems likely that they may also have to deny that our decisions are ever the true explanations of our behaviour. These consequences may be counter-intuitive, but they are by no means sufficiently so to warrant the rejection of dualism.

Questions and Readings

You may like to discuss/think about/write about some of the following questions:

(1) Try to imagine, in as much detail as you can, what disembodied existence might be like. How would you know, on the basis of your experience, that you were really disembodied?
(2) How convincing do you find the argument for the existence of the soul? What, in your view, is its weakest point?
(3) Is there anything in the nature of conscious experience which implies the existence of some underlying self which has those experiences?
(4) How much reason is there to think that all physical events have physical causes?
(5) How much reason is there to think that your decisions are sometimes the true explanation of your behaviour?

In thinking about the questions above, you might like to consult a selection of the following readings (capitalised names refer to collections of papers listed in the Bibliography):

David Armstrong, *A Materialist Theory of the Mind* (London: Routledge and Kegan Paul, 1968), Ch. 2.
Paul Churchland, *Matter and Consciousness* (Mass: MIT Press, 1984), Ch. 2, section 1.
René Descartes, 'Meditations on First Philosophy', 1 & 2, in *Descartes: Philosophical Writings*, E. Anscombe and P. Geach (eds.) (London: Thomas Nelson, 1954).
Peter Geach, *Mental Acts* (London: Routledge and Kegan Paul, 1957), sections 25 and 26. Reprinted in MORICK [1] and FLEW.

David Hume, 'Of Personal Identity', *A Treatise of Human Nature*, Bk. 1, Pt. iv, sect. vi (Oxford: Oxford University Press, 1888). Reprinted in PERRY, MORICK [2] and FLEW.

Norman Malcolm, 'Descartes's Proof that his Essence is Thinking', *Philosophical Review*, vol. LXXIV (1965). Reprinted in *Descartes*, Willis Doney (ed.) (London: Macmillan, 1967).

Norman Malcolm, *Problems of Mind* (London: Allen & Unwin, 1972), Ch. 1.

John Passmore, *Philosophical Reasoning* (London: Duckworth, 1961), Ch. 3.

Jerome Shaffer, *The Philosophy of Mind* (Englewood Cliffs: Prentice Hall, 1968), Ch. 3.

Sidney Shoemaker, 'On an Argument for Dualism', *Knowledge and Mind*, C. Ginet and S. Shoemaker (eds.) (Oxford: Oxford University Press, 1983). Reprinted in SHOEMAKER.

Sidney Shoemaker, *Self-knowledge and Self-identity* (Cornell: Cornell University Press, 1963), Ch. 2.

Peter Strawson, 'Persons', *Individuals* (London: Methuen, 1959), Ch. 3. Reprinted in CHAPPELL, GUSTAFSON, MORICK [1] and MORICK [2].

Richard Swinburne, 'A Dualistic Theory', *Personal Identity*, by S. Shoemaker and R. Swinburne (Oxford: Blackwell, 1984).

3   IDENTITY AND THE SOUL

i. The Concept of Identity

Our task in this chapter is to investigate in more detail the dualist conception of the soul as an individually existing thing, whose existence is independent of the existence of the body. We shall consider what answers a dualist might give to two related questions: (1) Under what conditions would a particular disembodied soul after my death be my soul? (2) What would fundamentally distinguish different disembodied souls from one another? Question (1) will form the topic of section ii, and question (2) will form the topic of section iii. But since they both in fact involve the concepts of identity and distinctness, we shall begin by trying to elucidate these. There are a number of points and distinctions to be introduced. Some of them may seem insignificant, but will later turn out to be of the highest importance. (Indeed our ultimate objective will be to construct, in section iii, a proof of the non-existence of the soul.)

(A) Qualitative vs Numerical Identity

Notice to begin with that there are two very different kinds of use of the words 'same' and 'identical'. Thus the question 'Is this the same car as was involved in the robbery?' is easily seen to be ambiguous. Is it being asked whether the car in question is similar to (is of exactly the same kind as) the one which was involved in the robbery? Or is it being asked whether it is the very same car? I propose to use the terms 'qualitative identity' (or 'qualitative sameness') and 'numerical identity' (or 'numerical sameness') to mark this distinction.

Qualitative identity has to do with similarities between a number of different objects, or between different temporal stages in the life of the very same object. It is this notion which is involved in the statements 'You are exactly the same as when I saw you last', 'I have just bought a new car identical to my old one', and in the question 'Are the twins identical?' Conversely, qualitative non-identity has to do with changes in the qualities of an object over time, or with the lack of similarity between different objects. For example: 'She has not been the same since she got married', and

'The vase you bought me as a replacement is not identical to the one you broke.'

Note that in order to be qualitatively identical, things do not have to be the same in every respect. They only have to share some restricted range of properties. Thus identical twins need only be similar in basic appearance and genetic potential; otherwise they can be as different as you please while still remaining identical. And identical cars need only be similar in make and appearance; they need not be owned by the same people, nor be in the same part of the country. In fact when the words 'same' and 'identical' are used in this way, what is really being talked about is qualitative similarity (indeed often, qualitative similarity in some restricted respect).

Numerical identity, on the other hand, has to do with the number of individual objects involved in some context. If x and y are numerically identical, then there is just one object involved (i.e. x and y are 'one and the same' object, they are 'the very same'). And if x and y are not numerically identical, then there are two objects involved (i.e. x and y are distinct objects). It is this notion which is at issue when a jury are considering their verdict in a court of law: is the accused the very same person as the person who committed the crime, or are they, on the contrary, two different persons? Note that they are not asked to judge whether the accused is similar to the criminal, nor whether they have changed since committing the crime. They are only asked to decide whether or not they are (are identical with) the criminal. This is a question of numerical, not qualitative, identity.

Clearly it is the notion of numerical identity which is involved in our two questions about the conditions for identity and distinctness amongst souls. Equally clearly, it is numerical identity of person which concerns us if we are interested in the possibility of an after-life. For of course I should not be greatly comforted to learn that after my death there will exist a person exactly like (i.e. qualitatively identical with) myself (e.g. a clone). Nor should I be greatly disconcerted to learn that after my death I shall continue to exist, but much changed (i.e. not qualitatively identical with my earlier self). All I really want to know is: shall I, my self, survive? So it is on the notion of numerical identity that we need to focus our attention.

(B) Leibniz's Law

This is a logical law governing the notion of numerical identity. It may be expressed like this: if two objects are numerically identical (are one and the same), then anything true of the one must be true of the other also. Thus: if the accused is (is identical with) the criminal, then if the accused has a mustache, so too must the criminal have a mustache. Expressed less paradoxically it is this: if two ways of referring succeed in referring to one and the same entity, then sentences that differ only in that the one way of referring has been substituted for the other will always share the same truth-value. Thus: if 'the accused' refers to the very same individual as does 'the criminal', then if 'The accused has a mustache' is true, so too must be 'The criminal has a mustache'.

Leibniz's Law may be represented in symbols thus: if $x = y$, then x has the property F if and only if y has the property F. The truth of this law is intuitively obvious. For if two objects are one and the same, then how could the 'one' have properties which the 'other' lacks? For if they really are one and the same, there is no 'one' and 'other' here, but only one thing, which may perhaps be being thought about or referred to in a number of different ways. (Hence the air of paradox in our initial statement of Leibniz's Law, when we used the phrase 'If two objects are identical . . .')

(C) Objections to Leibniz's Law

There might appear on the face of it to be some counter-examples to Leibniz's Law. Thus suppose that the police believe Mr Hyde to be the murderer. And suppose that Mr Hyde is in fact Dr Jekyll. It does not follow that the police believe Dr Jekyll to be the murderer, for they may not yet have discovered that Jekyll and Hyde are one and the same man. So is this not a case in which we have: $x = y$, and x is F, but y is not F? Similarly, from the fact that Jocasta is the mother of Oedipus, and the fact that Oedipus wishes to marry Jocasta, it does not follow that he wishes to marry his mother. For he does not yet know that Jocasta is his mother.

In fact these examples do not genuinely conflict with Leibniz's Law. For recall from section 1.iii that properties such as belief and desire are intentional: they always involve particular ways of representing the things which they are about. If we speak of the contexts created by such phrases as 'The police believe that . . .' and 'Oedipus wishes to . . .' as 'intentional contexts', then the important thing to realise is that words within an intentional context do not have their normal reference. Instead they refer to particular ways of representing, thinking or conceiving of those things.

Thus the name 'Mr Hyde', within the context of the sentence 'The police believe that Mr Hyde is the murderer', does not refer to Mr Hyde himself, but rather to the way in which the police think about or represent Mr Hyde. For it is not facts about Mr Hyde which make that sentence either true or false. (Indeed, as we saw in 1.iii, the sentence can be true even if no such person as Mr Hyde exists.) The only facts which are relevant, are facts about the police. And it can be a fact about the police that, represented in one way (as 'Mr Hyde'), they believe of Mr Hyde that he is the murderer, whereas represented in another (as 'Dr Jekyll') they believe of him that he is not.

Leibniz's Law tells us that if two ways of referring in fact refer to one and the same thing, then sentences which differ only in that the one way of referring has been substituted for the other must share the same truth values, so long as those sentences are genuinely about the things to which those ways of referring normally refer (i.e. so long as the sentences do not put those ways of referring within an intentional context). Then since the sentences 'The police believe that Dr Jekyll is the murderer', and 'Oedipus wishes to marry Jocasta' are not genuinely about Dr Jekyll and Jocasta, respectively, the examples we gave above are not genuine counter-examples to Leibniz's Law.

It is important to keep the application of Leibniz's Law distinct from the notion of qualitative sameness, discussed above. For one thing, Leibniz's Law states that numerically identical things will share absolutely all of their properties; whereas qualitative identity generally has to do with some restricted range of properties, as we saw. For another thing, numerical identity is entirely compatible with considerable change of properties over time (i.e. with qualitative non-identity). So the fact that numerical identity is governed by Leibniz's Law ('sameness of properties') does not mean that it implies qualitative identity.

Thus the accused person may be (may be numerically identical with) the criminal, although they have become quite different (in the qualitative sense) in the time which has elapsed between the crime and the trial. This does not refute Leibniz's Law, since the proper understanding of that law requires us to make suitable transformations of the tenses of the verbs involved. Thus if the accused is (is identical with) the criminal, and the criminal had dark hair, then it is now true of the accused that they *did* have dark hair. And if the accused is now white-haired, then it was true of the criminal at the time of the crime that they *would later be* white-haired. So despite the change (despite the qualitative non-identity) the two share the same properties, namely: 'having dark hair at the time of the crime' and 'having white hair at the time of the trial'.

(D) Transitivity, Symmetry and Reflexiveness

Other important features of numerical identity are that it is transitive, symmetric and reflexive. A transitive relation is one which reaches across chains of individuals who are related by the relation. Thus: if $x = y$, and $y = z$, then $x = z$. Again this is intuitively obvious. For if x and y are the very same thing, and y and z are the very same thing, then how could x not be the very same thing as z? A symmetric relation is one which, if an individual bears that relation to another, then the other bears the same relation to the first. Thus: if $x = y$, then $y = x$. A reflexive relation is one which everything bears to itself (if it stands in that relation to anything at all). Thus: $x = x$. Everything is identical with itself. These general features of identity, together with Leibniz's Law, will prove to be of some importance in our later discussions, both in this chapter, and in Chapters 5 and 7.

(E) Identity over Time, and Identification at a Time

We can distinguish two different kinds of judgement of numerical identity. On the one hand there are judgements of identity over time, which take the form: object x at time t(1) is the very same as object y at time t(2). And on the other hand there are judgements of identity at a time, which take the form: object x at time t is the very same as object y at time t. An example of the first form would be: 'The person now in the cells is the person who yesterday committed the murder.' An example of the second form would be: 'The tallest living person is the oldest living person.' I shall refer to judgements of the first form as 'judgements of identity (over time)', and to judgements of the second form as 'judgements of identification (at a time)'.

(F) Criteria of Identity and Identification

I shall argue that there must be more to judgements of numerical identity and identification than is given in Leibniz's Law. In the case of a judgement of identity, one must also judge some relation to exist between the earlier and the later objects which *constitutes* them as one and the same object. And in the case of a judgement of identification, one must also judge that there is some property of the objects *in virtue of which* they are one and the same object. There must, indeed, be 'criteria' of identity and identification. So to say that x is numerically the same as y will be to say, in part, that Leibniz's Law applies to them. But it will also be to say that x and y satisfy either the criterion of identity or identification for things of the kind to which they belong (depending upon whether what is in question is a judgement 'over time' or 'at a time').

I thus propose as a general thesis, that for every kind of object there must be such a thing as a criterion of identity for objects of that kind. The criterion will be a possible relation between earlier and later stages in the life of an object which would constitute them as one and the same thing. To illustrate: in the case of many types of physical object it is arguable that their criterion of identity is the relation of spatio-temporal continuity. That is: object x at t(1) is identical with object y at t(2) if and only if x has travelled in a continuous path through space to reach, at t(2), the place occupied by y. For example, suppose someone raises the question whether the human being now in the cells is the very same as the human who committed yesterday's murder. What would we take as settling the issue? I suggest the following: suppose a private detective to have witnessed the murder and to have trailed the culprit continuously ever since, never once taking their eyes off them for a moment. They would then be in a position to answer our question with complete certainty.

It is important to distinguish between a criterion of identity and mere evidence of identity. For example, in our judgements of identity of human being we often in fact rely upon such things as sameness of fingerprints. But clearly this forms no part of our conception of sameness of human being (of what 'same human being' means), since we acknowledge as a logical possibility that two different humans might have the same fingerprints. We have merely discovered empirically that sameness of fingerprints is reliable evidence of sameness of human being. A criterion of identity, on the other hand, is logically implied by statements of identity between things of the appropriate kind.

I also propose as a general thesis, that for every kind of object there must be such a thing as a criterion of identification for objects of that kind. This will be a possible property of those objects, such that sharing it would constitute them as one and the same object. To illustrate: in the case of physical objects it is arguable that their criterion of identification is spatial position. That is: object x, at a given time, is identical with object y, at the same time, if and only if x and y both occupy the very same region of space at that time. For example, consider what would conclusively settle the question whether the tallest person in the world is identical with the oldest person in the world. I suggest the following: send off one group of researchers to rank all living people in terms of height, and another group to rank them in terms of age. Then our question will be answered affirmatively if and only if the person who comes top of the one list occupies the very same region of space as the one who comes top of the other.

(G) Why must there be Criteria of Identification?

What argument is there for saying that there must exist criteria of identification in connection with every kind of individual thing? (For the sake of simplicity I confine myself to judgements *at* a time.) There are only two other possible alternatives. Either numerical identity simply *is* complete sameness of properties, none of these properties having any privileged status. Or there is indeed more to the notion of identity than complete sameness of properties, but the 'more' is nothing other than identity itself. I shall argue against these alternatives in turn. Although the issues are abstract, they are of the highest importance, both theoretical and practical. On this question will depend the possible existence of the soul.

Might numerical identity simply be sameness of properties? An argument against this is that there is no way in which we could ever hope to check through every single property of two objects in order to see whether or not they coincide. For there will simply be too many properties. It would seem that if we are ever to make judgements of identification with any confidence, then we must pick upon some property to constitute the identity-at-a-time of each sort of thing.

It might be replied that this argument relates only to what is necessary for us to have knowledge of identity, not to what is actually necessary for any given kind of individual thing to exist as such. It may indeed be the case — so the reply goes — that we have found through experience that some properties of things (e.g. spatial position) are very good evidence that the remainder of the properties of the things will also coincide. But it is quite another thing to claim that these properties form part of the very notion of physical-object identity. And it is another thing again to claim that there must be criteria of identification in connection with every kind of individual thing.

My response to this is that a criterion of identification is not merely required for knowledge of identity (though it is indeed required for that) but also by our very conception of what it is for an individual thing to have a property at all. It seems to me completely unintelligible that the coincidence of two descriptions (e.g. 'the desk in the corner' and 'the only item of furniture in the room') might consist in the bare fact that the things they refer to happen to share all of the same properties. For until we possess a criterion of identification we cannot even begin to assign properties.

For example, suppose that the desk is in fact red on one side and green on the other. Now are we dealing with two distinct objects here or only one? Are there two items of furniture, one of which is red and the other of which is green? Or is there only a single item of furniture, part of which is red and part of which is green? Lacking any conception of what distinguishes different items of furniture from one another (besides distinctness of properties) there is no way in which we can even begin to answer these questions. For here of course the idea of complete sameness of properties cannot help us. We know that there are distinct properties alright — namely red and green — but in the absence of a criterion for identifying and distinguishing items of furniture, we cannot even begin to decide whether they are properties of two different objects, or of different parts of the same object.

The general point to emerge is that we could not ascribe properties to things at all if our only conception of the identities of those things were given by complete coincidence of properties. Lacking any conception in advance of what distinguishes different things from one another, we should never know whether we were dealing with properties of distinct things, or of different parts of the same thing. Thus in the example above, what in fact determines that the colours are properties of the same object, is that the surfaces they apply to belong to an object occupying a single discrete region of space.

Similar considerations apply to the idea that there may be nothing to the identity and distinctness of things beyond this: their identity or distinctness. If we had no conception of what makes distinct items of furniture distinct, beyond the bare fact that they are

indeed distinct, then we still could not even begin to ascribe properties to them. Unless, that is, we were supposed to have some special
mental faculty which allows us to know by direct intuition whether
we are dealing with two distinct items of furniture or only one. But
this would pose even more problems than it solved: How do we
know that we have such a faculty of intuition? How do we know
whether it operates correctly? How are the mere facts of identity
and distinctness supposed to cause in us the appropriate intuitions?
And so on.

Since the alternatives are both equally unacceptable, I conclude
that there must exist a criterion if identification in connection with
every kind of individual thing. A similar argument will establish
that there must always exist a criterion of identity. It is these
criteria which provide us with our conceptions of what basically
distinguishes different things from one another, and of what
constitutes the continued existence of those things through time. In
the absence of such criteria, the world would be wholly unintelligible to us: we should be unable even to begin to ascribe properties
to things.

Conclusion

The two questions with which we began this chapter may now be
phrased more precisely. (1) What is the criterion of identity (over
time) for souls? (2) What is the criterion of identification (at a time)
for souls? In the sections which follow we shall proceed to take up
these questions in turn. But note an important general constraint
upon the success of the enterprise: any criteria we propose must
yield judgements broadly in line with our considered judgements of
personal identity and identification. For remember, the dualist
thesis is that souls are persons. So if the only available criteria were
wildly at variance with our considered judgements about ourselves,
then dualism would pass beyond all possibility of belief.

ii. Soul Identity

Our task in this section is to see whether or not we can construct an
adequate criterion of identity (over time) for souls. What we
require is a statement of the conditions necessary and sufficient for
the truth of judgements of the form: soul x at t(1) = soul y at t(2).
We need a relation between the soul at the earlier time and the soul

at the later time which can constitute them as one and the same soul. But this relation must yield judgements of soul-indentity broadly in line with our considered judgements of personal identity.

To start with we might try modelling our account as closely as possible upon that sketched earlier for physical-object identity, which took the form: physical object x at t(1) = physical object y at t(2) if and only if x is spatio-temporally continuous with y. The intuitive idea was of smooth motion between the place occupied by x at t(1) and the place occupied by y at t(2). Now motion consists of change in spatial position. So remembering that souls are supposed to be essentially thinking and experiencing entities, in the way that physical objects are essentially space-occupying entities, we might try the following:

Definition 1: Soul x at t(1) = soul y at t(2) if and only if x and y are linked by a smoothly changing series of thoughts and experiences.

We could construe this definition in such a way as to allow for periods of unconsciousness, by making the waking soul identical with the earlier soul whose experiences it resembles most closely.

Given the way in which our thoughts can jump from one thing to another, and given the radical discontinuities which can exist in our experiences, this account looks completely hopeless. Imagine falling asleep on an overnight train, your last thoughts before losing consciousness being of the repairs to the Statue of Liberty; then waking up the next morning in a completely different part of the country, thinking of the political situation in Guatemala. Obviously someone else may wake up with states of consciousness which resemble those you had the night before more closely than do your own. For example: someone who travelled on a train in the opposite direction, who happens to wake up thinking of the Statue of Liberty. So if we adopted the criterion of soul-identity proposed above, then we should have to say in a case of this sort that your soul had changed bodies.

What we need is a state of consciousness which can somehow bridge the discontinuities in thought and experience. The obvious candidate is memory. Thus although you awoke, in the example above, with an entirely new set of thoughts and experiences, you could of course recall if you wished much of what you had thought and experienced the previous day: where you were, what you did, what you saw. Then we might propose this:

Definition 2: Soul x at t(1) = soul y at t(2) if and only if y can, at t(2), remember something thought or experienced by x at t(1).

An account of this kind was first put forward by the English philosopher John Locke. We shall now spend the remainder of this section developing and refining it.

Obviously the proposal is not satisfactory as it stands, since identity is transitive, whereas memory is not. Thus someone might, as a child, steal apples from a neighbour's orchard, and then as a young woman recall that event while graduating with a degree in law. As an ageing judge she might still recall her graduation day, but have completely forgotten about the childhood theft. Then the situation could be represented diagrammatically thus:

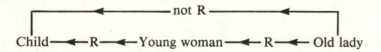

But now if we apply the definition above we should have to say that the young woman is the same person (soul) as the child, and the old lady the same person as the young woman, but the old lady is not the same person as the child. This would be absurd. Alternatively the old lady might still be able to recall the childhood theft, while having lost all memory of her day of graduation. Diagrammatically:

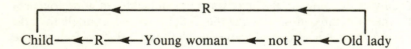

Then we should have to say that the old lady is the same person as the child, and the young woman is the same person as the child, but the old lady is not the same person as the young woman. This too would be absurd.

The solution to these difficulties is to extend the definition given above in such a way as to allow a series of overlapping memories to give identity of soul (and hence of person) as well as direct memories. We can do this by giving our account in two stages, first stating that direct memory gives identity, and the building on this to say that identity of soul carries across any series of souls linked together by direct memories. The neatest way to express this is as follows:

Definition 3: Soul x at t(1) = soul y at t(2) if and only if either (a) y can remember things thought or experienced by x at t(1), or (b) y is, by repeated applications of clause (a), identical with someone who is, again by clause (a), identical with x at t(1).

This definition applied to the examples above would have the consequence which we intuitively want. Namely that the child, the young woman and the old lady are all different stages in the life of the same person.

A more awkward difficulty is that memory itself presupposes personal identity, and so cannot be used in an account of the criterion of soul-identity without vicious circularity. Definitions and explanations are viciously circular, in general, if they take for granted a grasp of the very thing being defined or explained. Thus suppose you are explaining what a bachelor is to a non-English speaker. You say, naturally enough, that a bachelor is an unmarried man. But they reply that they do not understand the term 'unmarried'. If you respond that to be unmarried is to be either a bachelor or a spinster, then your explanations have become viciously circular. For they will be unable to understand your first definition until they understand your second. But they also cannot understand your second definition unless they already understand your first. (The second definition would have other faults as well: a two-year-old child can be unmarried, but is neither a bachelor nor a spinster.)

I shall argue that a definition of soul-identity in terms of memory must be like this. For I shall argue that 'Mary remembers experiencing E' implies 'Mary really did experience E', which in turn implies 'Mary is the very same person as the person who experienced E'. This of course brings us round to the very same relation — sameness of person, or soul — which we started out trying to define.

Notice first of all that memory is a species of knowledge. One of the distinctive features of knowledge, as opposed to belief, is that it implies truth. If I claim to know something, and what I claim to know is not in fact the case, then I do not really know it but merely believe it. (In contrast: if I claim to believe something, and what I claim to believe is not in fact the case, this does not show that I do not really believe it.) In the same way, if I claim to remember something that did not in fact take place, then I do not really remember it, but only seem to remember it. Thus: 'Mary remembers E' implies 'E really did happen.'

Secondly, notice that there are two very different kinds of memory. There is what might be called 'impersonal memory', or 'memory of fact', whose canonical form of expression is 'I remember that such-and-such'. (E.g. 'I remember that the Battle of Hastings was fought in AD 1066.') But there is also what might be called 'personal memory', or 'memory of experience', whose canonical means of expression is simply 'I remember such-and-such'. (E.g. 'I remember the Battle of Hastings.') This second kind of memory is the sort which was involved in our most recent definition of soul-identity. Yet it always involves an implicit claim to have done or experienced, yourself, the thing in question. (You cannot remember the Battle of Hastings unless you yourself were really there.) So if this implicit claim is false, then you do not really remember the thing after all, but merely seem to remember it. Thus: 'Mary remembers experiencing E' implies 'Mary is the very same person as the person who really did experience E.'

It may be worth noting a further feature of personal memory, which will prove to be of some importance later, namely that it is a causal notion. You only really remember event E, if the experience of E is the cause of your current belief. Suppose that I have an experience which leaves no trace in my memory at the time. But later a neuro-surgeon implants in my brain a state exactly like a memory of that experience. Here I think we should say that I do not really remember it. Although everything seems to me as though I remember it, and although I did in fact have such an experience, what I have is not really a memory, because it was not caused by the experience to which it relates.

Now consider the following example. Suppose I claim to remember falling out of a tree as a child and breaking my arm. I seem to recall my hand slipping on the branch, terror as the ground came up to meet me, then pain combined with astonishment at the strange angle of my arm in relation to my body. All this seems like yesterday. Yet it was not I who fell out of the tree but my sister. She afterwards described the experience to me so vividly that I had regular nightmares for some weeks, in which I dreamed that it was

I who fell. Somehow over the years this became transformed into a seeming-memory of having fallen out of the tree myself.

Clearly we should say in this case that I do not really remember falling out of the tree. For although my belief feels to me just like a memory (it comes to me as it were 'from the inside'), although what I believe is in fact a truth about someone (i.e. my sister), and although my belief is caused (via my sister's description) by the experience I claim to remember, it was not I who did and experienced those things. Since this is sufficient to disqualify it from being a genuine memory, personal memory of an experience must itself imply the identity of the rememberer with the person who underwent the original experience. In which case it is, as I claimed, viciously circular to define identity of soul in terms of personal memory.

The solution to the problem of circularity is to introduce a new concept of 'quasi-memory', which is to be like personal memory in all respects except that it does *not* imply personal identity. Thus someone quasi-remembers experiencing E if and only if: (a) they believe that an experience of E took place, finding it natural to describe this experience 'from the inside', (b) this belief is a true belief about someone (not necessarily themself), and (c) this belief is itself caused by an experience of E.

By employing the notion of quasi-memory, soul identity may be non-circularly defined as follows:

Definition 4: Soul x at t(1) = soul y at t(2) if and only if either (a) y can quasi-remember things thought or experienced by x at t(1), or (b) y is, by repeated applications of clause (a), identical with someone who is, again by clause (a), identical with x at t(1).

However, this now lets us in for a difficulty of another sort. The relation of quasi-memory can branch. But identity, because of its transitivity and symmetry, leaves no room for the possibility that two distinct persons might each be identical with a third. For instance both I and my sister may quasi-remember falling out of the tree. Then applying the definition above we should have to say that both I and my sister are, now, one and the same person, since each of us would be identical with the person who fell out of the tree; which is absurd.

We can apparently solve this difficulty by making our account a majoritarian one, since my sister will presumably have more quasi-memories about the tree-falling episode than I do myself. Thus:

> **Definition 5:** Soul x at t(1) = soul y at t(2) is and only if either
> (a) y can, at t(2), quasi-remember more things thought or experi-
> enced by x at t(1) than can anyone else at t(2), or (b) y is, by
> repeated applications of clause (a), identical with someone who
> is, again by clause (a), identical with x at t(1).

Now it might seem that the occurrence of the phrase 'than can anyone else' in clause (i) of this definition, would render the whole
account viciously circular. For who is 'anyone else' except: someone who is not identical with y? In which case, does not the definition itself employ the very notion which it tries to define? But in
fact the full phrase is: 'than can anyone else at the time of y's quasi-
memory'. This makes all the difference. For it only introduces the
notion of personal identification *at* a time, whereas we were concerned to define the notion of personal identity *over* time. There
would only be a vicious circularity if identification at a time itself
presupposed identity over time. And as we shall see in the next
section, it does not.

There is in fact a minor difficulty with Definition 5. For although
we might reasonably expect that my sister should quasi-remember
more details of the tree-falling episode than I do myself, this will
not necessarily be the case. (She may have forgotten all about it.)
Yet it would obviously be absurd to conclude, in that event, that I
am the person who fell out of the tree after all.

We can avoid this difficulty by insisting that in cases of conflict,
clause (b) of the definition should take priority. For presumably on
the day after the episode, my sister could quasi-remember a great
deal more about it than I could myself. (Indeed at that time I quasi-
remembered nothing, since I had only just been told about it, and
the nightmares had not yet begun.) And that person is, by clause
(a), identical with someone (i.e. my sister on the day after that) who
is, by clause (a), identical with someone who is . . . identical with
my sister now. We may thus let a series of overlapping majoritarian
connections take precedence over any single direct majoritarian
connection.

It is beginning to look as if the dualist can at least provide us with
a possible criterion of soul-identity. Yet it is easy to become puzzled
at the immense weight being placed on the concept of memory (or
rather quasi-memory) within the account. For is memory really so

very important? Is there any independent reason for thinking that memory has an important part to play in our concept of ourselves as individuals? Or has the account been constructed in terms of memory merely because it provides the dualist with a convenient means of bridging the discontinuities in consciousness?

By way of partial answer, notice that memory covers a great deal more than mere recollection of past events and experiences. Perhaps it really would be extraordinary to claim that such memories are so important to my existence as an individual that I should be counted as surviving just in case I retain them. But in fact 'memory' also covers memory of my desires and interests, memory of my short-term plans, long-term intentions and ties of affection. Without memory I should merely find myself desiring certain things, and taking an interest in certain things, without being able to distinguish between my life-long interests and desires, and my passing fancies. Indeed, perhaps the most important part of knowing who I am, is not memory of where I come from, what my name is, or what I have done and experienced in the past, but rather memory of what I care about and what I plan to do.

However, not everything which intuitively belongs to our sense of our own identities can plausibly be brought under the umbrella of 'memory'. What makes my present existence into part of a relatively coherent integrated life, is not simply memory of what I desired and intended in the past, but also that I find I still have many of those desires, intentions and ties of affection. (This point is easily missed, since we would normally understand the statement 'I remember what I want' in such as way as to imply that I still do want those things.) Indeed the whole business of forming plans and intentions for the future would be pointless if our desires were not, in general, relatively stable. No plans would ever get executed unless we still had the same desires once the time for planning was past, and the time had come for action. It may thus be more plausible to define soul-identity not merely in terms of connections of memory, but also in terms of connections of desire.

Desires, like memories, may be distinguished into impersonal desires on the one hand (such as my desire that a particular party should win an election), and personal, or 'self-referring', desires on the other (such as my desire that I should be rich). Self-referring desires, being for things to happen to my future self, presuppose the notion of personal identity over time, and so cannot be used to define it. But as in the case of memory, we can introduce a concept of quasi-desire (and of quasi-intention) in terms of which we may define personal identity without vicious circularity. Thus: a quasi-desire for a piece of chocolate is (a) a desire that an eating of chocolate should take place, where (b) that event is naturally represented by me 'from the inside'.

Also like memory, desire is a causal notion. Just as something only counts as a genuine personal memory if it is caused by the experience which it purports to be a memory of, so something only counts as a genuine desire if it is apt to cause (via the causation of action) its own satisfaction. If I want (really want) to eat a piece of chocolate, then I am in a state which is apt to cause an eating of chocolate to take place. (Note that this implies that a particular personal desire D should only be counted as the very same as an earlier desire C, if D is the 'causal descendant' of C. That is: if the existence of C is the direct cause of the later existence of D. For only if this is so can we say that by acting on the later desire D, the person is thereby satisfying desire C.)

Let us now introduce the concept of 'psychological connectedness' between persons at earlier and later times. Let us say that a person x at t(1) and a person y at t(2) are psychologically connected with one another to the extent that: (a) person y can quasi-remember x's thoughts, experiences, quasi-desires and quasi-intentions, (b) x and y have the same impersonal desires and interests, and (c) x and y have the same quasi-desires and quasi-intentions. (Where these clauses require that y's psychological states should be causal descendants of those of x.) We can then put this notion to work in a rather more plausible account of soul-identity, while preserving all the virtues of Definition 5, as follows:

Definition 6: Soul x at t(1) = soul y at t(2) if and only if either (a) y is, at t(2), more strongly psychologically connected with x at t(1) than is anyone else at t(2), or (b) y is, by repeated applications of clause (a), identical with someone who is, again by clause (a), identical with x at t(1). (Clause (b) to take precedence in cases of conflict.)

iii. Soul Identification

There are no insuperable obstacles in the way of providing an adequate criterion of identity over time for souls. Our question now, is whether it is possible to back this up with an adequate criterion of identification at a time. Recall that in section 3.i we argued that for every kind of object there must be something which determines whether two ways of referring to an object-at-a-time succeed in identifying one and the same object, or two distinct objects; this being the criterion of identification for objects of that kind. Then if it can be shown that there cannot be an adequate criterion of identification for souls, it will follow that souls cannot exist as distinct individual objects. This will be my overall strategy.

(A) General Points

It is important to note that criteria of identification are logically more basic than criteria of identity. Before we can begin to keep track of an object over time, we must be able to identify it — to pick it out from other individual objects of the same kind — in the first place. No one could have a conception of what constitutes the continued existence of an entity over time, unless they also had a conception of what would distinguish it from other entities of the same sort at any particular time during its existence. Someone could, on the other hand, have a conception of what individuates an entity at any particular time, without yet having any conception of what would constitute the continued existence over time of any one such entity. So in this sense criteria of identification are logically more fundamental.

In section 3.i we suggested that it might be spatial position which provides the criterion of identification for most kinds of physical object. Thus what ultimately determines whether 'The car in the garage' refers to the same or a distinct entity from 'The only car in town painted in black and white stripes', is whether or not the cars in question occupy the same or distinct regions of space. Now notice that spatial position can only be successful as a criterion of bodily identification, in virtue of the truth of the following three principles:

(i) Every physical object must always be in some place.
(ii) One physical object cannot be in two places — separated by a region of space in which no part of that object occurs — at once.
(iii) Two distinct physical objects cannot be in the very same place at the same time.

Principle (i) guarantees that you can always individuate an object by giving its spatial position. If it were possible for a physical object to exist without occupying any place, then it would have to be some other feature of it which distinguished it from other such objects. Principle (ii) guarantees that it is not necessary to mention more than one place in order to establish the identity of an object. If it were false, then occupancy of two distinct places would not be sufficient to establish that we were dealing with two distinct objects, and once again it would have to be some other feature of them which settled the issue. Principle (iii) guarantees that mention of a particular place is sufficient to distinguish one physical object from all others. If it were false, then it would have to be something other than occupancy of a particular place which determined whether we were dealing with just one object, or with more than one.

If souls exist as distinct individual entities — as they must do if souls are persons, since persons are distinct individuals — then there has to be a criterion of identification for them. There must be some range of properties, analogous to spatial positions for physical objects, which would enable us to pick out and refer to one individual soul rather than another. Or to put it another way: there must be something which fundamentally distinguishes souls from one another. There must thus exist some range of properties — call it 'Ø' — such that the following three principles hold:

(a) Every soul must always satisfy some property from the Ø-range.
(b) One soul cannot satisfy two different properties from the Ø-range at the same time.
(c) Two distinct souls cannot both satisfy the same property from the Ø-range at the same time.

Unless these three principles hold good, then we cannot be guaranteed to individuate any particular soul by saying 'It is the one which is F' (where F is some property from the Ø-range). In which case it would have to be some other property of souls which makes the difference.

(B) Bodily Criteria

It is obvious that connectedness with a particular body cannot provide the criterion of soul-identification, because of principle (a) above. If it is supposed to be logically possible that souls should exist unconnected with any body, as the dualist believes, then what fundamentally distinguishes souls from one another cannot be their association with different bodies. Connectedness with a particular body can at best be evidence of soul-identification, rather than a criterion of it. In fact we need a criterion which could serve to distinguish disembodied souls from one another, were it to turn out that disembodied existence does indeed occur.

Nor can we give our account in terms of connectedness with a particuar body, while allowing for the possibility of disembodied existence, by providing for appeals to past facts about the souls in question, namely which bodies they *were* connected with in this life. Thus we cannot say: soul x at t(1) = soul y, also at t(1), if and only if either (a) x and y are now connected with the same body, or (b) x and y were once connected with the same body, at some time prior to t(1). For the possession of a past (or future) property involves the identity of the object over time, and hence presupposes both criteria of identity and identification for objects of that kind. In which case the above account of soul-identification would be viciously circular. Thus: 'Soul x at t(2) was connected with body B at t(1)' says the same as 'Soul x at t(2) is the very same soul as the soul which is, at t(1), connected with body B'. And this presupposes that we already have a conception of what might enable us to identify both the earlier and the later soul.

The above argument generalises, to show that the criterion of identification for an object of any given sort cannot possibly involve either past or future properties without vicious circularity. Then if the criterion of soul identification cannot be bodily, and if it cannot involve either past or future properties, we must confine ourselves to present tensed properties whose application does not in any way presuppose a connection with a particular body. We are, in effect, thrown back on to consciousness-terms such as 'thought', 'quasi-memory', 'belief' and 'experience'. And then the question is whether it is possible to construct an adequate criterion of soul-identification out of such terms.

(C) Conscious Criteria

Consider the following proposal: soul x at t(1) = soul y, also at t(1), if and only if x and y are thinking exactly similar thoughts at t(1). This is obviously hopeless. There is no way in which it can satisfy principle (c) while at the same time remaining in line with our judgements of distinctness amongst persons. It is clearly possible for two distinct human beings to think exactly similar thoughts at exactly the same time. Indeed this does seem to happen quite frequently. So applying the proposed criterion of identification for souls, we should have to say that any two such human beings momentarily possess the same soul, thus becoming the very same person. (Note, moreover, that we cannot get around this difficulty by appealing to the fact that the thoughts in question may occur as part of two different trains of thought. For this would be to import past and future properties into the criterion of identification.)

Essentially the same difficulty infects the following proposal: soul x at t(1) = soul y, also at t(1), if and only if both x and y can, at t(1), quasi-remember exactly the same events and experiences. For again this either runs foul of principle (c) or yields absurd identifications. Thus two different human beings suffering from total amnesia would both have exactly the same quasi-memories (i.e. in both cases none at all). So we should either have to say that they would possess the same soul, and thus be the very same person; or it would have to be something other than quasi-memories which serves to differentiate them from one another.

It might seem that the following proposal can fare better: soul x at t(1) = soul y, also at t(1), if and only if x and y are both undergoing, at t(1), exactly similar experiences. For given that human beings always have different visual and aural perspectives on the world, it might seem impossible that two of them could ever have exactly the same experiences at the same time. But imagine two humans fitted-up with viewing-goggles and headphones, and otherwise anaesthetised, to whom we simultaneously play exactly the same clip of film with the same sound-track. Then surely these two individuals would undergo exactly the same experiences? For we should have cancelled out all differences in perspective.

A dualist might reply that this example only shows that it is possible for two different human beings to receive exactly the same visual and aural stimuli, not that the resulting experiences will be the same. And indeed this is correct: in general they would not be the same. For since the two subjects may have different memories, and different desires and interests, the stimuli will not have the same significance for them both. They may notice different things, concentrating their attention on different aspects of the experience. Or they may be distracted from different aspects of it by the thoughts which are occurring to them at the time. But all of this is only 'may' (or at most 'will') not 'must'. Suppose that the two subjects are both suffering from total amnesia, that both happen to have the same desires and interests, and that the same thoughts occur to them as the experience begins. It may then be perfectly possible that they should undergo exactly the same experiences. And we would then be committed to the absurd belief that they are in fact one and the same person (soul).

It might be objected on behalf of the dualist that these examples are purely imaginary, and are extremely unlikely to occur. But this would be to miss the point. Which is: that on any proposed account of the criterion for identifying souls — whether given in terms of some restricted range of states of consciousness (such as thought or memory), or whether given in terms of the complete set of such states — it will follow that it is logically impossible for two distinct souls to share exactly the same such states at the same time. Yet it is, on the contrary, surely conceivable that two distinct persons might possess qualitatively identical (exactly similar) states of consciousness at exactly the same time.

(D) A Proof of the Falsity of Dualism

Our argument against dualism may now be summarised as follows:

(1) The dualist believes that persons (selves) are non-physical souls.

(2) Persons are distinct individual entities.

(C1) So the dualist must believe that souls are distinct individual entities.

(3) There must be a criterion of identification in connection with every kind of individual thing.

(C2) So (from (C1) and (3)) if dualism is true, then there must be a criterion of identification for souls.

(4) Any possible criterion of soul-identification will entail that it is logically impossible for two distinct souls to possess the same states of consciousness, either in general, or for some restricted range of such states.

(5) It is, on the other hand, logically possible for two distinct persons to possess the same states of consciousness, either in general, or for some restricted range of such states.

(C3) So (from (C2), (4) and (5)) either no such things as souls exist, or souls are not persons.

(C4) So either way, dualism is false.

This argument gives every appearance of being a proof. The argument as a whole seems valid, and each of the premises (1)–(5) seems either indubitable in itself, or to have been adequately supported by arguments given previously.

It may be objected against this argument, that from the fact that we have failed in our attempts to frame an adequate conception of souls as individual entities, it does not follow that no such things can exist. For after all, there are surely all sort of things in the world for which we have as yet formed no adequate conception. But this objection mistakes the nature of our argument, on two counts. Firstly, it does not merely deal with our concepts and capacities, but with what is possible in the world. The claim was not merely that in order for us to have a conception of souls as individual things, we must be capable of distinguishing them from one another. It was rather that in order for souls to exist as individual things, there must be some properties (whether we know of them or not) which serve to render them distinct from one another. Secondly, the argument was not merely that we have not yet found an adequate criterion of identification for souls, but that there cannot be such a criterion. For it would have to be either bodily or mental. And as we have seen, neither can serve.

The last refuge of the dualist is to claim that there might be properties of souls which serve to individuate them, which are neither bodily nor mental, of a sort of which we as yet have no knowledge. But if we have no idea of the properties which individuate them, then we have no conception of souls as individual things. And then to believe that I am a soul, or to hope that I might survive physical death as a disembodied soul, would be just like 'believing' that there is a snark on the other side of the island, and 'hoping' to capture it. (See Lewis Carroll's poem, 'The Hunting of the Snark', which closes by revealing that the snark is a boojum. The point of the poem is that you cannot look for, nor hope to find, something which you have no conception of.) I should literally have no idea what I believe, nor what to hope for. I should be left merely with the words 'I am a soul, and the soul may survive the body', without having any idea what they might mean. You cannot believe what you cannot think. And the effect of the last refuge suggested above, is that we cannot think of souls as individual entities.

iv. The Argument for Dualism Reconsidered

We are faced with a paradox. In section 2.i we constructed an argument for the truth of dualism which gave every appearance of being a proof. Yet now in 3.iii we have constructed an argument for its falsehood which appears equally convincing. The correct conclusion to draw from this (since dualism cannot be both true and false) is that something, somewhere, must have gone wrong with one or other of those arguments. Our immediate problem is to find out what. My own view is that our recent argument against the truth of dualism is, as it appears to be, a proof; but that there is at least one mistake in the argument which we gave in its support.

The discussion in this section will proceed in three stages. In part (A) I shall expose a fallacy (an invalid step) in the argument of 2.i. In part (B) I shall show how a dualist can reformulate the argument in such a way as to avoid committing this fallacy. Then in part (C) I shall expose a fallacy in the reasons we gave in support of premiss (1) of the argument for dualism. Lacking any convincing reason for believing this premiss, we may reject it as false; and then we shall no longer have any proof of the existence of the soul.

(A) A Fallacy

Recall that one of the crucial steps in the argument of 2.i was as follows:

> (C1) It is logically possible that thinking things are not physical things.
> (3) All physical things are such that their physicality is a logically necessary attribute of them.
> (C2) So thinking things are not physical things.

This step is in fact invalid as it stands, involving a fallacy sometimes called by philosophers 'a modal shift'. (Modal terms are terms such as 'necessary', 'possible' and 'impossible'.) But in order to see how the premises (C1) and (3) can be true, while conclusion (C2) is false — i.e. in order to see how the argument is invalid — we need to investigate a phenomenon known to philosophers as 'scope'.

It can make all the difference to the truth or falsity of a judgement involving a modal term such as 'necessary', what the scope of the necessity is. What will often be crucial, is whether it is the whole sentence which falls within the scope of what is being judged to be necessary, or only part of it. On the first alternative, let us say that the necessity has 'wide scope', and on the second alternative, that it has 'narrow scope'. Then I shall claim that the argument above is invalid because the possibility in (C1) is wide-scope, whereas the necessity in (3) is narrow-scope.

Consider for example the sentence 'The thing of which Mary is thinking is, necessarily, physical.' This is ambiguous, depending upon whether we read it as saying: 'It is a necessary truth that the thing of which Mary is thinking is physical' (wide-scope); or rather as saying: 'The thing of which Mary is, in fact, thinking is necessarily-physical' (narrow-scope). Taken with wide-scope the judgement is false. For it comes to the same as saying: 'Mary can — as a matter of logic — think only of physical things.' This is obviously false, since Mary may think of the number 9, or the Greenwich Meridian. But taken with narrow-scope the judgement may be true. For if Mary is in fact thinking of the chair on which she is sitting, then that thing is necessarily-physical. For as we saw in section 2.i, we can make no sense of the idea that a particular chair might not have been physical, nor of the idea that it might cease to be physical while continuing to exist.

The difference between wide and narrow scope can be represented most clearly in terms of possible worlds. Suppose that we are dealing with a judgement of the form 'X is physical'. Then a judgement of wide-scope necessity will say: 'It is a truth about all possible worlds that if X exists in that world it is physical.' And a judgement of wide-scope possibility will say: 'It is a truth about some possible world that X exists in that world and is physical.' On the other hand a judgement of narrow-scope necessity will say: 'The thing which is X in our world, is physical in all possible worlds in which it occurs.' And a judgement of narrow-scope possibility will say: 'The thing which is X in our world, is physical in some possible world in which it occurs.'

In general, a judgement of the wide-scope necessity of 'X is physical' will only be true if the description 'X' describes the thing in such a way as to *imply* its physicality. Thus if 'X' is 'The chair on which Mary is sitting', then the wide-scope judgement will be true. It is a truth about all possible worlds that if there is a chair on which Mary is sitting, then it is physical. But if 'X' is 'The thing of which Mary is thinking', then the wide-scope judgement will be false. For even if Mary is in fact thinking of the chair, that thing is not described in such a way as to imply its physicality. It is not a truth about all possible worlds that if Mary is thinking about something in that world, then it is physical.

In general, a judgement of the narrow-scope necessity of 'X is physical' will only be true if the thing which is described by the term 'X' in the actual world belongs to one of those sorts of thing for which the criteria of identity and identification involve physical attributes. Thus if 'X' is 'The thing of which Mary is thinking', and Mary is in fact thinking of the chair, then the narrow-scope judgement will be true. For the chair is physical in all possible worlds in which it exists. But if Mary is in fact thinking of the Greenwich Meridian, then the narrow-scope judgement will be false. For the thing of which Mary is thinking (the Greenwich Meridian) is not physical in all possible worlds in which it occurs (in particular, it is not physical in the actual world).

Armed now with the distinction between wide and narrow scope, we can return to the crucial step in the argument for dualism. Since the possibility in (C1) is wide-scope, it should properly be represented thus:

(C1¹) It is a truth about some possible world that there exist thinkers in that world who are not physical.

But since the necessity in (3) is narrow-scope, it should properly be represented thus:

(3¹) All things which are in fact physical in the actual world, are physical in all other possible worlds in which they exist.

Now from these two premises together it simply does not follow that thinking things are not in fact physical things.

To see this, suppose that conclusion (C2) is in fact false. Suppose that the things which are, in the actual world, the thinking things, are all of them physical things. E.g. suppose that they are, in fact, physical brains. Yet it is still possible for (C1¹) to be true. It may be that in some other possible world thinking things are non-physical souls. And it is equally possible for (3¹) to be true. We merely have to conclude that the things which do the thinking in this world (brains) are physical in all other possible worlds in which they exist. Then since it is possible for the premises to be true while the conclusion is false, the argument from (C1¹) and (3¹) to (C2) is invalid.

(B) Avoiding the Fallacy

The dualist has a reply to the above criticism. It is that the arguments originally given in support of (C1), could equally well have been used to support a narrow-scope version of it, namely:

(C1*) The things which are, in the actual world, the thinking things, are non-physical in some possible worlds in which they occur.

Then this really could be put together with (3¹) to entail that thinking things are not in fact physical things. In brief, the argument would then be as follows:

(C1*) Thinking things are not essentially physical.
(3) All physical things are essentially physical.
(C2) So thinking things are not in fact physical things.

This argument is certainly valid: it commits no modal fallacy. The only issue outstanding is whether the dualist can indeed provide adequate support for premiss (C1*).

Recall the crucial role played, in the argument to (C1), by the apparent conceivability of disembodied thought and experience. It seems that I can imagine what it would be like to die, and cease to be embodied, but continue having thoughts and experiences. Indeed it seems that I can imagine what it might have been like had I never been embodied. We took this, at the time, to establish the truth of premiss (1), that it is logically possible for thoughts and experiences to occur in the absence of any physical thinker or experiencer. But it seems we could equally well have taken it to establish the stronger thesis that I, myself, am not an essentially physical thing. If it is conceivable that I might continue to exist without being physical, and conceivable that I might have existed without ever being physical, then I myself am not an essentially physical thing. It will follow that the thing which is me (the thinker) in the actual world, is non-physical in some possible worlds in which it occurs. Then if the disembodied existence of other actual thinkers is similarly conceivable, we shall have done enough to establish (C1*).

We seem to be able to show that I (the thinker) cannot really be a brain (nor indeed any other physical thing). For it seems conceivable that I might continue to exist without being physical;

but it is surely inconceivable that a particular brain might continue to exist without being physical. Then if we have our anti-Humean premiss, that it is impossible for thoughts and experiences to occur in the absence of some thinking experiencing thing, it follows that I am myself a non-physical thing. The argument for dualism can thus go through without committing any modal fallacy.

(C) Imagining vs Conceiving

The real weakness — indeed the only weakness — in the argument for dualism, lies in premiss (1), which states that it is conceivable that I might have disembodied thoughts and experiences. We argued for this on the basis of my being able to imagine having a sequence of experiences which do not in any way involve the experience of having a body. Now so far this is correct: it is indeed possible to imagine having such experiences. But it does not follow from this that it is really conceivable that I should have experiences which are not in fact the experiences of a physical thing. For I might have a sequence of experiences which do not involve the experience of having a body although I am, not disembodied, but merely hallucinating. Although I have experiences of moving through walls, of perceiving my own body from a perspective outside it and so on, it may be that I am all the time lying motionless in a hospital bed. From the fact that I can imagine a sequence of experiences which would, from my point of view, be indistinguishable from those of a disembodied being, it does not follow that disembodied experience is really logically possible.

There is a general moral to be drawn here about the limited usefulness of imagination in helping us establish what is logically possible, or genuinely conceivable. To imagine something is to represent to oneself the appearance of that thing: to have a visual mental image is to represent to oneself how something would look, to have an aural mental image is to represent to oneself how something would sound, and so on. So anything which goes beyond appearances — i.e. which is not simply a matter of the look of the thing, or the sound of the thing — does not strictly speaking belong to the content of the image itself. Rather it will have been added in thought. And there is no telling from the image alone whether its conjunction with that thought might not yield a contradiction.

Thus if I imagine a pig flying, what I really do is represent to myself how it would look to me if a pig flew: I imagine a sequence of experiences which I should naturally describe as being 'of a pig flying'. But this does not by itself show that it is logically possible for a pig to fly (though I have no doubt that such a thing is possible). The most that it shows is that it is possible to hallucinate a pig flying. For from the fact that those imagined experiences are logically possible, it does not follow that the thing itself is similarly possible.

Consider a somewhat more serious example: I can imagine a sequence of experiences which would, from my own point of view, be indistinguishable from having travelled back into the twelfth century, and which I should naturally describe in those terms. I can imagine stepping into a large box, and stepping out again a moment later to have experiences of a world in which people use oxen to draw wooden waggons and carts and so on. But it does not follow from this that time-travel is logically possible. For the thought 'And I should then be in the twelfth century' goes beyond anything which I have certainly imagined. All that I can be certain of having imagined, is a particular sequence of experiences. But these might be hallucinatory, or they might be experiences of a world which has miraculously changed in a moment into an exact replica of the world of the twelfth century. So from the fact that those experiences are logically possible, it does not follow that time-travel itself is logically possible.

Similarly then: when I try to imagine disembodied thought and experience all that I can be certain of doing, is imagining a sequence of expereinces which do not involve the experience of having a body. Then to this image I add the thought 'And as a matter of fact these are not the experiences of any physical thing.' But this thought is not strictly speaking part of the content of my image itself. And it may in fact be that its conjunction with what I imagine yields a contradiction. Certainly such experiences have been shown to be logically possible by my act of imagination. But it is quite another matter to claim that they could possibly be the experiences of a non-physical thing.

Although we have found an error in the argument for dualism, it is certainly not an obvious one. It has required no little labour to expose it, since we have had to draw a subtle distinction between imagining (which is confined to appearances) and conceiving (which can go beyond them). So it remains explicable that many intelligent people should have become convinced of the truth of dualism.

Conclusion

At last we have found an error in the argument for dualism: we have been given insufficient reason for believing that disembodied thought and experience are logically possible. But I cannot myself see any errors in the argument of 3.iii, the conclusion of which was that disembodied existence is not logically possible. So I conclude that dualism is false. Yet we are still left with the argument of 2.iii against the bundle theory of the mind, the conclusion of which was that conscious states must be the states of some individually existing thing. So it therefore follows that conscious states must be the states of some physical thing: either the living human organism, or some part thereof (e.g. the brain).

We have no option but to say that the person or self — the subject of thoughts and experiences — is a physical thing. This is a version of materialism. But it is, as yet, only weak materialism. For it does not follow from anything which has so far been shown that conscious states are themselves physical states. So although we have, in this chapter, provided sufficient reason for rejecting strong dualism, weak dualism remains a possibility: it remains possible that conscious states are non-physical states of a physical thing.

Questions and Readings

You may like to discuss/think about/write about some of the following questions:

(1) Could there be nothing more to the identity of two individuals than the fact of their identity? Or must there be criteria of identity and identification?

(2) If a person today is to be the very same individual as a person last year, is it logically *necessary* that they be linked together by a continuous chain of psychological connections?

(3) If a person today is to be the very same individual as a person last year, is it logically *sufficient* that they be linked together by a continuous chain of psychological connections?

(4) Could there be two distinct persons who possess exactly similar conscious states at the same time?

(5) When you imagine something, how much of what you imagine is certainly conceivable?

In thinking about these questions, you might like to consult a selection of the following readings (capitalised names refer to works listed in the Bibliography):

Joseph Butler, 'Of Personal Identity', *The Analogy of Religion*, appendix 1. Reprinted in PERRY and FLEW.

Gottlob Frege, 'On Sense and Meaning', *Translations from the Philosophical Writings of Gottlob Frege*, P. Geach and M. Black (eds.) (Oxford: Blackwell, 3rd ed., 1980).

Peter Geach, 'Reincarnation', *God and the Soul* (London: Routledge and Kegan Paul, 1969).

John Locke, 'Of Identity and Diversity', *Essay Concerning Human Understanding*, vol. 1, bk. II, ch. XXVII. Reprinted in PERRY and FLEW.

John Mackie, *Problems from Locke* (Oxford: Clarendon Press, 1976), Ch. 6.

Terence Penelhum, *Survival and Disembodied Existence* (London: Routledge and Kegan Paul, 1970), Chs. 2, 3, 5 and 6.

————, 'Personal Identity'. Entry in *The Encyclopaedia of Philosophy*, Paul Edwards (ed.) (London: Collier-Macmillan, 1967).

John Perry, 'Personal Identity, Memory, and the Problem of Circularity', in PERRY.

Sydney Shoemaker, 'Persons and their Pasts', *American Philosophical Quarterly*, vol. 7 (1970). Reprinted in SHOEMAKER.

Peter Strawson, *Individuals* (London: Methuen, 1959), Ch. 4.

Richard Swinburne, 'A Dualistic Theory', in S. Shoemaker and R. Swinburne, *Personal Identity* (Oxford: Blackwell, 1984).

David Wiggins, *Identity and Spatio-Temporal Continuity* (Oxford: Blackwell, 1967).

PART THREE:
STATES OF MIND

MIND AND BEHAVIOUR

i. Philosophical Behaviourism

Nothing in our critique of strong dualism has yet challenged the thesis argued for in section 1.iv, which we called the 'cartesian conception' of the meanings of terms referring to conscious states. This holds that those meanings are wholly concerned with the subjective feel of the corresponding states. Neither has anything yet challenged the thesis argued for in section 1.iii, that conscious states are themselves non-physical: weak dualism has survived unscathed.

In this section we shall discuss a philosophical doctrine which is designed to reject each of the above theses, holding both that the meanings of consciousness-terms are essentially tied to descriptions of physical behaviour, and that the states described by those terms are themselves physical ones. (The doctrine is thus a version of strong materialism: it not only holds that persons are physical things, but also that the conscious states of persons are physical states.)

(A) Introducing Behaviourism

The problem of other minds is still with us. So long as we believe that conscious states are non-physical, any argument by analogy to the existence of other minds must fail, foundering on the unique status of our own mental states amongst the items of knowledge. And so long as we adhere to the cartesian conception, there can be no valid arguments from the observed physical circumstances and behaviour of other human beings to descriptions of their states of mind. Then either way we shall lack sufficient reason to believe in the existence of any other conscious states besides our own.

It is worth reminding ourselves just how counter-intuitive this conclusion is. Imagine that you see a friend fall heavily in a skiing accident. You approach to find them with an obviously broken leg, groaning loudly, with their face contorted in apparent agony. Naturally you would have not the slightest doubt that they are really in pain. Just try, in a case of this sort, holding on to the thought 'This is merely the behaviour of a non-conscious automaton'! It is almost psychologically impossible to do. Of course this does not by itself show that the thought in question is false, since we may somehow be caused to believe something which we really have no reason to believe. But it does bring out just how difficult it would be to live with the conclusion that we have no knowledge of other minds.

Since we are indeed certain that other people besides ourselves have conscious states, and since all our judgements concerning those states are based upon observations of their behaviour, this gives us a powerful motive for saying that those judgements are, themselves, judgements about behaviour. This is the thesis of the philosophical behaviourist. Behaviourism (of the sort which I shall refer to as 'reductive', later distinguishing it from 'holistic') aims to solve the problem of other minds by providing an analysis — a definition, a translation — of all words referring to conscious states into purely behavioural terms. On this view, there simply *is nothing to* our conscious states over and above behaviour and dispositions to behave. And since the behaviour in question is all overtly physical, the behaviourist is also a strong materialist.

('Methodological' behaviourism, in contrast, is merely the approach adopted nowadays by most psychologists. They insist that scientists have no business trying to discover the workings of the mind by introspection of their own mental processes, but should confine themselves to what is publicly observable and testable: namely behaviour. They need not insist, as the philosophical behaviourist does, that introspectively observable mental processes are really mere dispositions to engage in overt physical behaviour.)

The philosophical behaviourist can claim, and with some justice, that our thesis of the logical independence of mental and physical states was granted far too readily. Certainly the truth of this thesis does not follow from the obvious facts that someone can be in pain without showing it, and can be exhibiting pain-behaviour without really being in pain. Nor does it follow, from the fact that descriptions of actual behaviour are neither necessary nor sufficient for the correct application of a counsciousness-term, that the meanings of such terms cannot be cashed purely behaviourally.

All that really follows, is that a behavioural analysis would have to be complicated, to take into account not only actual behaviour, but also 'dispositional' or 'hypothetical' behaviour. For it may still be true of the person who is in pain but does not show it, that they *would* acknowledge being in pain *if* we asked them, or that they *would have* groaned *if* they had not been aware of us watching them, and so on. And it may still be true of the person who exhibits pain-behaviour without really being in pain, that they *would* confess to be practising for a performance in a play *if* we asked them, or that they *would not* be behaving as they are *if* there were no one watching them, and so on. It is in such terms that the behaviourist may hope to frame their definitions.

So although we might initially be inclined to object against the behaviourist, that a person can surely feel a twinge of pain which they do not express at the time, and which they immediately forget about so that it never emerges in any way in their behaviour, this is really no difficulty. For it may still be true that if someone had asked 'How do you feel?' they would have replied 'I feel a twinge of pain.' And this is all that the behaviourist claims to need: the fact of the person feeling that twinge simply *consists in* the fact that they would give such a reply if asked.

However, what does begin to emerge is just how complicated a behaviourist analysis of words like 'pain' would have to be (at least if it takes the form of a direct translation into purely behavioural terms). It would have to proceed roughly as follows: someone is in pain if and only if, either (a) they exhibit characteristic pain-behaviour (think how complicated a detailed spelling-out of this would be) and would not later say 'I was only pretending' etc., or (b) they do not exhibit pain-behaviour but would say 'I am in pain' if asked, and would not later say 'I was lying' etc., or (c) they do not exhibit pain-behaviour and would say 'I am not in pain' if asked, but would have exhibited pain-behaviour if the circumstances had been different (i.e. if they had had no motive for pretending) . . . and so on. But naturally mere complexity cannot show reductive behaviourism to be false: the mind is indeed complicated.

(B) Arguments for Behaviourism

It is certainly an argument in favour of behaviourism that it can provide us with a solution to the problem of other minds. Not only that, but the solution can also be satisfying, in the sense that it leaves us in position to explain how we ever became ensnared by the problem in the first place. For the behaviourist can concede that no amount of actual observed behaviour will ever entail a description of a conscious state. This is so, because to attribute conscious states to a person will always involve commitments about what they would have done in various non-actual circumstances. (The analysis of a consciousness-term will always involve clauses of the form 'will do . . . if . . .') But it does not follow from this, that we have to fall back on some sort of argument by analogy. Nor does it follow that there is any special problem about achieving knowledge of other people's conscious states, any more than there is a special problem about knowing that a stick is brittle (disposed to break) based upon observations of its age and appearance, and the way in which it resists bending. (For to attribute brittleness, too, will always involve commitments beyond what is actually observed.)

Another argument for behaviourism which has been particularly influential may be summarised as follows:

(1) The cartesian conception entails that the language in which we each of us describe our own conscious states is a 'private' language, which cannot be understood by anyone else.
(2) But private language is impossible.
(C1) So the cartesian conception must be false.
(3) The only alternative to the cartesian conception is some form of behaviourism.
(C2) So behaviourism must provide the true account of the meanings of consciousness-terms.

This argument is certainly valid. I shall postpone discussion of the truth of the premises until Chapter 6.

(C) Reductive vs Holistic Behaviourism

Despite the strength of the above arguments, there are in fact devastating objections to reductive behaviourism. These arise most obviously in connection with the attempt to analyse beliefs and desires into purely behavioural terms. For a belief only disposes to action in the presence of certain desires. And a desire only disposes to action in the presence of certain beliefs.

For example, there is in fact no behaviour which is characteristic of someone who believes that the ice on a particular pond is thin. If they desire death by drowning, then their belief may lead them to go skating. If they desire someone else's death, it may lead them to say 'That is a good place to skate.' If they possess neither of these desires, then they will presumably do something else instead; but precisely what they do will depend upon their other beliefs and desires. Moreover, all this is only 'may' and not 'must'. Even if they desire death by drowning they are not guaranteed to go skating. On the contrary, their abhorrence of cold water may send them heading for the bathroom with a bottle of sleeping-tablets.

It looks as if a behaviourist analysis of belief will require clauses referring to various hypothetical desires. The clauses will specify the behaviour which may be expected of someone holding that belief, who also has the desire in question. (E.g.: someone with belief P will do E if they have desire x, and will do F if they have desire y.) But then when we come to the behaviourist analysis of desire, this will in its turn require clauses referring to various hypothetical beliefs. (E.g.: someone with desire x will do E if they believe P, and will do F if they believe Q.) We should then be forced to move in circles.

However, it is doubtful whether the sort of circularity which is involved here must be vicious, nor that it must totally undermine the behaviourist programme. For there are other areas in which groups of concepts are similarly intertwined, in such a way that it is impossible to explain any one of them without mentioning the others. For example the concepts of space and of physical object are interrelated in just such a fashion.

You cannot introduce the concept of a physical object to some-one without introducing the idea of occupancy of space. Indeed the criteria of identity and identification for physical objects palpably involve the concepts of spatial position and change of spatial position. But then on the other hand you cannot explain the concept of space without bringing in talk of physical objects. For it is arguable that space itself just *is* relations obtaining between physical objects, so that if there were no physical objects there would be no space either. At any rate you certainly cannot form any conception of particular places (e.g. the spatial position of London) except as relative to the place occupied by yourself ('London is over there'), or the places occupied by physical things with which you are already familiar ('London is due south of Leeds').

Philosophers describe concepts which are intertwined in this kind of way as being related 'holistically'. Other examples come from science, where a group of new concepts may be introduced at the same time as a new scientific theory, in such a way that each one of those concepts can only be defined in terms of other concepts belonging to that theory. So although it is by no means clear what account should be given of holistic relations in general, perhaps it can be said that holistically related concepts get their sense from their role within some wider theory or interlocking group of beliefs. Then the only way to get to understand those concepts, is to become immersed in the theory.

In any case, whatever is the proper explanation of the phenomenon, it would seem that holistic circles cannot be vicious ones. For we do after all possess concepts of space and physical objects, as well as the concepts special to various scientific theories. Nor does it follow that holistically circular definitions must be totally useless. On the contrary, they display the connections between the holistically related concepts, grasp of which will form an important part of understanding them. It is thus open to the behaviourist to defend their analyses of the concepts of belief and desire against the charge of vicious circularity, by claiming that those concepts are related holistically, being embedded in our common-sense theories for explaining human action (sometimes called 'folk-psychology').

It is not merely in connection with beliefs and desires that behaviourism should take a holistic rather than a reductive form. There is a strong case for thinking that holistic definitions should be preferred in connection with all terms referring to conscious states. Consider for example the term 'pain'. We noted that a reductive analysis of pain (that is to say, an analysis into purely behavioural terms) would have to be extremely complicated. But more than this, it can be shown that it would have to be infinitely long. In which case the reductive programme is doomed to failure from the start. The only way to close off the definition is to allow other consciousness-terms to occur within its scope (i.e. to allow it to become holistic).

A reductive analysis of the term 'pain' would, of course, have to include a description of the various kinds of apparent pain-behaviour (screaming, grimacing, saying 'Ow!' or 'It hurts' etc.). It must also, as we noted, include descriptions of the various kinds of behaviour which would reveal that the behaviour of the first kind was not genuine pain-behaviour (later doing the same thing on a stage, later saying 'I was only pretending', etc.) But notice that these second kinds of behaviour are themselves only apparent instances of their kinds (acting a part, making a truthful statement about one's past, etc.). For the pain-behaviour on the stage may actually be genuine, and not acting at all; and the statement 'I was only pretending' may itself be a lie; and so on. So clearly the analysis should include descriptions of a third kind of behaviour, namely: behaviour which would reveal that the behaviour of the second kind was not really genuine (later saying 'What I did on stage wasn't acting, I was really in pain', or saying 'When I told you I had only been pretending, I was in fact lying'). But now this behaviour in its turn is only apparent behaviour of *its* kind. And so on. Clearly we have embarked on an infinite progression. So there is no way in which a reductive analysis could ever be completed.

The above argument appears decisive against any attempt to analyse the meaning of the word 'pain' into purely behavioural terms. The only avenue of reply left open to the behaviourist, is to claim that all conscious states, and not just beliefs and desires, are interrelated holistically. A holistic analysis might proceed as follows: someone is in pain if and only if, either (a) they exhibit characteristic pain behaviour which is not a manifestation of beliefs and desires leading them to think that feigning such behaviour is the best thing to do in the circumstances; or (b) they do not exhibit pain-behaviour, but this is a manifestation of beliefs and desires which lead them to think that suppressing such behaviour is the best thing to do in the circumstances.

(D) 'For the most part' Behaviourism

There is in fact a difficulty with the above holistic analysis, which although minor in itself, leads to an important qualification of the form which holistic analyses should take. The difficulty is this: someone may think that feigning pain-behaviour would not be the best thing to do in the circumstances, and yet still go ahead and do it anyway. Then according to the definition above, that person would really be in pain, since they exhibit pain-behaviour which does not manifest beliefs and desires leading them to think that feigning such behaviour is the best thing to do in the circumstances. This is the phenomenon of weakness of will: someone may decide that the best thing to do would be X rather than Y, and then — without apparently changing their mind — go ahead and do Y all the same.

The best response for a holistic-behaviourist to make to this difficulty is to cast their definitions in a 'for the most part' form, since examples of weakness of will are rare. We might then say: 'Someone is in pain if and only if they normally either . . ., or . . .' This might be a perfectly defensible approach to take. For we do not have any very exact idea of what someone with a given mental state will be disposed to do, and the folk-psychology in which the holistic-behaviourist analyses are embedded is only rough-and-ready. This is in itself no objection to the behaviourist programme. For after all, you can know that a particular stick is brittle (disposed to snap) without having any precise idea of the circumstances in which it will break.

Conclusion

What emerges from our discussion is this: as a result of the holistic interrelation of beliefs, desires and other conscious states, the behaviourist is forced to give up the search for piecemeal reductive analyses. Since there is no *getting rid of* talk of conscious states in favour of talk of actual and possible behaviour, there can be no way of analysing statements about such states into purely behavioural terms. Now the question is: does this undermine the whole behaviourist programme? Does holistic behaviourism really deserve the title 'behaviourism'?

There were two main aims behind the attempt to reduce all talk of conscious states to talk about behaviour. The first was to provide a solution to the problem of other minds. The second was to establish a version of strong materialism, by showing that conscious states are, necessarily, either physical behaviour or dispositions to such behaviour. Now since holistic behaviourism is equally well placed in both respects, it does genuinely deserve to be classed as a version of behaviourism

Firstly, the only difficulty about arriving at knowledge of other minds, on the holistic-behaviourist account, is that we can only ever attribute single mental states to a person against a background of assumptions about their other conscious states. But this will be equally true of our knowledge of the states of any complex system. We can never test claims about the states of such a system individually, without presupposing other elements of our total theory. Yet the whole theory will be justified just in case it provides satisfactory explanations of the behaviour of the system, as well as reasonably accurate predictions of future behaviour. In this respect our folk-psychology (and hence our belief in other minds) would appear to be eminently justified.

Secondly, since the output of the total theory, combining together all the holistically defined concepts, is solely concerned with actual and possible behaviour, this is sufficient to show that beliefs, desires and the rest simply are themselves dispositions to behaviour. It is merely that they are dispositions which can only operate in conjunction with other such dispositions. So this is still a version of strong materialism.

ii. From Behaviourism to Functionalism

This section will fall into three parts. In part (A) I shall present an objection to behaviourism, whether reductive or holistic. In part (B) I shall explain a new theory, to be entitled 'Functionalism', which overcomes the objection. Then in part (C) I shall introduce the problem which will concern us in section iii. Namely: what are behaviourists and functionalists to say about the sort of awareness which each one of us has of our own conscious states?

(A) Activity and State vs Disposition

Everyone admits that it is possible to feel a twinge of pain which goes unexpressed at the time, and which the person then completely forgets about. As we saw, the behaviourist will claim that the having of such a twinge merely consists in the fact that certain hypothetical sentences become true of them at the time. E.g. that if anyone were to ask the person how they feel, they would reply 'Just now I feel a twinge of pain.' But this account seems to get everything back-to-front. How can the pain itself merely consist in the disposition to make such a reply? Surely the pain is, rather, the positive state which is the cause of that disposition. Surely they are disposed to make that reply *because* they are in pain (rather than their disposition *being* the pain).

Another example: suppose someone wakes up one morning and thinks to themself 'It must be time to get up', this thought remaining unexpressed in either speech or action, perhaps because they straight away fall asleep again. Now the behaviourist will have to say that the person did not actually *do* anything at the time, since no observable behaviour took place. All that really happened is that they acquired when they woke up a certain disposition-to-behave (e.g. to say 'That it must be time to get up' in response to the question 'What are you thinking?') which in fact remained unactualised.

One way of articulating precisely why we find this sort of account so strange, is to ask how it is possible for a hypothetical sentence to be true ('If asked . . ., then they will say . . .') unless there is some categorical sentence which makes it true ('They are . . .'). For how can a thing have a dispositional property (a disposition-to-behave) unless there is some positive fact about it which explains, or constitutes, that disposition? Thus how can it be true that a particular glass is brittle ('If struck with moderate force, then it will break') unless there is some categorical fact about the glass which explains or constitutes its brittleness (presumably to do with its molecular structure)?

The behaviourist may reply that the positive change which takes place in the person when they wake up, which constitutes their acquisition of the disposition to behave, will be a change which takes place in the brain. Of course we do not know in detail what this change is, but then neither do we know exactly what it is about the glass which makes it brittle. Yet this reply seems inadequate. For we would ordinarily believe that the positive change which takes place in someone, which explains the truth of the hypothetical sentence, 'If asked . . ., then they will say . . .', is nothing other than their act of thinking itself. Surely it is that act which *explains* the disposition, rather than itself *being* the disposition.

These points converge on the following objection: we need to insist that thinking is an activity, which we are aware of engaging in at the time when we engage in it. And we know that we sometimes engage in that activity privately. Then it cannot be right to analyse words which refer to activities ('think', 'imagine', etc.) in such a way that in certain circumstances (i.e. private thinking) they merely refer to behavioural dispositions. We need to insist that when someone thinks something privately to themself, they are actually doing something positive at the time. When someone engages in a private train of thought, it cannot be right to say that what really happens is that they merely acquire a whole series of dispositions-to-behave which remain unactualised.

Although I have focused here on the behaviourist's treatment of unexpressed pains and acts of thinking, the objection is really quite general. Our ordinary view is that conscious states are the causes of (rather than identical with) our behaviour and behavioural dispositions. Thus when someone screams and groans in pain we normally think that the pain itself is not the behaviour but the cause of the behaviour. And when someone is not exhibiting pain-behaviour but is disposed to do so (would do so is we were to ask them about their feelings perhaps) we do not think that the disposition is itself the pain. Rather: if it is true that they would answer 'I am in pain' if asked how they are feeling, then this is *because* they are in pain. So conscious states cannot in general be identified with behavioural states — whether actual or dispositional — since they are rather the causes of those states.

(B) Functionalism

The best response for a behaviourist to make to the above objection, is not to fight it but to absorb it, altering their theory accordingly. Instead of saying that pain is, by definition, a sort of behaviour and/or disposition to behave, they should say that pain is, by definition, the cause of that sort of behaviour and/or disposition. And instead of trying to analyse an unexpressed act of thinking as the mere appearance at that time of a particular disposition-to-behave, they should analyse it as the event which causes that disposition to occur. Nor should a train of thought be analysed as a sequence of dispositions-to-behave making their appearance one after the other, but as a sequence of actual events, each one of which is the cause of a particular disposition.

Construed in this way, behaviourism would no longer be attempting to analyse unexpressed pains and acts of thinking into the wrong category, namely the category of disposition rather than the category of event. Nor would those pains and acts of thinking which *are* expressed, be identified with their behavioural manifestation, but rather (as we would intuitively believe) with the private events which cause that behaviour. Such a theory would still deserve the title 'behaviourism', since the aim continues to be to provide an analysis (either reductive or holistic) of all words referring to mental states into purely behavioural terms (together with the term 'cause'). An appropriate title for the theory might be 'causal-role behaviourism'.

Causal-role behaviourism is a better, more plausible, theory than behaviourism. But if we are now analysing mental states in terms of their behavioural effects, our position may be strengthened still further by allowing into the analysis descriptions of their physical causes as well. If it is plausible to claim that an essential part of knowing the meaning of the word 'pain', is knowing that pain is normally the cause of certain kinds of behaviour and behavioural disposition, then it is equally plausible to claim that one will need to know that pain is generally caused by various kinds of injury or violence to the body. Similarly, if it is plausible to include in the analysis of the phrase 'sensation of red' the fact that such sensations are often the causes of certain kinds of behaviour (e.g.

picking up a red book in response to the request 'Bring me the red one'), then it will be equally plausible to include such facts as that sensations of red are generally caused by exposure to something red within one's field of vision.

We are now proposing that mental states should be analysed in terms of their normal causal role, mediating between a specified input — e.g. injury — and a specified output — e.g. pain-behaviour. But if we are analysing mental states in terms of their normal causes as well as their normal behavioural effects, then it is no longer appropriate to describe the theory as a version of behaviourism. A better title would be 'functionalism', since we should in fact be analysing mental states in terms of their functions. Thus the normal function of pain is to be the causal intermediary between a specified bodily cause and a specified sort of behavioural effect.

It is worth noting that some mental states will turn out on analysis to be closer to the input end, and some closer to the output. Thus a sensation of red will be close to the input and at some distance from the output: its characteristic cause is a physical event (light striking the retina, etc.), but its characteristic effects include other mental states (such as forming the belief that there is a red thing in the environment) and it will only have effects on behaviour indirectly, via these other mental states. A decision, on the other hand, will be close to the output and at some distance from the input. The characteristic effect of a decision is, fairly immediately, a bodily movement. But its characteristic causes will include other mental states such as thoughts and desires, and it will only be linked to the physical input via these other mental states.

So as with behaviourism, functionalism will be most plausible in a holistic form, allowing us to mention other mental states amongst the causes and effects of the state under analysis. Also as behaviourism, its analyses should be cast in a 'for the most part' form. (Of course some pains are not caused by tissue-damage, and some — for example a slight twinge — need not issue in any disposition to pain-behaviour.) An example will make clear why this should be so.

Compare the mind with any complicated machine, such as the motor-car. We have concepts, such as 'gear-box' and 'carburettor', for describing the various parts of a car. These concepts are functionally defined, their meanings being given in terms of the causal roles of the parts within the overall functioning of the machine.

Thus gear-boxes can be made out of many diverse materials, and present a wide range of appearances. All that is essential, is that they should occupy the characteristic causal role of a gear-box. But of course there can be no saying what the function of a gear-box is without mentioning any other parts of the engine, since it only has its function when in conjunction with those other parts. Moreover its function should be described in 'for the most part' terms, since engines do not always work as they ought.

Similarly then with the mind: we believe that human behaviour characteristically results from the causal interaction of many different mental states, some of these interactions taking place at some distance from the behaviour itself. And we believe that these mental states in turn, are caused in complex ways by other mental states and by the impact of the physical environment on the body. Small wonder then, that there can be no describing the function of any given mental state without mentioning other such states, and that mental states do not always occupy precisely the causal roles which they normally would.

Note that functionalism inherits at least one of the major advantages of behaviourism, in that it too can provide us with a satisfying solution to the problem of other minds. For we have knowledge of the relevant inputs and outputs, and we are surely entitled to assume that there exists a causal intermediary between them. If 'pain' means 'state which is normally caused by tissue damage and which normally causes a disposition to pain-behaviour', then we can surely know that other people have pains. But because of the occurrence of the term 'normally' in the definition, there can be no valid deduction from observations of tissue damage and ensuing pain-behaviour to the existence of a pain: for it is always possible that this is one of the unusual cases. So we can still explain how it was that we became ensnared by the problem of other minds in the first place.

(It may be worth remarking that the existence of 'for the most part' definitions puts us in position to challenge one of the main premises in the argument giving rise to the problem of other minds, namely the claim that all arguments are either deductive or inductive. For if pains are defined in terms of their normal causal role, then the connection between pains and their normal causes and effects is certainly not an inductive, contingent, one. It is not something which we discover empirically, but something which we fix when we fix our concept of pain. But then on the other hand, the occurrence of the term 'normally' in the definition means that the argument from normal causes and effects to the existence of a pain is not deductively valid either. The connection is a 'loose logical' one.)

Note, however, that functionalism is in principle neutral between weak dualism and strong materialism. For nothing is said in the theory about whether the causal intermediaries are themselves physical or non-physical. In fact it is usual for functionalists to be strong materialists, for reasons similar to those which will emerge in Chapter 5. But they do not have to be. So here is one half of the claimed logical independence of weak dualism from the cartesian conception of meaning, mentioned, but not argued for, in section 1.iv. Since it is possible for the cartesian conception to be false (i.e. if functionalism is true) while weak dualism remains true, weak dualism does not itself entail the cartesian conception.

(C) 1st Person vs 3rd Person

Both behaviourism and functionalism are at their most plausible when providing third-person analyses of mental states (e.g. 'That person is in pain'). For we do after all judge of the truth of such statements by observing people's physical circumstances and behaviour. But can they provide even half-way plausible accounts of the meanings of first-person descriptions (e.g. 'I am in pain')? For I certainly do not judge that I myself am in pain by observing my own physical circumstances and behaviour! Yet the term 'pain' is surely not ambiguous between its first- and third-person uses. I do not mean one thing when I talk about my own pains (a state with a particular qualitative feel), and something quite different when I talk about someone else's pain (a state occupying a particular causal role).

Now a behaviourist would have to respond by saying that the utterance 'I am in pain' is itself just a piece of pain-manifesting behaviour. It is like saying 'Ouch!' Like a groan or a grimace it evinces pain without describing it. Then of course I would not need to infer the truth of the sentence 'I am in pain' from observations of my behaviour, since the utterance of that sentence itself would be a piece of behaviour of the appropriate kind. Indeed the distinctive thing about the utterance would be that it verifies itself. (Compare: 'I am now speaking English'.)

This response is inadequate, however, on at least two counts. Firstly, 'I am in pain', unlike 'Ouch!', surely is genuinely descriptive. For instance it can occur in conditionals just like any other descriptive statement: just as I can say 'If she is in pain, give her more analgesic', so too can I say 'If I am in pain, give me more analgesic'. (Contrast: 'If ouch, give me more analgesic'.) Moreover when we think of the kinds of complex descriptions which we can offer of our experiences, it becomes quite implausible to try and construe all our utterances as mere behavioural manifestations of the corresponding states. Think for example of saying to your doctor 'This pain is most unusual: it alternatively throbs and stabs, and in between fades almost to a tickle.'

Secondly, even if the statement 'I am in pain' were a non-descriptive behavioural manifestation of pain, I should still strictly have to infer the fact that I am in pain from observations of my behaviour (included in which would be the utterance of the sentence 'I am in pain'). If pain is, by definition, either pain-behaviour or a disposition to such behaviour, then I should need to reason as follows: I have just uttered the sentence 'I am in pain', which is an example of normal pain-behaviour; I have no reason to believe that I possess beliefs and desires which would lead me to produce such behaviour as a pretence; so very likely I am in pain. Of course this would be absurd. I do not need — not even 'strictly speaking' — to reason from my utterance to my pain. On the contrary, I make that utterance precisely because I am aware that I am in pain.

As a result of this brief discussion of the behaviourist's treatment of the first person, we can lay down three general constraints which any adequate functionalist account must meet. Firstly, it must explain how we do not, in our own case, need to reason from observations of our own physical circumstances and behaviour to descriptions of our own conscious states. Our knowledge of our own minds is somehow immediate and non-inferential. Secondly, it must allow for the fact that utterances like 'I am in pain' are genuinely descriptive, and are either true or false (unlike 'Ouch!' which is neither). Thirdly, it must explain how first-person descriptions of mental states have the same sort of content — the same sort of meaning — as third-person descriptions. The word 'pain' is not ambiguous, meaning one thing when I describe my own pains, and something different when I describe those of other people. In the next section we shall consider a number of different functionalist accounts, each of which meets these three general constraints. It is a further advantage of functionalism over behaviourism, that no behaviourist theory can even get this far.

iii. First-personal Problems

I shall discuss three distinct proposals whereby functionalism may hope to overcome the difficulties with the first-person, outlined at the end of section 4.ii. Since none of them is entirely adequate, I shall conclude that functionalism is a (partly) false theory of the manner in which we conceive of the mind. Not all expressions referring to mental states can be analysed in purely functional terms.

What is common to each of the three proposals, is that both first-person and third-person statements about the mind are said to have some sort of content: the same causal-role-describing meaning: but there are claimed to be two different modes of knowledge of that role. The third-person mode of knowledge is by observation and inference: observing the normal causes and effects of a particular mental state, we reason to the existence of the normal causal intermediary. But the first-person mode of knowledge is by observation alone: each one of us is caused to have direct knowledge of the states with the causal roles in question, through introspection.

So on each of the three accounts my first-person judgements and statements are genuine judgements, and genuine statements; not mere behavioural effects of the mental states in question. And when I judge that I am in pain my judgement has exactly the same content which it has when I judge that someone else is in pain. Namely: that there is occurring a state whose normal cause is tissue-damage, and whose normal effects include dispositions to pain-behaviour, as well as the disposition to judge that one is in that state. But I do not need to base my judgement upon observations of tissue-damage or behaviour, because it is part of the content of what I judge, that a disposition to make such a judgement is amongst the normal effects of the state which I am judging about. So if I find myself inclined to judge that I am in pain, then this is by itself sufficient reason to believe that I am in pain.

So much for what all the proposals have in common. It should be clear that their common features enable each one of them to meet the general constraints laid down at the end of the last section. I shall now explain and discuss the different proposals in turn, making clear as I proceed how they differ from one another.

Proposal (A)

On each of the first two proposals, my knowledge of my own mental states is genuinely perceptual. Contrary to the sort of view expressed in section 1.iv, my mental states are not themselves states of awareness. Rather they are distinct from but characteristically cause such awareness. So in this respect no distinction is being drawn between the senses of the phrase 'aware of' as it occurs in 'aware of a pain' and 'aware of a man in the distance'. In both cases the objects of the awareness (a pain, a man) are distinct from the awareness itself; and in each case the awareness is characteristically caused by its object.

On each of the first two functionalist proposals, our introspective knowledge of our own mental states (construed as functional states, defined in terms of their normal causal role) is genuinely perceptual. By introspection we arrive at judgements about our own mental states; those judgements qualifying as knowledge because they are almost always correct; and qualifying as perceptual because they are themselves caused by the mental states in question.

The distinctive feature of the first proposal, is that introspection is held to lack any phenomenological content. There are no such things as private sensations or 'feels' on the basis of which we judge. Rather, we just have the capacity to get it right most of the time, by direct 'intuition'. In fact proposal (A) might be represented diagrammatically thus:

$$\text{Tissue damage} \rightarrow \left\{ \text{PAIN} \right\} \begin{array}{l} \rightarrow \text{Intuitive awareness of pain} \\ \rightarrow \text{Disposition to pain-behaviour} \end{array}$$

On this account, all that exists are the states occupying their respective causal roles (together with their normal causes and effects), and the judgements caused by the states which they describe.

Compare my knowledge of the position of my own limbs. It is clear that the content of a first-person judgement of limb-position is exactly the same as of a third-person judgement. If I say 'My legs are crossed' this obviously has the same sort of meaning as when I say 'That person's legs are crossed.' But in my own case I do not have to discover the arrangement of my limbs by looking and seeing, nor by feeling with my hands. But then neither (arguably) do I go by any sensations characteristic of bodily position. For it is doubtful whether there really are any such sensations. (There are tactile sensations of course. But I can normally state the position of my limbs without relying upon them.) Rather, I just have the capacity to get it right most of the time, my judgements somehow being caused by the limb-positions which they describe.

The main objection to this version of functionalism, is precisely that it leaves wholly out of account the way things feel to me. Judgements that I am in pain are surely quite unlike judgements about the position of my limbs. For they are not just intuitive. I certainly do not merely find myself thinking, on no apparent basis whatever, 'There is a state occurring whose characteristic cause is tissue damage and whose characteristic effects include a disposition to pain-behaviour.' On the contrary, if such a thought occurs to me at all, it does so precisely because I *feel* the state in question. So far from being merely intuitive, judgements that I am in pain are made on the basis of my felt awareness of pain.

Any account of the mind which tries to treat all mental states as if they were without phenomenological content, must surely be rejected as inadequate. There really is such a thing as what pains and sensations of red feel like. I know from my own experience what they feel like, and I know that they feel completely different from one another. I do not merely have a bare ('intuitive') capacity to distinguish them. Rather, I distinguish them from one another on the basis of their different, and distinctive, qualitative 'feels'.

However, not all mental states have phenomenological content. The mind is not uniform. Beliefs, desires and thoughts are quite different from experiences like pains and sensations of red. If I believe that it will rain tomorrow, want it to be sunny, and am thinking about what to do if it is not, then I may know myself to be in these states. But I do not know this on the basis of what it feels like to be in them. For it does not feel like anything to believe that it will rain tomorrow. There is no such thing as the qualitative 'feel' of a belief or a thought.

I can see no good reason why this version of functionalism should not be accepted as an account of those mental states which are not experiences, or which do not (unlike felt emotions) have an experiential aspect. To have a particular belief is to be in a state occupying a particular causal role, amongst whose normal effects is a disposition to believe that one is in that state. What is distinctive about a conscious (as opposed to an unconscious) belief, is that it has among other things the capacity to cause a second-order belief, namely the belief that one has that belief. Similarly, a particular thought is an event occupying a distinctive causal role, which generally causes the belief that such an event is occurring.

Proposal (B)

The second proposal is an obvious development of the first. It is that in the case of experiences, we have introspective knowledge of the states which occupy the appropriate causal roles via the awareness of the distinctive qualitative feels which they cause in us. So I do not simply find myself inclined to judge — apparently groundlessly — that I am in pain. Rather, I am caused to be aware of the distinctive feel of pain, and judge that I am in pain on that basis. Diagrammatically:

$$
\text{Tissue damage} \rightarrow \left\{ \text{PAIN} \right\} \begin{array}{l} \rightarrow \text{Awareness of the qualitative feel of pain} \\ \rightarrow \text{Disposition to pain-behaviour} \end{array}
$$

Note that on this version of functionalism, as on the previous one, there is a distinction being drawn between the pain itself, and our awareness of it. Yet the awareness of pain is no longer thought of as some kind of contentless intuitive knowledge, but rather as a particular sort of qualitative feel, caused by the pain itself. In fact it is being claimed that experiences are functionally-defined states, amongst whose characteristic effects are their distinctive qualitative feels.

One difficulty with this account is that the problem of other minds immediately raises its head once again. For although I may surely know, in the case of other people, that they are in a state whose cause is tissue damage, and whose normal effects include a disposition to pain-behaviour, how can I know that the qualitative feel which that state causes in them is anything like the feeling which similar states cause in myself? The assumption in the definition above is that the qualitative feel of pain is the same across all different experiencers. But how do I know this? If nothing, for me, counts as a pain which does not cause this qualitative feel (the feel which I call 'the feel of pain') then it seems I cannot know that other people have pains. So this version of functionalism only finds a place for qualitative feels at the expense of losing what seemed to be the distinctive advantage of behaviourist and functionalist accounts of the mind. Namely: of explaining how we can have knowledge of the mental states of others.

The functionalist may try to surmount this difficulty by denying that the particular character of the feeling which any individual person has, is of any relevance to the question of whether or not they are in pain. All that matters is that there is some feeling which pain causes in them, on the basis of which they may correctly judge that they are in pain. Diagrammatically:

Tissue
damage → { PAIN } → Awareness of some qualitative feel or other
→ Disposition to pain-behaviour

Then so long as I know that other people have states caused by tissue damage which cause a disposition to pain-behaviour, and which cause some qualitative feeling in them (not necessarily the same as in me), I should know that they have pains. On this account, although pains do cause qualitative feels, the distinctive natures of those feelings are semantically redundant.

This suggestion may be rejected out of hand. Nothing could be a pain which did not normally have (or cause) the distinctive feel of pain (that is to say, the feel which I refer to in my own case as 'the feel of pain'). If I imagine that in the case of someone else the state which is caused by tissue damage and which causes pain-behaviour, causes in them a feeling which (were I to be aware of it) I should describe as 'a sensation of red', then I have imagined someone who does not in fact have pains.

What our experiences feel like — their distinctive qualitative character — is surely essential to their identity. For example, suppose that you were trying to get across to a congenitally blind person the concept of 'a sensation of red'. You can tell them all about the normal causes and effects of this experience. And you can tell them that it causes a distinctive qualitative feel. But none of this will get across the essential thing; namely: what it actually feels like to experience a sensation of red. And until they know this, they surely do not know what 'sensation of red' means.

A further difficulty with proposal (B) — on either version of it — is that it would be possible upon occasion to be completely mistaken about the nature of our experiences. It would be possible that the distinctive qualitative feels on which we base our judgements, should sometimes be caused in some other way; in which case it would be possible to hallucinate pain (to feel as if one were in pain when one was not). And it would also be possible that the state occupying the causal role of pain may sometimes fail to cause the appropriate feeling. Then it may seem to me that I am not in pain — perhaps it seems to me that I am experiencing nothing, or perhaps a tickle — when in fact I am. But in my view neither of these is a genuine possibility. I want to say that if everything feels to someone as though they are in pain, then they are indeed in pain; and if everything feels to them as though they are not, then they are not. But I shall postpone further discussion of this matter until the next section, where it will be treated more thoroughly.

What delivers the decisive blow against proposal (B) as a general account of the mind, is that there would remain some mental states which could not be defined in terms of their causal roles, namely the qualitative feels themselves. For the whole point of this proposal is that we are to know of the occurrence of our functionally-defined mental states through an immediate ('straight off') recognition of the feelings which they cause in us. So even if these feelings do have causal roles of some sort, they are certainly not identified or conceived of in terms of their causal role. Then even if proposal (B) were correct as regards the analysis of words such as 'pain', 'after-image' and 'experience of red' (and whether or not this is so will depend upon whether it is possible to be mistaken about such states), it would not cover descriptions such as 'feel of pain', 'awareness of an after-image', or 'felt-quality of an experience of red'.

Proposal (C)

An obvious strategy for dealing with the problems which arose with proposal (B), would be to deny that pain is normally the cause of our awareness of its qualitative feel; insisting instead that pain is in fact identical with our awareness of that feeling, provided that it occupies a distinctive causal role. Diagrammatically:

$$\text{Tissue damage} \rightarrow \left\{ \begin{array}{c} \text{Awareness of the} \\ \text{qualitative feel of} \\ \text{pain = PAIN} \end{array} \right\} \rightarrow \begin{array}{c} \text{Disposition to} \\ \text{pain-behaviour} \end{array}$$

This is, after all, our common-sense view. We believe that it is the felt quality of our experiences which cause us to cry out, rather than that the awareness of that felt quality, and the crying out, are both caused by some further underlying state (the pain).

Although this proposal still leaves us with the problem of other minds (for how do I know that the state acting as the causal intermediary between injury and crying in other people, has the same qualitative feel as the state occupying that causal role in myself?), it does have two important advantages. Both derive from the fact that introspection is no longer being viewed as a genuine species of perception. The awareness of pain is no longer being thought of as something distinct from, but caused by, the pain itself; rather the awareness of pain *is* the pain. So there is no room for the possibility of either hallucinating pain or its absence. Neither are there any states left over, which cannot themselves be defined in functionalist terms.

Under proposal (C), conscious experiences are to be defined as a conjunction of qualitative feel with causal role. It would be on the basis of their feel that I would know of the existence of my own conscious states, but it would be on the basis of their causal role that I would (supposedly) know of those of other people. Then on such an account pain is, by definition, both a state with a particular distinctive feel, and which normally is caused by tissue damage and causes a disposition to pain-behaviour. But the main trouble with this account is that it appears at least logically possible for the two elements of the conjunction to come apart.

Even if the feel of pain is, in our world, the state occupying the characteristic causal role of pain, there appear to be other possible worlds in which this is not so. It seems we can imagine worlds in which that feeling normally has quite different causes and effects. (Equally, we can apparently imagine worlds in which the causal role of pain is occupied by some quite different feeling.) What would we say about such a world? According to the definition above, if there occurs a state with the feel of pain, but normally occupying some different causal role, then it is not really a pain (for only one half of the definition is satisfied). But I should want to describe this case by saying that it is a world in which pains have quite different causes and effects. For surely, anything which feels like a pain is indeed a pain. (Again this will be argued in greater depth in the next section.)

Proposal (C) could only be adequate, in my view, if we could demonstrate some sort of necessary connection between the two elements of the conjunction. Only if we can tie the feel of pain logically to its causal role can we do justice to our intuition that anything with the feel of pain is a pain, by declaring that the possible world, apparently imagined above, is in fact impossible. And only if we can tie the feel of pain logically to its causal role does it appear likely that proposal (C) can help us with the problem of other minds. For otherwise how are we to infer, from our observations of the normal causes and effects in other people, that there intervenes a state with the qualitative feel of pain?

None of this appears at all likely: there just does not seem to be the sort of necessary connection which we need. But appearances can be deceptive, and I shall return to the matter in section 6.iv.

Summary

Proposal (A) could only be adequate if experiences, as well as thoughts and beliefs, lack any distinctive qualitative feels. Proposal (B) (and indeed proposal (A)) could only be adequate if it were possible to be mistaken about the nature of one's own experiences. And proposal (C) could only be adequate if some kind of necessary connection were to exist between the feels of our experiences and their distinctive causal roles. The difficulties with proposal (A) are insurmountable, as are the difficulties with proposal (B). (Though we shall consider further what scope there is for error about our own experiences in the next section.) Proposal (C) we shall return to at the end of Chapter 6; but at the moment it, too, appears implausible.

iv. Errors in Mind

Two of the versions of functionalism discussed in the last section treat introspection as a genuine species of perception. Our awareness of our own mental states is said to be distinct from, though characteristically caused by, the existence of those states. It follows from this that we may sometimes be in error about our own states of mind: I may think that I am in pain when I am not, and I may deny that I am in pain when in fact I am. This idea will be subjected to critical scrutiny in part (B) of this section. But we shall begin in part (A) by considering an even more radical version of the thesis. Namely: that I may be mistaken in thinking that I have experiences — or at least experiences of the kinds which I think I have — at all. As we shall see, the two issues are in fact closely connected.

(A) Radical Error

Recall from section 4.i, the holistic interrelatedness of our concepts for classifying mental states. In trying to explain this phenomenon we noted that those concepts are embedded within a wider network of beliefs about the mind, involving many such concepts. These are mostly beliefs about which sorts of mental state are causally related with which, and about the causal relations between mental states and physical circumstances and behaviour. This network we referred to as 'folk-psychology'. Now there are some who say that our common-sense folk-psychology is a primitive scientific theory. The network of beliefs in which our everyday mental concepts are embedded, is said to constitute our first tentative steps on the road to a completed science of the mind.

If this were correct, then there would be no particular reason to think that folk-psychology should survive through future scientific discovery and change. On the contrary, there is every reason to think that it will not. For there are many phenomena — ranging from weakness of will to the more exotic forms of mental illness — which we are powerless to explain in terms of our everyday beliefs and concepts.

It seems reasonable to suppose that any future completed science of the mind will work with quite different assumptions and concepts from those employed in folk-psychology. Then if our folk-psychology were intended as a scientific theory, it would eventually have to be rejected as a false theory of the mind. In that case it would turn out that there are no such things as desires, pains, mental images or sensations of red: we should be radically in error about our own mental states. Our belief in such entities would one day come to seem just as crude and primitive as a belief in witches or phlogiston now seems to us. In a sense, the mind as we (think we) know it would one day be eliminated. (Indeed in one of its versions this view is known as 'Eliminative Materialism', since it holds that the beliefs and concepts which are to replace folk-psychology should deal exclusively with physical phenomena.)

Now I agree that future science will probably not respect the classifications of mental states which we currently make. And I agree that future psychology may look completely different from our present folk-psychology. But it only follows that folk-psychology will thereby have been shown to be false, rather than continuing to be true alongside the new science, if it did purport to be a scientific theory in the first place. And it will only follow that there are no such things as pains or sensations of red, if we currently use the terms 'pain' and 'sensation of red' with the intention of dividing up mental phenomena in the way that Nature herself divides them. That is to say: if we have committed ourselves, in the use of those terms, to classifying mental states in the way in which a future completed science would classify them. Otherwise our current psychological concepts can legitimately continue to exist alongside the new ones.

The important point to grasp is that not all ways of classifying the world purport to 'divide nature at the joints'. Not all concepts attempt to classify things in the way that a completed science would classify them. Nor does every network of beliefs and causal explanations constitute a scientific theory. For there are many other points of view from which we can select a set of concepts, and start to classify things, besides the scientific.

Think for example of our concepts for classifying items of furniture, such as 'table', 'chair' and 'lamp'. These concepts obviously do not purport to be scientific ones; the purposes for which they have been selected are more social than scientific. Moreover it is clear that the loose network of beliefs and causal explanations in which these concepts figure ('You cannot sit at the table because the chair is too high', 'The lamp is not powerful enough to illuminate a table of that size') does not itself purport to be a scientific theory, although it presupposes a certain amount of (low-level) scientific knowledge. So it would be absurd to suggest that future science may discover that there are really no such things as tables and chairs. It may then be, that our concept of 'pain' is more like our concept of 'chair' than it is like our concepts of 'plant' or 'fish'.

Of course it is true that pains and sensations of red occur naturally, whereas tables and chairs are human artefacts. But this need not mean that the points of view from which we classify them are not equally social rather than scientific in orientation. Compare our classification of foodstuffs: we classify these into spices, vegetables, pulses, grains and so on. Like experiences, these items are naturally occurring. Also like experiences (on the functionalist view) they are defined in terms of their functions. Thus: a spice is any product of a plant (this is why salt is not a spice) which is capable of altering the tastes of food in certain characteristic ways. Moreover they figure in causal explanations ('It tasted bad because it contained too much spice', 'The bread is heavy because the wheat was coarse-ground') and form part of a wider network of common-sense beliefs.

It is obvious that the term 'spice' is not intended to divide nature at the joints. (For instance: a chilli is a spice, though a green pepper is a vegetable; despite the fact that the two belong to the same biological family.) Nor does the network of beliefs in which it is embedded constitute a scientific theory. So there can be no question of future science discovering that there are really no such things as spices. We classify together the items we call 'spices' because they belong together from the point of view of our practical interest in taste and cooking, not because we think they belong together from the point of view of scientific theory.

Something similar is true in connection with our use of the terms 'belief', 'pain' and 'sensation of red'. We do not intend that they should divide nature at the joints. Nor is the folk-psychology in which they are embedded a scientific theory. Rather, the classifications reflect our various social interests and purposes (trying to change someone's mind, asking for and rendering sympathy, and so on), against a background of loosely structured common-sense beliefs. So there is no threat to folk-psychology, nor its concepts, from the future development of science.

This is not to say that our mental classifications will never change in the light of future scientific discoveries. But any changes will be pragmatically-based replacements of our current modes of classification, rather than direct falsifications of them. The old modes of classification will still remain available, and if used will still be capable of yielding true judgements. It will merely be that, our purposes and practices having changed under the impact of scientific discovery and technological change, there may be other modes of classification which subserve those purposes better than do our present ones.

For example, scientists may one day discover that there is a particular type of tickle, and a particular type of pain (each of which is discriminable from the other types) which are a sign of the onset of certain kinds of serious illness. It would be entirely natural to respond to this discovery by changing our mode of classification, classifying together as 'the same sensation' feelings which we had previously distinguished from one another. But this would not show that there are no such things as tickles or pains; nor that my current judgement, that I have a pain in my foot, is false.

(B) Local Error

I have argued that there is no real possibility of us being radically in error about our own conscious states. But there apparently remains the possibility of local error. Although I am certainly not mistaken in thinking that pains really occur, I may perhaps occasionally be mistaken in thinking that I am or am not in pain at that particular time. However I shall argue that this view (at least as it regards our experiences) depends upon essentially the same fallacy: that of thinking that our interest in psychological classifications is a scientific one.

My intuitions are very firmly to the effect that the things which functionalists generally claim as possibilities are not really possible at all. I want to say that if everything seems to someone as though they are in pain — if they are aware of the distinctive qualitative feel of pain — then they are indeed in pain; even if that feeling is somehow caused by a state which results from light striking the retina, and which causes a bout of giggling. Equally, I want to say that if everything seems to someone as though they are *not* in pain — if they are not aware of any pain — then they are not really *in* pain; even if the tissues of their hand are being damaged, and they find themselves jerking that hand away from something hot and nursing it.

On one version of functionalism, when I make judgements about my own pains, I think 'through' the qualitative feel (as it were) to the underlying cause (whatever it may be). Then what my judgement is really about (the pain) is not the qualitative feel itself, but rather the underlying cause of that feel. Now this would be an entirely appropriate mode of thinking if we were doing science. Indeed it may be that some psychologists already do use terms like 'pain' and 'sensation of red' in the way that this sort of functionalist describes. Since they are interested in the underlying causes of our conscious states rather than their distinctive feels, this would be an eminently sensible thing to do.

However our everyday classifications of mental phenomena are not, in the way in which most of us employ them, merely primitive science. For as I have said already, the purposes for which we make use of those classifications are more social than scientific. To adopt the scientific perspective towards other human beings or towards oneself — the perspective from which it becomes appropriate to think 'through' the qualitative feel of an experience to the underlying cause — is in a sense to regard those beings as mere objects: as complicated systems whose functioning we try to explain and predict, in the way that you might try to explain and predict the functioning of a machine. But most of the time we regard human beings (including ourselves) as subjects, with their own subjective view of themselves and the world. Here it is important for us to try to see things from their point of view: to understand how things seem and feel to them. From this perspective it is the qualitative feel of pain which matters, and the nature of the underlying cause is of no immediate relevance.

For everyday purposes (the purposes which matter most to us in our own daily lives) we have no motive to employ concepts of experience in the way that this sort of functionalist describes. When we make judgements about a pain or a sensation of red, we are not judging about the underlying cause of a particular feeling. Rather, our judgement is about the qualitative feel itself. And in this there does not appear to be any room for error, at least not in judgements of immediate recognition (see the 'certainty thesis' of section 1.iv).

However, as we noted in the last section, the mind is not uniform. Since beliefs (and most desires) do not have any felt characteristics, our first-person judgements about them cannot be judgements of recognition. Nor can those judgements be primarily concerned with qualitative feel, since the states in question do not possess any distinctive feel. Even more significant, perhaps, it is part of our ordinary conception of these states that they are relatively long-term, continuing to exist when we are no longer aware of them. Experiences, on the other hand, are episodic: when you cease to be aware of a pain or a sensation of red the experience ceases. These features combine to make it possible that we should sometimes be mistaken about our conscious beliefs and desires.

For example, suppose that someone who previously had believed in the existence of the soul were to become convinced of the falsity of their belief after reading this book, this change of mind entering consciously into their thoughts on a number of occasions. Then you ask them one morning what they believe, and they — forgetting their change of mind — sincerely profess to be a dualist. Then later in the day they are back once again, stoutly maintaining the truth of materialism. Might we not naturally describe this as a case in which someone makes a mistake about what they believe? For it does not seem very plausible to say that they changed their mind in the morning, and back again in the afternoon, in both cases without being aware of having done so. Rather, we should say that they believed in materialism throughout, but that on that one morning they momentarily forgot what they really believed. There will be many examples of this general sort.

I can see no reason why we should not embrace a functionalist account of self-consciously held beliefs and desires. We can say that we conceive of them as states occupying distinctive causal roles, amongst whose normal effects will be a disposition to cause the second-order judgement that one is in such a state. It will then be possible occasionally that the sencond-order judgement should be caused inappropriately by some other state, so that we believe falsely that we have a particular belief or a particular desire.

Note that this concession to functionalism does not destroy the distinction between conscious and unconscious beliefs and desires. If we conceive of the states as characteristically causing self-aware-ness of them in the subject who has them, then although we may sometimes make mistakes, each person is in a position of special authority with respect to their own beliefs and desires. This is the conception of (conscious) belief and desire which subserves our everyday needs and purposes: we want to know how the subject sees themself, in order that we may try to reason with them, or change their mind. But from a scientific perspective what interests us is to be able to explain the person's behaviour. From this point of view it does not matter over-much whether the beliefs and desires appealed to in the explanation are self-consciously held or not. We may then employ a concept of (unconscious) belief and desire, as mere behaviour-determining states.

Conclusion

No version of functionalism can, it seems, provide a complete account of the mind. Although it can offer an adequate analysis of our concepts of belief and desire, our concepts of experience remain recalcitrant. Until returning to the issue in Chapter 6, I propose to continue as if the cartesian conception provided the correct account of the latter range of concepts. That is to say: I propose to assume that the meanings of terms such as 'pain' and 'sensation of red' are wholly concerned with the qualitative feel of the states they describe. So although it may be true that these states do occupy causal roles, this will be true as a matter of contingent fact, and not out of logical necessity.

Questions and Readings

It will help focus your thoughts if you discuss/think about/write about some of the following questions:

(1) Could there be people who feel pain but never exhibit pain-behaviour?
(2) Is the statement 'I am in pain' a description of my private sensation? If not, what is it?
(3) What sort of knowledge is it, to know what a particular experience feels like?
(4) Is it possible to hallucinate pain?
(5) Might scientists discover that there are really no such things as pains and mental images?

There is a vast literature on the issues of behaviourism and functionalism. You might like to consult a selection of the following (names in capitals refer to items listed in the Bibliography of collected papers):

David Armstrong, *A Materialist Theory of the Mind* (London: Routledge & Kegan Paul, 1968), Chs. 5, 6 and 15.
David Armstrong and Norman Malcolm, *Consciousness and Causality* (Oxford: Blackwell, 1984).
Paul Churchland, *Matter and Consciousness* (Mass.: MIT Press, 1984), Ch. 3.
Peter Hacker, *Insight and Illusion* (Oxford: Oxford Univeristy Press, 1972), Ch. IX.
David Lewis, 'An Argument for the Identity Theory', *Journal of Philosophy* 63 (1966). Reprinted in a LEWIS and ROSENTHAL.
————, 'Mad Pain and Martian Pain', in BLOCK. Reprinted in LEWIS.
Norman Malcolm, *Problems of Mind* (London: Allen & Unwin, 1972), Ch. 3.
Thomas Nagel, 'What is it Like to be a Bat?', *Philosphical Review* 83 (1974). Reprinted in BLOCK, NAGEL and HOFSTADTER.
Hilary Putnam, 'Brains and Behaviour', in *Analytical Philosophy*, Second Series, R. Butler (ed.) (Oxford: Blackwell, 1863). Reprinted in PUTNAM.
————, 'The Nature of Mental States', in *Art, Mind and Religion*, W. Capitan & D. Merrill (eds.) (Pittsburgh: University of Pittsburgh Press, 1967). Reprinted in BLOCK, ROSENTHAL and PUTNAM.
Richard Rorty, 'Mind-Body Identity, Privacy and the Categories', *Review of Metaphysics*, XIX (1965). Reprinted in BORST, ROSENTHAL and HAMPSHIRE.
Gilbert Ryle, *The Concept of Mind* (London: Hutchinson, 1949).
Jerome Shaffer, *The Philosophy of Mind* (Englewood Cliffs: Prentice-Hall, 1968), Ch. 2.

5   MIND AND BRAIN

i. Mind/Brain Identity

With the failure of behaviourism, one attempt to establish strong materialism has failed. Since we cannot analyse descriptions of conscious states into descriptions of physical behaviour, it remains possible that such states are in fact non-physical states of a physical being. Moreover, with the partial failure of functionalism, the cartesian conception of meaning has been left intact, at least with respect to words referring to conscious experiences. Even the partial success of functionalism, with respect to words like 'belief' and 'desire', has done nothing to establish strong materialism. For the states occupying the causal roles in question may in fact be non-physical ones.

But even if strong materialism is not a necessary truth, it may be true as a matter of empirical fact. For even if descriptions of conscious experiences are logically independent of all descriptions of physical states (as the cartesian conception implies) it may in fact be the case that those descriptions are descriptions of the very same things. This is just what the thesis of mind/brain identity affirms. It holds that just as a particular cloud is, as a matter of fact, a great many water droplets suspended close together in the atmosphere; and just as a particular flash of lightning is, as a matter of fact, a certain sort of discharge of electrical energy; so a pain or a thought is (is identical with) some state of the brain or central nervous system.

The identity-thesis is a version of strong materialism: it holds that all mental states and events are in fact physical states and events. But it is not, like behaviourism and functionalism, a thesis about meaning: it does not claim that words such as 'pain' and 'after-image' may be analysed or defined in terms of descriptions of brain-processes. (This would be manifestly absurd.) Rather, it is a contingent thesis about the things in the world which our words refer to: it holds that the ways of thinking represented by our terms for conscious states, and the ways of thinking represented by some of our terms for brain-states, are in fact different ways of thinking of the very same (physical) states and events. So 'pain' does not mean 'such-and-such a stimulation of the neural fibres' (just as 'lightning' does not mean 'such-and-such a discharge of electricity'); yet for all that, the two terms in fact refer to the very same thing.

This section will fall into three parts. In part (A) I shall provide a general argument for the truth of the identity-thesis; in part (B) I shall distinguish between two different versions of that thesis, and will argue that one of them is more plausible than the other; then in part (C) I shall discuss the extent to which the identity-thesis can help us with the problem of other minds.

(A) An Argument for the Identity-Thesis

Recall the difficulties raised in section 2.iv concerning the causal interaction of mind and body. They were raised there as difficulties with strong dualism, but in fact they can equally well be raised against weak dualism. Indeed they can be developed into a strong argument in support of the mind/brain identity-thesis.

As we noted in section 2.iv, we believe very firmly that some mental states and events are causally necessary for the occurrence of some physical ones. For example, I believe that if I had not been conscious of a pain in my foot (mental event), I should not have gone to the doctor (physical event). My awareness of the pain was, I believe, a causally-necessary condition of my later visit to the doctor. But as we also noted, it seems most unlikely that we shall ever need to advert to anything other than physical-physical causality when we investigate the detailed causal nexus behind any given physical event. On the contrary, it seems likely that there will always be physical events providing us with a sufficient causal explanation of any particular bodily movement. For example, as we trace the causes of my legs moving me in the direction of the doctor's surgery, through events in the muscles of my legs and feet, through events in the nerves of my spinal column, into events in the cells of my brain, it seems most unlikely that the chain of physical causation will eventually run out. So it is unlikely that we shall be forced to appeal to any non-physical event in order to provide a satisfactory explanation of my visit to the surgery.

Now the only way in which we can hold on to both beliefs — the belief that some mental events are causally necessary for the occurrence of some physical ones, and the belief that it is unnecessary to appeal to anything other than physical events in providing causal explanations of other physical events — is by believing that some mental events *are* physical ones. Then somewhere in the chain of physical causes of my visit to the doctor there will be a brain event which is (is identical with) my awareness of a sensation of pain.

This argument for the general truth of the mind/brain identity-thesis may be summarised as follows.

(1) Some conscious states and events are causally necessary for the occurrence of some physical ones.
(2) In a completed neuro-physiological science there will be no need to advert to anything other than physical-physical causality.
(C) So some conscious states and events are (are identical with) physical (brain) states and events.

The argument is valid. And although its conclusion only claims that some conscious states are physical, it can easily be developed in such a way as to entail the stronger conclusion, that all are. For almost every kind of conscious state can sometimes be causally necessary for a physical one. Sometimes a particular bodily movement would not have taken place if: I had not made a particular decision; I had not thought a particular thought; I had not been aware of a particular sensation; I had not had a particular after-image; and so on. Then since it seems extremely unlikely that some conscious states are physical while some are not, it follows that all are.

Premiss (1) forms an important part of our common-sense view of ourselves and the world. We believe that conscious processes can make a difference to the world. Indeed as we saw in section 2.iv, we also believe the stronger thesis that conscious events form part of the true causal explanations of many physical events. Then the only way in which we can hold on to this belief, while denying the identity-thesis, is by denying premiss (2). We would have to deny that all physical events have purely physical causes.

Yet premiss (2) forms an important part of our scientific world-view. The more science progresses, the more likely it seems that all physical events will ultimately be explicable in purely physical terms. On the basis of what we know already, it would be quite extraordinary if it were to turn out that a physical event, such as one particular brain-cell firing off an electro-chemical impulse to another, sometimes has no physical cause. It would be even more extraordinary if this event were to prove to be, not random, but caused by something non-physical. The existence of non-physical causes of physical events would require us to recognise whole new species of causal relations and causal laws.

Given its validity and the strength of its premises, the argument above could reasonably be taken as a proof of the identity-thesis, were it not for the myriad objections which can be raised against that thesis. (Some of these have already been presented in section 1.iii, in the guise of arguments for the truth of weak dualism.) In later sections we shall consider a number of them, many of which involve apparent breaches of Leibniz's Law ('identical things share identical properties'). Despite the strength of the argument in its support, the identity-thesis will only be rationally acceptable if we can reply adequately to each of the objections.

(B) Type vs Token Identity

There is an important distinction to be drawn between type-identity and token-identity. The thesis of mind/brain type-identity holds that each general type of mental state — for instance pain, or the sensation of red — is identical with some general type of brain-state. So whenever a pain is felt it will be identical with a particular instance of some general type of brain-state, the same type of brain-state in each case. The thesis of mind/brain token-identity is much weaker. It holds only that each particular instance of pain is identical with some particular brain-state, those brain-states perhaps belonging to distinct kinds. It holds that each particular occurrence of a mental state will be identical with some particular occurrence of a brain-state, but that there may be no general identities between types of mental state and types of brain-state. Note that the argument for the identity-thesis sketched above is indifferent between these two versions of it.

There is some reason to think that the thesis of mind/brain token-identity is the better theory. One argument would be this. We know that there is a considerable degree of redundancy in the human brain. For instance, although speech is normally controlled from a particular region in the left-hand hemisphere, someone who has had that region damaged can often recover their ability to speak, with a little practice. So a particular decision to speak may sometimes be identical with an event in one part of the brain, while sometimes it may be identical with an event in quite a different part. Now it does not immediately follow from this that the brain-events are of different types: this will depend upon what counts as a 'type' of brain-event. But there seems at least no particular reason to assume that the events will all be of the same type.

The case can be made even stronger if we recall that many creatures besides human beings may possess conscious states. If not only mammals, birds and reptiles, but perhaps also non-biological systems such as computers can possess mental states, then it is obviously false that there will always be the same type of physical state in existence whenever there exists an instance of a given type of mental state. For the structures of these creatures will be very different from one another, and from the structure of the human brain. (This topic will be pursued further in Chapter 8.)

Supposing that the thesis of token-identity is the true theory of mind/brain identity, then there must surely be something more to be said, at the physical level, about what is common to all the different kinds of physical event which are (are identical with) pains. Consider the following analogy. The true theory of clouds is very likely a version of token-identity thesis. For clouds can be made up out of many other kinds of droplet besides water droplets. Thus rain clouds, dust clouds and clouds of industrial smog are all clouds. Yet there must surely be something common to all these different sorts of collections of particles which explains how they are all clouds. And indeed there is: what is in common is a functional property of the collections in question, having to do with their weight relative to the surrounding atmosphere, and the way in which they reflect light to give the characteristic appearance of a cloud. So the true theory of clouds is a version of token-identity thesis, coupled with an account of the function, or causal role, of the different physical tokens.

Similarly then for mental states: the best version of strong materialism is a token-identity thesis, coupled with an account of the causal-roles of the different types of mental state. Now we concluded Chapter 4 by accepting functionalism as an analysis of terms referring to dispositional states like beliefs and desires, but with the cartesian conception still intact in connection with terms referring to conscious experiences. If this is correct, then the functionalist element in strong materialism will be partly a necessary truth (where the states in question are dispositional), but it will be a contingent truth where the states in question are pains and sensations of red. For if the cartesian conception provides the correct account of the meaning of terms like 'pain', then the characteristic causal role of pain is something which we have to discover empirically, by observation and experiment.

(C) The Identity-Thesis and the Problem of Other Minds

Can the thesis of mind/brain identity, if true, provide us with a solution to the problem of other minds? Recall from section 1.ii, that an argument by analogy to the existence of other minds was obstructed by the claimed uniqueness of my own states of consciousness. But if the identity-thesis were true, then my experiences would not be especially unique: they would in fact be physical states like any other. So an argument by analogy could go through after all, as follows:

(1) I know of the existence of conscious experiences from my own case.
(2) All of my conscious experiences are in fact brain-states.
(3) Other human beings possess brain-states similar to mine.
(C) So other human beings possess experiences similar to mine.

Of course this argument is not strictly valid, since it purports to be a species of inductive argument. But it does appear to be rationally convincing. Moreover premises (1) and (3) are obviously true, while Premiss (2) merely states the identity-thesis. So if we could know that thesis to be true, the argument as a whole would carry conviction.

If the identity-thesis is true, then there is no longer any problem about knowing that other experiences exist: I can know this to be true on the basis of an argument by analogy. But can I know the particular experiences which people possess on particular occasions? If I see someone injured and groaning, I can know that they possess *some* conscious experience. But can I know that they are aware of the sensation with the distinctive qualitative feel which I describe, in my own case, as 'pain'? Indeed is the argument by analogy sufficiently strong to rule out the following sort of possibility: the conscious state which in their case is caused by injury and causes groaning has the qualitative feel which, were I to be aware of it, I should describe as a tickle?

Recall the example of the black boxes found on the seashore, which we used in section 2.ii. Since the boxes all perform the same functions, we are entitled to conclude that they all contain states occupying the same causal roles, namely mediating between a specified input (e.g. a red button being pressed) and a specified output (e.g. a red light flashing). But the states occupying those causal roles may have only that in common: their causal role. In other respects they can be as different as you please. Similarly then in the case of human beings: when I observe the injured person exhibit pain-behaviour, I am entitled to conclude that there is some state in them occupying the same causal role occupied, in my own case, by the sensation of pain. And in virtue of the likely truth of the mind/brain identity thesis, I am also entitled to conclude that the state occupying that causal role is very likely a conscious one. But it seems left open that it might be quite different in other respects (in particular, with respect to its qualitative feel) from the state which I call 'pain'.

But what of considerations of simplicity? Is it not a great deal simpler to suppose that in all of us the same causal roles are occupied by the same feelings? And are not simpler theories in general more reasonable? But in fact the difference in the degree of simplicity here is only marginal. For what really does the work, in our explanations of the behaviour of ourselves and others, is the supposition that we all possess states which occupy distinctive causal roles. What explains how you can respond appropriately to the command 'Bring me a red flower', is the fact that you have learned to discriminate objects on the basis of some-experience-or-other, and associate with that experience the term 'red'. Any hypothesis about the particular distinctive feel of your experience is really redundant to the explanation: I do not in fact need to employ any such hypothesis.

I can see no reason why it should be thought more likely that human beings all have the same experiences occupying the same causal roles, even given the truth of strong materialism. For we know already that they differ from one another in all sorts of subtle ways. It is rather as if we had found a set of black boxes which not only share many of their features, but are each of them in many ways unique. None of them look quite alike or have the same physical dimensions, and their responses to any given stimulus (e.g. the pressing of a red button) will often differ quite markedly from one another. Now in cases where we were for some reason confident that all of the boxes had states occupying the same causal roles, could we also be reasonably confident that those states would be similar in other respects? Surely not. In light of the many differences existing between the boxes, it seems just as likely that the physical mechanisms underlying any given causal role will be subtly different in each case. Equally then in the case of human beings: since we already know that they differ from one another in many ways, there is no particular reason to think that they will all have exactly similar brain-states/sensations occupying similar causal roles.

All this is supposing that we only know of the general truth of the mind/brain identity-thesis. The situation would surely be different if we also knew some particular identities. If I knew that pains in myself were always identical with a particular type of brain-state, and then discovered that the states which occupy that causal role in you are also of that type, then I should have to conclude that you too feel pain in those circumstances. There can, for the materialist, be no differences at the level of consciousness which do not reflect differences at the level of the brain.

Note however that we do not in fact know of any particular identities as yet (and certainly not if we discount all evidence presupposing that we do already have knowledge of one another's sensations, such as experiments in which subjects have to report their experiences). So if I had to rely upon knowledge of particular identities, I certainly would not yet know under what conditions other people experience similar sensations to myself. Indeed it would be doubtful whether I ever could know this. For if I am not simply to take for granted knowledge of other people's experiences, I should have to discover the identities in question purely through experiments upon myself. For it is only in my own case that I can assume knowledge of particular sensations.

I conclude that the identity-thesis can only provide us with the general knowledge that other people possess conscious experiences of some sort. I suppose it is some kind of argument in support of the thesis that it can even get us this far, but it is hardly very strong. For the commonsense view is that we already know a great deal more than the bare fact that other people besides ourselves have experiences. On the contrary, we think we can often know what other people are feeling on particular occasions. So we need to look elsewhere for a completely satisfying solution to the problem of other minds. This will be our task in Chapter 6.

ii. Preliminary Difficulties

In the last section we presented an argument in support of the identity-thesis which would have been convincing if considered purely on its own terms. Over the next three sections we shall reply to all the main objections which have been raised against that thesis, beginning with some of the less serious ones. They will get more serious as we go along.

(A) Certainty

Our first objection derives from Descartes, who deployed a similar argument in support of strong dualism. It runs as follows:

(1) I may be absolutely certain of my own experiences, when I have them.
(2) I cannot have the same degree of certainty about the existence of any physical state, including my own brain-states.
(C) So (by Leibniz's Law) my conscious experiences are not in fact identical with brain-states.

Although both the premises in this argument are true, the argument itself commits a fallacy (is invalid). For as we noted in section 3.i, Leibniz's Law only operates in contexts which are not intentional. And it is obvious that the context created by the phrase 'X is certain that . . .' is an intentional one.

For example, the police may be certain that Mr Hyde is the murderer, while they have no inkling that Dr Jekyll is the murderer, despite the fact that Jekyll and Hyde are one and the same man. And Oedipus may be certain that Jocasta loves him without believing that his mother loves him, despite the fact that Jocasta is his mother. So from the fact that I have complete certainty about my own conscious states without having certainty about my own brain-states, it does not follow that my conscious states are not brain-states. For just as one and the same woman may be presented to Oedipus in two different guises — as Jocasta, and as his mother — so perhaps one and the same brain-state may be presented to me under two different aspects: in a third-person way (as a brain-state), and via the qualitative feel of what it is like to be in that state.

(B) Privacy

This second argument is a variation on the first. It runs as follows:

(1) Conscious states are private to the person who has them.
(2) Brain-states are not private: like any other physical state, they form part of the public realm.

(C) So (by Leibniz's Law) conscious states are not in fact identical with brain-states.

However, the term 'private' is ambiguous: something can be private in respect of knowledge (only I can know of it), or it can be private in respect of ownership (only I can possess it). Taken in the first way, the argument is the same as that above, and commits the same fallacy. But taken in the second way, premiss (2) is false.

It is true that only I can 'own' my conscious states: no one else can feel my pain, or think my thought. But it is equally true in this sense that only I can own my brain-states. For no one else can possess my brain-state either. Any brain-state which they have will be, necessarily, their own brain-state, not mine. Conscious states are certainly not unique in respect of privacy of ownership. The same is true of blushes and sneezes as well as brain-states: no one else can blush my blush or sneeze my sneeze. Indeed it seems that in general the identity-conditions for states and events are tied to the identities of the subjects who possess them.

(C) Value

A thought can be wicked. A desire can be admirable. But no brain-state can be either wicked or admirable. We may therefore argue as follows:

(1) Conscious states are subject to norms: they can be good or bad, wicked or admirable.
(2) No purely physical states are subject to norms: no brain-state can be either wicked or admirable.
(C) So (by Leibniz's Law) conscious states are not identical with brain-states.

We might immediately be inclined to quarrel with premiss (2). For can a particular stabbing not be wicked? And what is a stabbing if not a physical event? But it may be replied that it is not the stabbing itself — considered merely as a physical event — which is wicked, but rather the intention behind it. And in general, physical states and events are only subject to norms if they are intentional (or at least foreseen).

This reply is sufficient to save the truth of premiss (2), but at the cost of revealing the same fallacy in the argument as was involved in the argument from certainty. For if it is only things which are intended (or foreseen) which can be wicked, then the context created by '. . . is wicked' will be an intentional one. For example, if the fact that it is wicked of Mary to have a particular desire implies that she either intentionally adopted that desire, or at least foresaw that she would continue to possess it if she took no steps to eradicate it, then it is no objection to the identity-thesis that it is, on the other hand, not wicked of her to be in such-and-such a brain-state. For you can foresee E (that you will marry Jocasta) without foreseeing F (that you will marry your mother), even though E is identical with F. And certainly she neither intended nor foresaw that she should be in that particular brain-state.

(D) Colour

An after-image can be green, a pain can be sharp and piercing. But it is hardly likely that any brain-state will be either green or sharp and piercing. There will then be many arguments which take the following sort of form:

> (1) I am experiencing a fading green after-image.
> (2) No brain-states are green.
> (C) So (by Leibniz's Law) my after-image is not identical with any brain-state.

One mistake in this argument is that it treats my after-image as though it were a particular individual thing, having greenness as a property. Now it is true that the sentence 'I experience a green after-image' has the same grammatical form as the sentence 'I pick up a green book', which creates the impression that greenness is a property of the after-image in just the same way that it is a property of the book. But this impression is misleading. For the book in question might have had some other colour, while remaining the numerically-same book. But can we make any sense of the idea that the very same after-image which I have now, might have been red?

Of course what is true, is that I might now have been experiencing a red after-image rather than a green one. But can we make sense of the idea that it might have been this very same after-image (which happens to be green) which would then have been red? I suggest not. Rather, the greenness is essential to the identity of that particular after-image. The reason being that it is a mistake to treat the fading after-image as if it were a kind of object or individual thing.

It is rather an event, or happening. And the greenness is in fact part of the event of experiencing-a-fading-green-after-image, as opposed to being a property *of* it.

This reply on its own is not sufficient to rebut the argument. For it seems certain that greenness is not part of the event of undergoing-such-and-such-a-change-in-brain-state. So how can that event be identical with the event of experiencing-a-fading-green-after-image, if greenness really is part of the latter event? For must not identical events have identical parts? For example, if the battle of Waterloo is (is identical with) the battle which lost Napoleon the war, then if a particular cavalry charge is part of the battle of Waterloo, it must also be part of the battle which lost Napoleon the war. For they are the very same battle (the very same event).

The second mistake in the argument is to think that an experience can be green, or a conscious event have greenness as one of its parts, in anything like the same sense that a physical object can be green, or a physical event have greenness as one of its parts. Experiences are not literally green in the way that grass is literally green. Rather, the 'greenness' of my green after-image consists in my having an experience which is like the experience of seeing a green patch (and it is the patch which is green, not the experience). Then if to have a green after-image is to be in state like the state one is in when one sees a green patch, and if the possession of that after-image is identical with some brain-state, it will indeed follow that the brain-state too is like the state one is in when one sees a green patch. But there is no difficulty about this. For the latter state too will be identical with some brain-state. And it seems entirely plausible that there should be some resemblance between the two brain-states.

The point can be put like this: green after-images are experiences *of* green, rather than things (or events) which *are* (or which contain) green. A green after-image is, as it were, an event of being-under-the-impression-that-one-is-seeing-a-green-patch. If this is so, then the after-image can be identical with a brain-state without breaching Leibniz's Law, so long as the brain-state too can in this sense be 'of' green. If green after-images represent green, rather than literally being green, then there will be no· difficulty here so long as it is possible for brain-states to represent. This question will be pursued under section 5.iii below.

(E) Felt Quality

This objection arises out of the last one. Even if after-images are not literally coloured, still they do literally have phenomenal (felt) characteristics, which we describe by means of the colour-terms ('sensation of red', 'sensation of green', etc.). For example there is the qualitative 'feel' which is common to the experiences of having a green after-image and seeing green grass. Indeed as we insisted against certain kinds of functionalism in section 4.iii, all experiences have distinctive qualitative feels, which we are each of us aware of in our own case. But can any brain-state have a distinctive feel? For example, think of a particular brain-state — say one group of brain cells firing off impulses to another group — and ask yourself 'What is the distinctive feel of this event?' It is hard even to get a grip on the question. How can any brain-event feel like a sensation of red, for example? Surely only another sensation can, in the required sense, *feel like* a sensation of red.

The argument sketched above may be summarised as follows:

(1) All experiences have distinctive felt qualities.
(2) Brain-states do not have distinctive felt qualities.
(C) So (by Leibniz's Law) experiences are not in fact identical with brain-states.

Once again we have been misled by grammatical form, this time into thinking of the qualitative feel of an experience as being genuinely a property of it. (Thus we say 'The pain has a distinctive feel' just as we say 'The car has a distinctive colour'.) It would be more accurate to say that the experience itself *is* (is identical with) a distinctive qualitative feel. The experience of pain is not different from the feel of pain. Rather they are one and the same. So it is entirely irrelevant whether or not a brain-state can possess (have as a property) a particular qualitative feel. Since the experience itself is identical with its qualitative feel, the real question is whether or not a brain-state, too, can be identical with a qualitative feel. And we have as yet been given no reason for thinking that this cannot be so.

(F) Complete Knowledge

Someone could know all physical facts about the brain without knowing what the different experiences feel like. Thus no amount of information about brain-processes will ever allow a congenitally blind person to know what a sensation of red feels like. But if there is information about feelings which would not be conveyed by any amount of information about the brain, then feelings cannot themselves be brain-states. The argument is as follows:

(1) Complete knowledge of physical states would not imply knowledge of what experiences feel like.
(2) If experiences were physical states, then complete knowledge of the physical would imply complete knowledge of experiences.
(C) So experiences are not physical states.

Although this argument, like the argument from certainty, involves an intentional term (the context created by the phrase 'X knows that . . .' being an intentional one) it does not commit the same fallacy. This is because the premises speak of complete knowledge, knowledge from all points of view. Oedipus certainly could not have complete knowledge of Jocasta without knowing that she is his mother. (So if he does know everything about her, but does not know that she is his mother, then she is *not* his mother.)

Both of the premises in the above argument are true. But the argument is invalid, because of a shift in the meaning of the term 'knowledge'. Knowing what an experience feels like is not propositional (factual) knowledge, but rather practical (recognitional) knowledge. It is a matter of knowing how to do something rather than knowing that something is the case. Knowing what a sensation of red feels like is a matter of being able to recognise it when you have one: it is a practical skill. Now of course no amount of factual information will necessarily give you a practical skill. As the name suggests, this will generally require practice. So the sense in which premiss (1) is true is this: no amount of factual knowledge about the brain will necessarily enable you to recognise your experiences when you have them.

Premiss (2), on the other hand, is only true if restricted to factual knowledge (practical knowledge being excluded). If Jocasta is Oedipus's mother, then if he has complete knowledge of (all facts about) Jocasta, he must have complete knowledge of his mother. But it does not follow that he must be capable of recognising her when he sees her. He may have been told every fact that there is to know about his mother (the exact length of her nose, the colour of her eyes, the number and colour of hairs on her head, and so on) and yet still not be able to recognise her. This will depend upon how good he is at translating factual information into visual imagery. If he is particularly bad at it, he may have to identify his mother by ticking-off all the facts piece-meal ('length of nose . . . yes; colour of eyes . . . yes;' and so on).

It is thus entirely consistent with the identity-thesis that you cannot teach a blind person what sensations of red are like by telling them facts about the brain. Although sensations are brain-states, knowing what they are like is a matter of being able to recognise them ('straight off') when you have them. And it is hardly surprising that people cannot acquire such a recognitional skill by being given the bare facts; they will of course need practise in having those states.

iii. Further Difficulties

In this section we shall consider two of the arguments we originally presented in support of weak dualism (and hence, by implication, against the thesis of mind/brain identity) in section 1.iii. These are the arguments from intentionality, and from spatial position.

(A) Intentionality

Recall from section 1.iii the claim that conscious states are unique in being intentional. Our argument was as follows:

(1) Conscious states are intentional, or representational, states.
(2) No merely physical state (e.g. of the brain) can be intentional in its own right.
(C) So (by Leibniz's Law) conscious states are not identical with brain-states.

This argument is valid, and premiss (1) is obviously true. So everything turns on the acceptability of premiss (2).

There is a general philosophical problem about representation. Much of the philosophy of language is concerned with the question: how is it possible for anything to represent — or be *about* — anything else? So it may be that the difficulty we experience in trying to understand how an arrangement of cellular connections could represent anything, is merely a specific instance of the general difficulty of understanding how anything at all can represent anything. In any case the problem of representation is not made any *less* of a problem by supposing that the states which do the representing are non-physical ones.

Perhaps the claim that physical states can be representations-in-their-own-right cannot be made entirely convincing in the absence of a solution to the general problem of representation. Nevertheless we can at least get an inkling of how intentionality can be embodied in a physical system, in advance of a solution to that problem. For by looking at systems which are, manifestly, purely physical — e.g. computers and computer-controlled machines — we can begin to see how they can display some of the distinctive features of intentional states. If we can see the beginnings of intentionality embodied in a physical system such as a computer, then there is no reason in principle why full-blown intentionality (beliefs, desires and the rest) should not be embodied in the biological computer which is the human brain.

One distinctive feature of intentional states is that they represent things in one way rather than another. For a crude analogue of this, imagine a computer linked to a video-camera and mechanical arm. The computer is programmed to scan the input from the camera, and to grab with its arm any yellow object. In order for the grabbing-operation to be successful it must also be able to interpret from the input the shapes, sizes and spatial positions of those objects. But the computer does not select objects on the basis of their shape or size, but only on the basis of their colour.

Now suppose that the only yellow objects which are ever presented to the machine are in fact lemons, its purpose being to select lemons from a passing array of fruit. Of course lemons do also have a characteristic shape, but the computer is indifferent with respect to shape. It initiates a grabbing motion only in response to the yellow colour. Then there is almost a sense in which the machine might be said to desire the yellow objects which it grabs, but not the lemon-shaped objects, even though the yellow objects are all lemon-shaped.

Of course I do not want to say that such a machine would literally have a desire for yellow objects. Though quite what is missing here, which would be present in the case of a genuine desire, is not easy to see. Perhaps (as we suggested in section 2.iii) we can only make sense of something having a particular desire against a wider background, a network of other desires and beliefs. Or perhaps only a being which is alive, which has needs (and which may consequently be said to have 'a good') can have desires. Some of these possibilities will be explored in section 8.iv. The important point for our purposes here is that we have found an analogue for the intentionality of desire in the concept of 'differential response'. Just as Oedipus will respond differently to one and the same woman presented to him now as Jocasta, now as his mother; so the machine will respond differently to one and the same bit of fruit presented to it now as a yellow thing (its shape being obscured), now as a lemon-shaped thing (its colour being obscured).

The other distinctive feature of intentional states, is that they can be directed at non-existent objects. And it is apt to seem unintelligible how any physical system could do this. Here again my strategy is to construct, by way of reply, a crude physical analogue for this aspect of the intentionality of desire. Thus consider the sort of behaviour which might be displayed by a Cruise missile. It is programmed to take photographs of the terrain beneath it at various points along its route, to scan those photographs for landmarks in order to check its position, and adjust its direction accordingly. Now suppose that as a result of an error, it is programmed to find a distinctively-shaped lake at a particular point on its route, but that no such lake exists. As a result, the missile circles round and around the area, until finally it runs out of fuel and crashes. Here we might almost say 'The missile was searching for a lake which did not exist.'

Note that the intentionality displayed in the Cruise missile's 'desire' is not merely derivative from the thoughts and intentions of the computer-programer. True enough, that 'desire' was caused to exist by the programer. But its intentionality — its directedness on a non-existent object — is actually displayed in the behaviour of the missile itself. For it has entered a cycle of behaviour which we know will only be terminated if it succeeds in photographing a lake with a particular distinctive shape; but we also know that no such lake exists.

I conclude that there is no reason in principle why a merely-physical system should not display the various features characteristic of intentional states. So we have been given no reason for supposing that beliefs and desires are not themselves physical (brain) states.

(B) Spatial Position

Recall from section 1.iii the following argument:

(1) All brain-states must occupy some particular position in space.

(2) It is nonsense (meaningless) to attribute any particular spatial position to a state of consciousness.

(C) So (by Leibniz's Law) conscious states cannot be identical with brain-states.

This argument is valid. Premiss (1) is obviously true. So everything depends upon the truth of premiss (2). I shall not waste time quibbling that some conscious states (e.g. pains) are apparently attributed spatial positions. For the identity-thesis extends to all conscious states without exception. And in any case it is unlikely that some conscious states are identical with brain-states and some not. I shall focus on the hardest case for the identity-theorist; namely, thoughts.

An identity-theorist might be tempted to respond to the above argument by conceding that our ordinary concept of thought makes attributions of spatial position to them nonsensical, but by rejecting that ordinary conception as mistaken. They may insist that every thought (properly conceived of) does in fact have a place, namely the place of its identical brain-state. But for them to take this line would be a mistake. For then the thesis of mind/brain identity would no longer represent a contingent discovery, but would be something which we have stipulated as true through a change of meaning.

In fact we should be entitled to reply to the identity-theorist as follows. 'If you mean the word "thought" as we usually do, then your thesis is false; indeed necessarily false. But if, on the other hand, you wish to give the word a different meaning for your own special purposes, then you are perfectly entitled to do so. But don't pretend that you have made a momentus discovery, or that you are saying anything which conflicts with what the weak dualist believes. All you have done is given a new definition.' (It is rather as if someone were to give new definitions of the words 'red' and 'green', in such a way that it then makes sense to ascribe those words to numbers; and were then to announce, as if they had discovered something terribly important, 'Contrary to what has always been believed, every even number is red and every odd one green.')

A more promising strategy for the identity-theorist would be to suggest that we have again been misled by the grammatical form of phrases like 'my thought of my mother' into conceiving of a thought as if it were a special kind of individual thing or object.

For obviously, if a thought were really a physical object like a grain of sand or a brain-cell, then it would have to occupy some precise position in space. So perhaps we need to be reminded that a thought is an action, and an action is a species of event (a 'happening'). And then the general question becomes: what are the criteria for attributing spatial positions to events?

Often the place of an event can be pinned down no more precisely than the place of the subject of that event. And in such cases requests for more precise specifications will seem nonsensical. Thus the place of the event of Mary-growing-older is wherever Mary is. And the question 'Is the event of Mary-growing-older taking place two inches behind her right eye?' seems just as nonsensical as the parallel question about the event of Mary-thinking-of-her-mother. Yet for all that the process of ageing is a purely physical one.

Now we only need to be reminded of these facts to realise that we do in fact attribute spatial positions to thoughts; namely: whenever we say where the thinker of that thought is. And the fact that requests for more detailed specifications of the spatial positions of thoughts sound nonsensical, need not show that thoughts themselves are non-physical. Thinking, like ageing, may be a physical process whose subject is the whole human being.

However, the position of an event is not always simply the position of its subject. An event can also take place in part of its subject. Thus the position of Mary's-left-big-toe-turning-blue is not simply wherever Mary is. It is, more precisely, wherever her left foot is. For if Mary is lying on a river-bank with her left foot in the water, then the event takes place in the water; whereas Mary herself is not in the water.

It seems likely that the physical event which is, according to the identity-theorist, the event of Mary-thinking-of-her-mother, takes place in some particular region of her brain. So we still have a problem, if the closest we can get to the spatial position of Mary's thought is the spatial position of Mary. If the brain-event can be two inches behind her right eye, whilst it is nonsensical to describe the thought of her mother as occurring two inches behind her right eye, then the thought and the brain-event cannot be identical.

The correct way for an identity-theorist to respond, is by denying that it is nonsensical to ascribe precise spatial positions to thoughts. The only real evidence which the objector has for this claim, is that most of us would be left gaping, our minds completely blank, if asked whether Mary's thought is two inches behind her right eye.

But this does not show that the question is literally meaningless. It only shows firstly, that it is not the sort of question which itself points you in the direction in which you have to look for an answer. (Contrast: 'Where is the dam cracking?' It is part of the ordinary notion of a crack, that in order to find them you have to search in specific locations.) And secondly, that we can have no idea where to look for an answer until we have acquired some further information.

Suppose you were asked 'In what specific region of her body is the event of Mary-catching-a-cold taking place?' This too would have a tendency to make your mind go blank, partly because it is no part of the ordinary concept of a cold that in order to establish whether someone has a cold you have to search in specific locations within the body. But on reflection you may realise that what you are really being asked is: 'In virtue of changes in what parts of Mary's body is it becoming true that she has a cold?' This at least is a question you can understand. But if you know nothing of viruses, or medicine generally, you may not even know what sorts of things would be relevant to the discovery of the answer. Yet when you are told that colds are viruses, and that viruses enter the body at specific locations, then you know what would constitute an answer. Note, moreover, that it would be hardly very plausible to say that the term 'a cold' had changed its meaning for you when you acquired this information.

The question about the specific location of Mary's act of thinking about her mother is essentially similar. The first step in dispelling the puzzlement which it causes is to realise that what we are in fact being asked is: 'In virtue of changes in what specific region of Mary is it becoming true that she is thinking of her mother?' The next step is to learn that each conscious event is identical with some brain-event. Then we know that in order to answer the question, we should first need to discover which brain-event is identical with Mary's thought, and then discover where that brain-event is occurring. Yet we do not need to regard our acceptance of the identity-thesis as altering the meaning of the term 'thought', any more than our acceptance that colds are viruses alters the meaning of the term 'a cold'. We may thus deny the claim made in premiss (2) of the argument above.

iv. Necessary Identities

In this section we shall deal with a particularly serious difficulty for the thesis of mind/brain identity, which turns on the claim that a statement of identity, if true, is true necessarily: it is a truth about all possible worlds. For then if, as seems plausible, the thesis of mind/brain identity is merely contingent (i.e. not a truth about all possible worlds), it will follow that it is not true at all. The argument closely parallels those we considered (and dismissed) in sections 2.i and 3.iv in support of strong dualism.

Thus far in this chapter we have assumed the thesis of mind/brain identity to be contingent: although it may be true in the actual world, there are other possible worlds in which it is false. Now what is certainly the case is that it is not a conceptual truth: it is not true in virtue of the meanings of the terms involved. But perhaps some necessary truths are not conceptual truths. Perhaps some truths are truths about all possible worlds without being true in virtue of meaning. For example, consider once again the identity between Jekyll and Hyde (supposing them to have been a real historical character). The truth of 'Jekyll is Hyde' is certainly not merely a matter of meaning; for the police had to discover it by empirical investigation. But it is, for all that, a necessary truth. Since it is in fact true that Jekyll is identical with Hyde, things could not have been otherwise. For if Jekyll is Hyde, then there is only one thing involved rather than two. It is not as if there were two logically distinct things, which happen to be related to one another in a particular way in the actual world ('being identical with one another'), but which could exist unrelated in some other possible world. Rather there is only one thing, which must remain identical with itself in all possible worlds in which it occurs.

In general where we have a true identity-statement which involves two names for the same thing, we cannot say 'This thing is identical with that thing in the actual world, but there are other possible worlds in which they are not identical.' For if the identity-statement is true, there is in reality no 'this' and 'that'. There are not two things, but only one. And it is impossible to conceive of a world in which that thing is not identical with itself.

So it might be said that the thesis of mind/brain identity, if true, will be a necessary truth; but a necessary truth which we have to discover empirically, not by conceptual analysis. It might be said that if pain is a brain-state, then it is necessarily a brain-state. Now this can be turned into a powerful argument against the identity-thesis. For it certainly seems that the identity-thesis might have been false. Surely we can conceive of possible worlds in which people's experiences are not brain-states. For example: a possible world in which someone feels pain, although there is no electrical or other activity taking place in their brain at all.

However, pain is not an individual thing in the way that Jekyll and Hyde are individual things; it is rather a general kind of thing. So the sentence 'Pain is a brain-state' does not claim an identity between two individuals. What it really says is this: 'Each individual pain is identical with some individual brain-state.' (Even the thesis of mind/brain type-identity can be construed as saying this, merely adding the rider: 'and the brain-states with which the individual pains are identical all belong to a single type'.) There are then two alternative ways in which we can take the statement 'If pain is a brain-state, then it is necessarily a brain-state', depending upon whether we read the necessity with wide-scope or with narrow-scope. Thus:

(a) If each pain is identical with some brain-state, then it is true in all possible worlds that each pain is identical with some brain-state. (Wide-scope)

(b) If each pain is identical with some brain-state, then the things which are, in this world, the pains, are identical with those brain-states in all possible worlds in which they occur. (Narrow-scope)

So our first question is: which if either of these two theses is true?

There is no reason whatever to believe thesis (a) to be true. For compare: if each executed person is identical with some particular murderer, then it is true in all possible worlds that each executed person is a murderer. From the fact that all the pains in this world are identical with brain-states, it certainly does not follow that all the pains in all other possible worlds are identical with brain-states.

Thesis (b), in contrast, is true. This will be like: if all executed people are murderers, then the people who are, in fact, executed, are identical with the people who did in fact commit those murders in all possible worlds in which they exist. This is true, since in order to make it false you would have to suppose that there were really two distinct persons involved in each case (the executed person, and the murderer) rather than just one. Similarly then with thesis (b): if the particular pain I now feel is identical with some particular brain-state, then there is only one state involved, not two. And that state must be identical with itself in all possible worlds in which it occurs.

The claim that the identity-thesis is, if true, necessarily true, is only defensible if the necessity is taken with narrow-scope. So there is no prospect of developing a convincing argument against the identity-thesis, unless we can also establish a narrow-scope version of the claim that it (the identity-thesis) is not in fact a necessary truth. Confining ourselves to the case of pain, we should need to establish premiss (2) in the following argument:

> (1) If each pain is identical with some brain-state, then the things which are, in this world, the pains, are identical with those brain-states in all possible worlds in which they exist.
>
> (2) Each pain in this world is, in some other possible worlds in which it exists, not identical with any of those brain-states.
>
> (C) So it is not the case that each pain is identical with some brain-state, even in this world.

Since this argument is valid, and since premiss (1) is true, we shall have sufficiently refuted the identity-thesis if we can establish premiss (2).

Now premiss (2) can in fact be made to seem extremely plausible. For not only can I imagine a world in which pains, in general, are not identical with brain-states (which would only give us the wide-scope version: 'there are possible worlds in which pains are not brain-states'); I can also apparently imagine a world in which the very same pain which I feel at the moment is not identical with any brain-state. For example, in connection with any particular candidate brain-state, can I not imagine my current pain existing while that brain-state does not occur? Then since this exercise can be repeated for all other candidate brain-states, and all other pains, we have apparently done enough to establish premiss (2).

Of course we would be in a position to challenge premiss (2) had we accepted a functionalist account of pain. For what I imagine, when I claim to imagine my pain existing in the absence of any relevant brain-activity, is the feeling of pain. But for most kinds of functionalist, the feeling of pain is not the pain itself. On the contrary, the pain itself is said to be the cause of that feeling, probably a particular brain-state. So to imagine the feeling continuing in the absence of the brain-state is, for this sort of functionalist, merely to imagine that feeling being caused by something other than pain.

But since we have rejected functionalism, this reply is no longer open to us. Since we have agreed to identify pain with its feel, to imagine that feeling existing is to imagine the pain itself.

We have finally arrived at an extremely powerful argument against the identity-thesis. On the one hand it seems that the very same conscious states which I now enjoy might continue to exist, or might have existed, in the absence of any relevant brain-activity. But on the other hand it seems that if these conscious states are in fact brain-states, then they will have to remain brain-states (i.e. identical with themselves) in all possible worlds in which they occur. It therefore seems that the identity-thesis must be false.

The only adequate response to this argument parallels the response we made to the argument for strong dualism (in section 3.iv): we must deny that we have really succeeded in imagining what we think we have imagined. In particular, we have to deny that we have really imagined this very same pain, which I feel now, existing in the absence of the relevant brain-activity. All we have in fact imagined is a pain which is qualitatively identical with this one existing in the absence of brain-activity (which only gives us the wide-scope thesis). The illusion arises because there is no difference, so far as the content of our image goes, between imagining the very same pain, and imagining an exactly similar pain. The difference only emerges when we add to our image the thought 'And this would be the very same pain.' But the addition of this thought would, in the presence of the identity-thesis, render the whole story impossible.

Compare: I can apparently imagine a particular individual person — say Ronald Reagan — existing in the twelfth century. That is: I can imagine someone who looks like Ronald Reagan dressed in armour, saying things in very old-fashioned English and so on. But all that I have certainly established here, in virtue of what I have imagined, is that there might have existed someone qualitatively indistinguishable from Ronald Reagan in the twelfth century. It does not follow that Reagan himself — the very same man who is currently President — might have existed then. Indeed, most philosophers would wish to deny that this is possible.

I conclude that there is no convincing argument against the identity-thesis based upon the necessity of identity. There is certainly a sense in which the identity-thesis is a contingent truth (wide-scope). There is also a sense in which that thesis is, if true, necessarily true (narrow-scope). But there is no good reason to believe the narrow-scope version of the claim that identity-thesis is *not* necessary, which is what we need if the argument is to be successful. What the objector needs to establish — that this very same pain could exist without being physical — goes beyond the content of what we can show by means of our imagination. The most that imagination can show is that a qualitatively similar pain could exist in the absence of relevant brain-activity.

Conclusion

In section 5.i we presented an argument for thinking it likely that all conscious states are identical with brain-states. Then in the sections following we have replied to all the various possible objections to this idea. Since there is good reason to believe the identity-thesis to be true, and no good reason to believe it false, the case for that thesis is rationally convincing. We should therefore embrace the thesis of mind/brain identity, and declare ourselves to be strong materialists.

Questions and Readings

You may like to discuss/think about/write about some of the following questions:

(1) How strong are the arguments for thinking that all conscious states are identical with brain-states?
(2) Is it possible for a brain-state to be a distinctive qualitative feel?
(3) Can any merely-physical system display the distinctive features of intentionality?
(4) Does it make sense to ascribe spatial positions to thoughts? How do you tell whether something 'makes sense'?
(5) Can you imagine turning into a pillar of salt (like Lot's wife) while your headache continues? If so, what consequences would this have for the identity-thesis?

In thinking about these questions, you may like to consult a selection of the following readings (capitalised names refer to collections listed in the Bibliography):

Kurt Baier, 'Smart on Sensations' *Australasian Journal of Philosophy* XL (1962). Reprinted in BORST.

Donald Davidson, 'Mental Events', *Experience and Theory*, L. Foster and J. Swanson (eds.) (London: Duckworth, 1970). Reprinted in DAVIDSON and BLOCK.

Saul Kripke, *Naming and Necessity* (Oxford: Blackwell, 1980), Lecture III.

———, 'Identity and Necessity', *Identity and Idividuation*, M. Munitz (ed.) (New York: New York University Press, 1971). Excerpt reprinted in BLOCK.

David Lewis, 'An Argument for the Identity Theory', *Journal of Philosophy*, 63 (1966). Reprinted in LEWIS and ROSENTHAL.

Norman Malcolm, *Problems of Mind* (London: Allen & Unwin, 1972), Ch. 2.

Colin McGinn, 'Anomalous Monism and Kripke's Cartesian Intuitions', *Analysis*, 37 (1977). Reprinted in BLOCK.

Thomas Nagel, 'What is it like to be a Bat?', *Philosophical Review*, 83 (1974). Reprinted in NAGEL, BLOCK and HOFSTADTER.

Ullan Place, 'Is Consciousness a Brain Process?' *British Journal of Psychology*, XLVII (1956). Reprinted in FLEW, CHAPPELL, MORICK (2) and BORST.

Jerome Shaffer, 'Could Mental States be Brain Processes?' *The Journal of Philosophy*, LVIII (1961). Reprinted in BORST.

———, *Philosophy of Mind* (Englewood Cliffs: Prentice Hall, 1968), Ch. 3.

J. J. C. Smart, 'Sensations and Brain Processes', *Philosophical Review*, LXVIII (1959). Reprinted in CHAPPELL, ROSENTHAL and BORST.

6   PRIVACY AND MEANING

i. Private Language

Let us begin this chapter by reviewing the status of the problem of other minds. We ended Chapter 4 by partially (but only partially) accepting functionalism as an account of the meanings of terms referring to conscious states. Since we have accepted that beliefs, desires and dispositional (as opposed to felt) emotions are functionally-defined states, we shall no longer be troubled by the problem of other minds with respect to them. Our knowledge of such states in others will be by inference from their normal causes and effects, many of which we can observe. However, we also concluded Chapter 4 by rejecting functionalism as an account of the meanings of terms referring to sensations. We seem to have no real option but to accept that the meanings of such terms are wholly concerned with the qualitative feels of the corresponding states (in effect, to accept the cartesian conception with respect to them). So the problem of other minds, as it relates to our knowledge of the sensations of other people, remained untouched.

In Chapter 5 we argued for the likely truth of the mind/brain identity-thesis, not just with respect to beliefs and desires, but for all conscious states including sensations. This then warranted an argument by analogy to the conclusion that other people very likely experience some conscious sensation or other when they are pricked with a pin, or when they look at a red light. But the argument remained relatively weak: it was not strong enough to give us knowledge of the particular sensations which other people experience on specific occasions.

Recall the suggested possibility of colour-spectrum inversion, with which we began our discussion of other minds in section 1.i. Since you like me are able to discriminate objects on the basis of their colours, I can (in the light of the likely truth of the mind/brain identity thesis) reason by analogy that there is probably some conscious sensation in you which forms the basis of your discriminatory ability, just as there is in me. But what reason have I for thinking that those sensations will be similar to my own? Perhaps the sensation underlying your ability to discriminate red objects is similar to the sensation underlying my ability to discriminate green objects, and vice versa.

The point can be put like this: given the truth of the mind/brain identity-thesis, an argument by analogy establishes that there are conscious sensations in you occupying similar causal roles to the conscious sensations in me. But given the cartesian conception of terms referring to such sensations, there is no logical connection between any particular feeling and any particular causal role; so quite distinct feelings may, in different people, occupy similar causal roles. Moreover, given that there already exist many known differences between us, there seems no real reason to assume that our sensations will all feel the same. I therefore cannot know what particular experience you have when you look at a red object: I only know that you experience some sensation or other.

My aim in this chapter will be to provide a complete solution to the problem of other minds, via a refutation of the cartesian conception. But first, in part (A) of the present section I shall consider (and reject) a proposed analysis of the concept of knowledge, under which I could after all be said to have knowledge of the sensations of others. Then in part (B) I shall argue that it follows from the cartesian conception, that the language in which I describe my own sensations is 'private', being intelligible to myself alone.

(A) The Causal Theory of Knowledge

So far in this book we have been working implicitly with a conception of knowledge as justified true belief. We have, in fact, been taking for granted something like the following analysis:

> Someone knows that P if and only if (a) it is true that P, (b) they believe that P, and (c) they have sufficiently good reason for their belief that P.

It is this concept which has been employed throughout our discussion of other minds. We have assumed that, if I lack any good reasons for thinking the sensations which others feel when they are injured and cry out to be qualitatively similar to those which I should feel myself in similar circumstances, then I cannot be said to know that they are similar (even if, as a matter of objective fact, they really are).

However some philosophers have proposed an alternative analysis of knowledge. They have said that a true belief should be counted as knowledge so long as it is reliably caused by the fact which it is about. Thus:

> Someone knows that P if and only if (a) it is true that P, (b) they believe that P, and (c) their belief that P is, in the circumstances, reliably caused by the fact that P.

Then suppose that other people do in fact have the very same sort of feeling as myself when they are injured and cry out, this feeling being part of the cause of their pain-behaviour. Their pain-behaviour in turn causes me (unreflectively) to believe that they have the same sort of feeling which I myself would have in similar circumstances. If the above analysis were correct, I could then be said to know what the sensation feels like in other people which occupies the causal role of pain. For (a) it is true that they feel what I feel, (b) I believe that they feel what I feel, and (c) this belief of mine is reliably caused by the fact that they feel what I feel. For as a matter of fact, if they had felt some other sensation when they were injured they would not have exhibited pain-behaviour, and I should consequently not have come to believe them to be in pain.

Now it would be plausible to claim at least that the appropriate kind of causation of belief is an additional necessary condition for knowledge, alongside truth, belief and justification. For example, suppose that, unknown to myself, I have had a small radio-receiver implanted in my brain. This enables scientists to make me experience certain kinds of visual hallucination. They can send an appropriate message to the radio-receiver, which then stimulates certain cells in the visual centre of my brain. Suppose then, that I as walk into my office one day they cause me to hallucinate a glass of water standing on my desk; and it so happens that there really is a glass of water there. I should want to say in this case that I do not really know that there is a glass of water on the desk. Although my belief is true, and although I have sufficiently good reason for it (the same reasons as I have in the case of normal perception) I do not really know it. For my belief is not caused by the glass of water in question, but rather by a radio-message sent out by scientists in a nearby building. So: knowledge that P is at least justified true belief which is suitably caused by the fact that P.

However, this relatively weak claim is of no help to us with the problem of other minds. What we need is the stronger thesis, that reliable causation can be substituted for the justification-condition in the analysis of knowledge (as in the account sketched earlier). So, is the existence of a suitable causal ancestry for a true belief sufficient to qualify it as knowledge, irrespective of any justification which the believer may have? In my view no, as the following example will show.

Suppose that Russian scientists have invented a form of artificial telepathy. They are able to implant a small radio-transmitter in a person's brain, which can somehow transmit all of their private thoughts. These signals can then be picked up by a receiver in the brain of someone else, and translated into suitable beliefs of the form 'That person is thinking such-and-such'. Now the Russians have managed to get at Margaret Thatcher, and have implanted one of their transmitters in her brain. But they have implanted the receiver in me by mistake, rather than in one of their agents as they intended. (Suppose I went into a private hospital for a routine operation, and somehow got mixed up with the Russian agent. I came out — unknown to myself — with a brain-implant, and they came out without their wisdom teeth.) So I wake up one morning to find myself with a whole stream of beliefs about Mrs Thatcher's thoughts. I find myself thinking 'Mrs Thatcher is considering a reshuffle of her cabinet' and such-like.

In this example I have true beliefs about Mrs Thatcher's thoughts which are reliably caused in the circumstances by the fact that she has such thoughts. But can I therefore be said to know what she is thinking? It is surely obvious that I cannot. For I have not the slightest reason to think that my beliefs are in any way reliable. (At least this is so initially. After a while I may discover, from reading the newspapers, that my beliefs actually fit quite well with her subsequent behaviour.)

A large part of the point of classifying something as knowledge, as opposed to mere true belief, depends upon it being reasonable for the person in question to place reliance upon it. Knowledge is something which you can rely on. Yet in the example above, suppose I were to find myself believing 'Mrs Thatcher has just decided to slash the duty on alcohol'. Would it then be reasonable for me to place my life's savings into shares in breweries and distilleries? Obviously not. From my point of view this would be a mad gamble on a totally unreasoned, and unreasonable, 'hunch' about Mrs Thatcher's intentions.

What the example shows is that true beliefs — even true beliefs which are reliably caused by the facts with which they are concerned — can only count as knowledge if they are reasonably held. So the problem of other minds remains as it was: since I lack any good reason for my intuitively-held beliefs about the sensations which other people experience on particular occasions, these beliefs cannot be counted as knowledge (not even if they are, as a matter of fact, true, and caused by the facts which they are about).

(B) An Argument for the Existence of Private Language

We have established that if conscious experiences are defined wholly in terms of their distinctive qualitative feel, then we none of us know what sensations other people feel on particular occasions. But if we lack any knowledge of other people's sensations, then it follows that the language in which each one of us describes our own experiences is a private one, which is intelligible to ourselves alone. For when I say that I am in pain, I mean to describe an experience with a distinctive qualitative feel. So if you do not know what feeling I am describing, then you do not know what I mean by 'pain'. Equally, since I do not know what experience you are describing when you say that you are in pain, I do not know what you mean by 'pain' either.

It might be objected to this argument, that from the truth of the cartesian conception it only follows that we do not *know* whether or not other people describe the same sensations as ourselves when they use the same words. It does not follow that we do not in fact describe the same sensations. So it may really be the case that we all have the very same sort of feeling whenever we truthfully say that we are in pain. It would merely be that — the problem of other minds remaining only partially resolved — we cannot know that this is so.

This objection is unsuccessful however. For understanding is a species of knowledge, in the following sense: in order to understand what someone means by a term, you must know what they mean. So even if we do in fact describe the same feeling by means of the word 'pain', if we do not know that this is so, then it will still follow that we do not understand one another in the use of that word: it will still follow that the language in which we describe our sensations is a private one.

Suppose we overhear someone in the street say something in a language which sounds like Russian. Then knowing no Russian ourselves, we take bets as to what they have said. I guess that they said 'For dinner tonight we have caviar'; whereas you guess that they said 'In a little over a week we fly home.' Suppose it later transpires that I was right. Could I then claim to have understood the original statement? Obviously not. Although I formed a true belief about what had been said, I certainly did not know it. Since my belief was based purely upon guesswork, rather than good reason, I neither know nor understood the meaning of the original statement. (Note that this would remain the case even if my belief was in fact reliably caused — unknown to me — via the sort of artificial telepathy discussed above.) Now my position with respect to the statements of others about their own sensations appears essentially similar: being unable to know what feelings they are describing I am reduced to guesswork; and then even if I happen to get it right I shall not have understood them.

The argument here summarises as follows.

(1) The meanings of sensation-terms are wholly concerned with the qualitative feels of the corresponding states.

(2) If (1) is true, then no one knows what feelings other people experience on particular occasions.

(C1) So when people describe their own conscious experiences, no one else is able to know what they mean.

(3) Understanding implies knowledge: if you do not know what someone means, then you do not understand them.

(C2) So the languages in which we describe our own conscious experiences are private: they are intelligible to no one except ourselves.

This argument is valid. Premiss (1) is the cartesian conception, restricted to sensation-terms in accordance with the conclusions of Chapter 4. The truth of premiss (2) has emerged from our discussion of the problem of other minds. And premiss (3) has just been sufficiently established.

In the next section I shall present an argument suggesting that conclusion (C2) cannot possibly be true, because there can be no such thing as a private language. It would then follow that premiss (1) — the cartesian conception — must be false. (Always supposing that the other premises are, as they appear to be, true.) However, it might be questioned whether we really need to *argue for* the absurdity of conclusion (C2). For is it not just obviously absurd to claim that we do not understand one another when we talk about pains and tickles, or sensations of red? Surely we do succeed in communicating about such matters! Then since it is impossible to have a valid argument with true premises and a false conclusion, it will follow that premiss (1) is false if the other premises are not.

But this would be to move too swiftly; for it might be possible to explain how we can come to be under the illusion that we understand one another. If so, then we cannot simply rely upon our common-sense belief in the reality of communication, since this belief may itself be the result of such an illusion. And indeed, such an explanation is readily to hand. For notice that since the sensations which each of us describes by the term 'pain' at least occupy the same causal role, the fact that we do not understand one another would not matter for practical (public) purposes.

Thus whatever your sensation may feel like to you, it is at least true that it is normally caused by injury, and alleviated by analgesics. So when you say 'Help me: I am in pain', and I respond by giving you some aspirin, I shall have given you something which will satisfy you; and you will accordingly feel that you have been understood. This would be sufficient to explain how we so naturally come to believe that we understand one another (supposing that belief to be false). For it makes no difference to our practical lives whether we understand one another or not, provided that the sensations in question occupy similar causal roles. (But note, this does not mean we understand one another after all. For it makes all the difference to me — in private — whether what I feel is a pain or a tickle, since these states have quite distinct qualitative characteristics.)

We therefore have no option but to try to *demonstrate* the absurdity of the claim that we speak a private language, if we are to show the cartesian conception to be false. This will be our task over the next two sections.

ii. Against Private Language

Can there be private meanings? Is it logically possible for someone to speak a language which is intelligible to no one but themselves? Of course someone might invent an uncrackable code: they would then express their thoughts in a code which not even the CIA, with all its computers, could break. But this would not be a private language in the sense in which I understand it. For the person would presumably possess the key to their code, which they could reveal to us if they chose to do so. Moreover, there could certainly be a language which only one person does in fact understand. For if I were the only person left alive after the nuclear holocaust, then English would be just such a language. Perhaps there could even be a language which only one person *ever* understands. Perhaps Tarzan growing up alone in the jungle might invent, or somehow get into the way of speaking, a language which is unique to himself. For it is certainly not a necessary truth that language has to be taught.

I mean by 'private language' one which the speaker is incapable of explaining to anyone else, even if there are other persons to explain it to, and even if both teacher and pupils try their hardest. The language in which I describe my own sensations will be just such a language, if the meanings of its terms are wholly concerned with the qualitative feels of the corresponding states. For then no matter how hard I try, I shall not be able to get across to anyone else which feelings I describe by means of those terms.

In this section I shall present an argument that there cannot be such a language: that it is logically impossible for someone to speak a language which is private in the above sense. The argument will be built up in three main steps.

(A) Conceptual Capacities

I claim firstly, that any meaningful use of a sign implies that the speaker has the capacity to use that sign in a regular, rule-governed, way. To concentrate for the sake of simplicity upon predicate-terms: any meaningful predicate represents a general rule of classification. For example, the meaningful use of the colour-predicate 'red' involves a rule for classifying shades of colour. And anyone who uses the word with *that* meaning must be capable (at least in principle) of making the appropriate classifications. Now so much is obvious: meaningful use of a sign presupposes a background of conceptual capacities, these capacities involving the ability to use that very same sign on other occasions in an orderly rule-governed way.

What is less obvious, and more important, is that everything may seem to someone as though they have the capacity to use a sign regularly when in fact they do not. For consider the following example. Imagine that scientists have discovered a drug which has selective effects upon language-use. It causes the subject's use of a term, or class of terms, to become entirely random, while leaving them with the impression that everything is in order. For instance, perhaps it affects their use of the colour-terms; but it does this, not by affecting their eyesight, but rather by continually shifting their sense of which shades of colour belong with which. Someone under its influence will use these terms in an entirely haphazard manner: applying the word 'red' now to shades of green, now to shades of blue, now to jet-black, and so on. But these applications are made with all the feelings of obviousness and inevitability which you or I would experience on classifying a ripe tomato as 'red'.

Here I think we should say the following. Although people who are under the influence of the drug feel that their use of the colour-terms is rule-governed and meaningful, in fact it is not. So when they say of an object 'This one is red', there is in fact nothing that they mean (even if the object does happen to be red). Since their use of the sign does not reflect a capacity to classify shades of colour in any regular manner, it is in fact meaningless; despite the fact that it feels to them to be entirely meaningful.

What this example shows is that it is possible to be mistaken about whether or not one's use of a sign is meaningful. Since it is conceivable that my usage may seem to me to be meaningful when it is not, seeming-meaningfulness does not entail actual-meaningfulness. There is then a genuine question here, as to how the private linguist is to know that their use of the signs in their private language is genuinely meaningful. In a public language we can perhaps know this because it is possible to get others to learn, and check upon, our modes of classification; and because they enable us to interact with the physical world in coherent predictable ways. But the private linguist is concerned only with the qualitative feels of their own private experiences. Can they construct from such materials sufficient reason to believe themselves to be classifying those feelings in a genuinely orderly way?

(B) Knowing One's Own Capacities

I shall now argue that there is no way for a private linguist to acquire such knowledge. I shall argue that a putative speaker of a private language cannot know whether or not they are capable of using their signs in a regular way; so they cannot have knowledge of their status as linguists. The case will be built up in two stages: arguing firstly, that nothing a private linguist might be aware of can by itself constitute the capacity to use a sign regularly; and secondly, that nothing they might be aware of can provide sufficient evidence of such a capacity.

There are three things which could be present in the consciousness of a private linguist when they use their signs, which might plausibly be thought to constitute a capacity to use those signs in a regular way. (I ignore obviously absurd candidates, such as definitions or lists of rules. For of course these would themselves have first to be understood.) Either: (a) a mental image, or (b) a series of examples, or (c) an intention. Let us take each of these candidates in turn.

(a) No mental image can by itself constitute the capacity to use a sign regularly, for the image still needs to be applied. And someone might, while yet retaining the image, go on to apply it in an entirely random way. Thus in order to teach someone the meaning of the word 'horse', for instance, it is obviously not sufficient merely to present them with a picture of a horse. For there is nothing in the picture itself which shows what is to count as a relevant similarity. So someone who is given that picture may go on to apply it quite randomly, because they hit upon different similarities as being relevant on different occasions (now 'having four legs', now 'being brown in colour', now 'having a tail' and so on). Images and pictures can at most form *part* of a person's capacity to use a term regularly, when conjoined with the capacity to apply them in one way rather than another. But this capacity cannot itself be an image, or else there will have to be an infinite series of images, each one explaining how the next one is to be applied.

(b) Similar considerations apply to any sample or series of samples. Suppose that by way of explanation of the term 'red', you present someone with a number of samples of red objects. Again the samples cannot contain within themselves the conditions of their own application: the person still needs to know what counts as a relevant similarity, and their sense of this may shift randomly in connection with different cases. A series of samples, like an image, can only constitute part of the capacity to use a term, when conjoined with the capacity to apply those samples themselves in a regular way.

(c) Although intentions may be plausible candidates to constitute our conceptual capacities, they cannot by themselves provide the private linguist with the knowledge that they do possess such capacities. For notice that intentions are like beliefs and desires (and unlike sensations) in that they lack any distinctive qualitative feel, and can continue to exist while you are no longer aware of them. So we should say that an intention is a functionally-defined state, amongst whose normal effects will be a disposition to think that one has that intention. They are therefore the kinds of conscious states about which it is possible to be mistaken. All that the private linguist can be immediately certain of, is their current thought that they are intending to use one of their private terms in a particular regular way. Since it is possible for this thought to be caused by something other than the intention, the private linguist must first discover that their thoughts (about their intentions to use their private signs in regular ways) are generally manifested in appropriate action. That is to say: they must first discover that they do indeed classify their private sensations in a regular manner.

This now brings us to the second stage in our argument that a private linguist cannot know their status as a linguist. If nothing which is immediately present to the consciousness of a private linguist (such as an image, a series of sensations, or the thought that they have a particular intention) can by itself constitute the capacity to use a term in a regular way, then there appears to be only one way left open for them to know that they do possess such a capacity. They will need to know that they have in fact used that term regularly in the past, and will have to be able to see that their current use is a continuation of that regularity. They will need to recall for comparison some of their past applications of the term, and will need to be able to discern a genuine regularity running through both their past and their present usage.

But even supposing that the private linguist can know that their memory of their past usage is reliable (and there are perhaps special problems about this), how are they to know that they are not in the same position as the person who has taken the use-randomising drug? For example, let us grant them an accurate memory of all the past sensations which they have described as 'pain'. Still it can only be said that it now *seems* to them that there is a genuine regularity in that past usage, and that it now seems to them that their present sensation is part of the same regularity. They may in fact have been using the term 'pain' randomly, despite their feeling of regularity. In the same way, it may be amongst the effects of the randomising drug, that a subject will feel that their use of the term 'red' has been normal and regular, even when all the shades of colour which they have in fact classified as 'red' are placed before them.

It therefore appears that there is no way for a putative speaker of a private language to know that they mean anything by the signs which they use. For nothing immediately present to consciousness can by itself constitute the capacity to use those signs regularly; and their memory of past usage, too, is insufficient evidence.

But why should it be supposed to follow from this that private language is impossible? For might not someone speak what is in fact a meaningful private language without them (or us) being able to know that they do? Why should lack of knowledge that a sign is meaningful be thought to entail that it is not meaningful? For might not the private linguist in fact be using their signs in a regular way, although they cannot know that they are? This brings us on to the final stage in the argument against private language, in which I propose to show that meaning (like understanding) is a species of knowledge: in order to mean something by a sign, you must be capable of knowing that you do.

(C) Knowledge and Meaning

We have already argued, in the last section, that understanding is a species of knowledge: we argued that in order to be said to understand the statements of another person, you must know what they mean by them. Well suppose we could establish a similar thesis with respect to each speaker's own meaning: suppose we could show that in order to mean something by a statement, you must at least be capable of knowing that you mean something by it. It would then follow from the fact that a private 'linguist' cannot know whether or not they mean anything by their private statements, that they really do not mean anything. And it would therefore follow that private language is impossible.

(It would obviously be too strong to claim that meaningful use of a sign requires *actual* knowledge that it is meaningful, rather than the mere *potential* for such knowledge. For presumably a child learning its first language means something by its utterances, at a time prior to acquiring the general concept of meaning. At that stage it will certainly not know that its utterances are meaningful, since it will be incapable of even formulating such a thought. It will, however, be in a position to know this as soon as it acquires the appropriate concepts: it has the potential for such knowledge.)

Consider the following development of our earlier example of the use-randomising drug which yet leaves you with the feeling that everything is normal. Suppose that you yourself know all about the effects of this drug, having been one of the experimental subjects on whom it was originally tested. Now someone places in front of you ten glasses of identical-looking liquid, and tells you that nine of them contain the drug, the remaining one containing a placebo. They ask you to choose and drink from a glass, which you do; in fact choosing the placebo. Then your use of the colour-terms will in fact remain unaffected, but you yourself do not know this. On the contrary, you have good grounds for thinking that your subsequent usage will probably be random. So this is a case in which your use of the term 'green' will in fact be regular, but in which you yourself do not know that it is. Then do you, or do you not, subsequently mean anything by it?

One reason for denying that you subsequently mean anything by 'green', is that the colour-terms will have become, at least temporarily, completely useless to you. For you now cannot reasonably draw inferences from your past beliefs involving those terms; nor is there any point in forming intentions which involve them. To elaborate: suppose that prior to drinking the liquid you had been trying a new brand of sweets, and had made the discovery that the green ones taste revolting. Now someone offers you one of those sweets, which you are inclined to describe as 'green'. Should you take it or not? You have no way of knowing. Since you have no reason to think that your present use of the term 'green' is in any way connected with your past use, you have no idea what to expect. Similarly, if you had been considering what colour to paint your living-room walls, there is now no longer any point in trying to form a sensible intention on the issue. For supposing that you were to settle that green (what you are now inclined to call 'green') would be a suitable colour, who knows what shade of colour you would select as green by the time you arrive at the paint-shop?

Now in fact in this example you would soon discover that your use of the word 'green' was regular, and would thus discover that you had taken the placebo. For you would soon discover that you could rely upon past beliefs and future intentions. You would try the 'green' sweet and it would indeed be revolting. You would come back from the shop with 'green' paint and it would indeed create exactly the effect you had wanted. And so on. We should then be entitled to say that you had meant something by 'green' all along, despite not having known that you did, because you were capable of discovering that your use of the term was regular. But as we argued in part (B) above, the private linguist does not have such a capacity. If the private linguist cannot discover that their use of their signs is meaningful, then they can never rely upon past discoveries and future intentions.

The reasons why meaning should be regarded as requiring (the capacity for) knowledge, and the reasons why understanding too requires knowledge, are closely parallel; and it will be instructive to compare them. One of our most basic sources of interest in communication (linguistic understanding) is that it enables us to acquire new information from other people. Indeed most of what we know, we have learned from the statements of others. But for this to be possible we must know what their statements mean. Thus suppose you utter the words 'It rained yesterday in Leeds.' This gives me reason to take on board the belief that it did indeed rain yesterday in Leeds; but only if I have reason to believe that by that utterance you meant: that it rained yesterday in Leeds. If I don't know this, then I don't know what belief I should add to my stock of beliefs as a result of your statement.

Another basic source of interest in communication, is that we want to be able to co-ordinate plans and intentions. But again this will only be possible if we know what other people mean when they state their plans and intentions. For if we are reduced to guessing, then even if we happen to guess right it will not have been reasonable for us to rely upon it.

Now similarly in the case of idiolectic meaning (that is to say, meaning which is purely for my own purposes): the most basic point of having a language is to be able to use it. I want to be able to collect information, construct theories, frame plans and intentions, and so on. But this will only be possible if I can know that my use of the signs of my language is regular rather than random. If it is to be reasonable for me to rely upon some belief which I have formed in the past, then I must first know that my current usage of the terms in which that belief is expressed, is in line with my past usage at the time when the belief was formed. And if it is to be reasonable for me now to form an intention for the future, I need to be confident that when the time comes for me to act on that intention, my use of the words in which it is expressed will be in line with my present usage. In short: in order to be able to make use of my language, I need to be capable of knowing that I can hold on to my own thoughts, as they are expressed in that language.

In connection with both communication and idiolectic meaning, it is our most basic interests in the phenomena in question which determine where the boundaries of the concepts should be drawn. (This remark will become clearer in section 7.iv, where I introduce a doctrine I call 'conceptual pragmatism'.) The boundary between understanding and failing to understand the words of another should be drawn in terms of knowledge of what they mean. For only so can successful communication reasonably be given the kind of role which it has in our lives. And the boundary between meaning and failing to mean anything by a sign, should be drawn in terms of the speaker's capacity to know that their use of that sign is regular rather than random. For only if they can acquire such knowledge, can that sign be of any rational use to them.

Summary

The full argument for the impossibility of private language may now be set out as follows:

> (1) Meaningful use of a sign implies the capacity to use it in a regular (rule-governed) way.
> (2) A putative speaker of a private language cannot know whether or not they are capable of using their signs in a regular way.
> (C1) So a putative speaker of a private language cannot know whether or not their use of their signs is meaningful.
> (3) Meaning requires knowledge: meaningful use of a sign requires (the capacity for) knowledge that one's use of that sign is meaningful.
> (C2) So a putative speaker of a private language cannot use the signs of their 'language' meaningfully. (I.e.: private language is impossible.)

This argument is valid. Premises (1) and (3) have in my view been sufficiently established. So it appears that if there is a weakness anywhere, it must lie with premiss (2). This will form the topic of the next section.

iii. A Cartesian Counter-attack

This section will fall into two parts. In part (A) I shall present a cartesian counter-attack to the argument of the last section, specifically an attack upon premiss (2). This will prove successful. But then in part (B) I shall show how the argument can be modified, so as to leave us still with a proof of the falsity of the cartesian conception.

(A) Public vs Private Language

The cartesian should respond to the argument of the last section by claiming that it was much too strong: that if it were successful, then an exactly parallel argument would prove the impossibility of public language. But since this conclusion is absurd (indeed self-defeating: for *in what language* is it to be expressed?), there must be something wrong with the original argument.

The claims expressed by premises (1) and (3) of the argument against private language were quite general: that meaningful use requires classificatory capacities, and that meaningful use requires knowledge that one has a classificatory capacity. Each of these claims will hold equally for public language as for private. It was premiss (2) which purported to be specific to private language: that a private linguist cannot know whether or not they possess any (private) classificatory capacities. Our argument in support of this premiss was that (a) nothing present to the consciousness of a private linguist can by itself constitute such a capacity, and (b) that nothing they can remember about past use can provide sufficient evidence of such a capacity. But these points would hold equally for public language. So if there were nothing further that a public speaker could know about themselves which a private speaker could not, then it would follow that if the argument for premiss (2) were sound, we could none of us know that we possess any classificatory capacities at all.

The only real difference between public and private language, is that in the case of public language other people can check up on my abilities to classify things. But there are at least two difficulties which stand in the way of us exploiting this difference to explain how it is that a public speaker (and only a public speaker) can know that they possess any genuine classificatory capacities.

Firstly, even if other people agree that the speaker is not classifying things randomly, the individual speaker has still to classify the agreement of the rest of the community as 'agreement'. If it is to be the fact that other people generally classify things in the same way that I do, which is to be the ground of my knowledge that I myself possess a genuine classificatory capacity, then I must first be able to classify us all as: classifying things in the same way. So either I have to take for granted that I really do possess this particular classificatory capacity (and if this one, why not others?), or I shall be forced to go round in circles: judging that I agree with the rest of the community in my use of the classification: classifying things in the same way.

Secondly, we noted at the outset of the last section that the 'publicity' of a language should not be taken to imply that there actually exists more than one speaker of it. So we had better not now argue that the crucial difference between public and private language is that in a public language you can get other speakers to check up for you that you are using your signs in a genuinely regular way. For if we took this line, then the argument against private language would equally show that neither Robinson Crusoe (before the arrival of Friday), nor Tarzan, nor myself as the only survivor of a nuclear holocaust, could really speak a language. And this would be absurd.

I conclude that there is no difference between public and private language which can explain how we know that we possess public (but not private) classificatory capacities. Then supposing that the rest of the argument against private language stands firm, there must have been something wrong with the argument for premiss (2); or else we should have to conclude that public language, too, is impossible. And indeed there was: we were too restrictive about the sort of evidence which someone might have for the claim that they possess genuine classificatory capacities. We insisted, in effect, that they must have separate evidence which is directly relevant to each single capacity which they possess. But why should this be so? Why should not their evidence be that they possess a whole system of classificatory capacities? And why should not this evidence be allowed to be indirect?

In fact the real source of our knowledge that we possess classificatory capacities has already been hinted at towards the end of the last section, when we commented on how a public speaker would soon discover that they had taken the placebo rather than the use-randomising drug. It is that our judgements fit together into a coherent network of relatively stable beliefs.

For example, in order to suppose that my use of the colour-terms were really random, I should have to suppose either: that the world itself were randomly changing while miraculously keeping in step with my changed inclinations for the use of those terms; or: that my randomly changing inclinations were somehow miraculously keeping in step with one another. I believe, for example, that red tomatoes are generally ripe, that green ones are generally unripe, and that black ones are generally rotten; these beliefs having been confirmed on many different occasions. Now if we were to try to suppose that it is only my use of the colour-terms which is random (my judgements of 'ripe' and 'rotten' being genuinely regular), then we should have to suppose that there is in fact no correlation between the colour of tomatoes and their degree of ripeness, but that my shifting inclinations for the use of the colour-terms does miraculously match their degree of ripeness. Thus on each occasion when I call a tomato 'red' I should judge truly that it is ripe. But sometimes it would in fact be red, sometimes green, sometimes blue, and so on.

If on the other hand we were to try to suppose that it is not just my use of the colour-terms, but also my use of the terms 'ripe' and 'rotten' which is random, then we should have to suppose that two randomly shifting systems of classification can miraculously keep in step with one another to produce a stable network of belief. Thus on one occasion when I call a tomato both 'ripe' and 'red' it would in fact be ripe and red, on another occasion it would be rotten and green, on yet another occasion it would be unripe and blue, and so on. And again we should have to suppose that there is in fact no regular correlation between colour and degree of ripeness.

Of course all this passes beyond the possibility of belief. By far the simplest, most reasonable, explanation of my use of the colour-terms is that I do indeed inhabit a world of objects which have relatively stable colours, and that I am indeed genuinely capable of classifying those things in terms of their colours. And in general, the most reasonable explanation of my use of the signs of my public language is that I inhabit a relatively coherent, stable, predictable world, and am genuinely capable of classifying the things in that world.

Now this is completely devastating of the argument against the possibility of private language. In order for a private linguist to know themselves to possess genuine classificatory capacities, it is only necessary that their private language should be embedded within a coherent system of relatively stable beliefs. And for this to be possible, it is only necessary that the private world which they describe with their language should itself be to some extent coherent, stable and predictable. So far as I can see there is nothing in the concept of 'privacy' which shows that these things cannot be so.

(B) The Argument against Private Language Redirected

Our original purpose was to demonstrate the falsehood of the cartesian conception. The strategy was to proceed by means of two steps: arguing first (in section 6.i) that it entails that the language in which each of us describes our own sensations is private to ourselves; then arguing second (in section 6.ii) that private language is impossible. It is this second step which has now failed. But notice that we were trying to prove more than we needed to: it would have been sufficient if we could have shown that we do not *in fact* speak a private language. That there may or not be persons who speak private languages in other possible worlds is irrelevant; for the cartesian conception entails that each of us speaks a private language in the real world.

The argument of the last section was thus to some extent a blind alley: we were in any case trying to prove something much stronger than we really needed. However, that effort was not entirely wasted. What we have shown is that language is only possible within a coherent regular world. It is this coherence which ultimately forms the basis of any reasonable belief in our own classification capacities; and we have shown that the reasonableness of that belief in turn is necessary if there is to be genuine language. So the language in which I describe my own sensations (construed as the cartesian conception would have it) is only possible if those sensations themselves form part of a relatively stable regular realm. It can only be the case that we do indeed speak a private language (as the cartesian conception entails) if the language of sensation is embedded within a coherent system of belief.

Now there may seem to be no special problem about this. For do I not in fact possess a whole battery of beliefs about the relations which exist between my sensations and my physical circumstances and behaviour? I believe, for example, that the distinctive feeling which I call 'pain' is generally caused by tissue-damage and causes in me a disposition to pain-behaviour. If I were to try to suppose that my use of the sensation-terms were merely random, then I should have to suppose that the causal relations between my sensations and the physical world were equally random. For example, I should have to suppose that tissue-damage causes in me now one sort of sensation and now another, these changes miraculously keeping step with my disposition to describe them all as 'pain'.

Notice, however, that almost the whole of the network of beliefs in which my sensation-concepts are embedded has to do with the relations between my private sensations and the public world. There is no comparably stable network amongst those sensations themselves. Indeed here I possess hardly any general beliefs whatever. My sensations are followed now by one sort of sensation, now by another: sometimes they change this way, and sometimes they change that. Sometimes pains are preceded by sensations of touch, sometimes not. Sometimes intense pains cause feelings of nausea, sometimes not. And so on. So if I were confined to the world of my sensations alone, then I should be hard pushed to provide myself with any evidence that I do genuinely possess the ability to classify them. Since everything is constantly shifting, I should have no particular reason to think that it is the world (of my sensations) which is shifting, rather than my attempts to describe it.

Now this can be turned into a convincing argument against the cartesian conception. For the whole point of that conception is that there are to be no logical connections between any given sort of sensation and any given causal role. The cartesian may believe that many sensations do in fact have causal roles; but this is to be entirely contingent and inessential. Since our sensations are not classified in terms of causal role, there must be possible worlds in which they occupy quite other roles, or indeed no role at all. Given this, the cartesian must surely accept that our ability to classify our sensations is logically independent of whether or not they occupy any distinctive causal roles. There would then be possible worlds in which we retain our abilities to speak and make judgements about our sensations, but where those sensations are not connected in any regular way with the public realm. But this conclusion we have now established to be false. We have just shown that if we were confined to the shifting sands of our sensations themselves — those sensations being unconnected in any coherent way with the physical realm — we should be unable to speak of them at all. The cartesian conception must thus be false, since it entails a false conclusion.

Putting together points which have emerged both in this section and the last, our argument against the cartesian conception may now be summarised as follows:

(1) If the cartesian conception is true, then there are other possible worlds which are like this one in every respect (in particular, in which we retain our capacity to speak about our sensations), except that the sensations in that world do not occupy any regular causal roles.

(2) There is not enough stability within our sensations for some-one to be able to know that they are genuinely capable of classi-fying them, if they are confined to the evidence provided by those sensations alone.

(3) But meaning requires knowledge: in order for someone to mean something by a term, they must be capable of knowing that there is a genuine classificatory ability underlying their use of it.

(C1) So the cartesian conception entails a falsehood. Namely: that there are possible worlds in which we retain our ability to speak about our sensations although they do not form part of any coherent stable realm.

(C2) So the cartesian conception is false.

This argument is valid, and each of the premises has been adequately supported by argument. It is therefore rationally convincing.

What we have shown is that our abilities to speak and make judgements about our sensations are necessarily tied to certain regular public causal roles. Although there may be other possible worlds in which people speak private languages (in which sensa-tions are unconnected with the physical world, but nevertheless form a coherent stable system of their own), our world is not one of them. Indeed with the realm of our sensations being the shifting quicksand which it is, it would be logically impossible for us to have a language dealing with it, unless those sensations occupied (as they do) distinctive causal roles.

iv. Meaning and the Mind: Function and Feeling

We have finally refuted the cartesian conception of the meanings of sensation-terms. Now this might seem to give us the strongest pos-sible argument in support of either behaviourism or functionalism. However, from the fact that the meanings of those terms cannot be wholly a matter of qualitative feel, it does not follow that they must therefore be wholly a matter of behaviour or causal role. There remains the possibility outlined as proposal (C) in section 4.iii above: that sensation-terms should be analysed as a conjunction of qualitative feel with causal role.

This is the view I shall now defend. But note at the outset that there is a strong general argument for thinking that something along these lines must be correct. For we still have the arguments of 4.iii and 4.iv that no adequate functionalist analysis of the sensation-terms can leave out the element of qualitative feel. But we also have the argument of the last section, that their meaning cannot be wholly a matter of qualitative feel either. Then the only remaining alternative is to combine the two forms of account.

(A) A Necessary Conjunction

We are suggesting that the term 'pain', for example, should be analysed somewhat as follows: someone is in pain if and only if both (a) they are in a state having a particular distinctive feel, and (b) that state normally is caused by tissue-damage and causes a disposition to pain-behaviour. Each of the two parts of the definition would state a condition logically necessary for the occurrence of pain, but neither by itself would be logically sufficient.

Our main objection to this form of account was that it seemed logically possible for the two parts to occur separately; and yet we wanted to insist that for someone to feel pain was sufficient for them to be in pain. To elaborate: although it may be true that the feeling of pain occupies a distinctive causal role in the actual world, it seems conceivable that there might be other possible worlds in which it occupies some quite different causal role, or none at all. Thus I seem to be able to imagine a world in which the distinctive feeling of pain is caused by stroking the skin, and causes a disposition to giggle. Then according to the definition above, this would be a world in which there is no pain. But as we argued in sections 4.iii and 4.iv, if everything feels to someone as though they are in pain, then surely they really are in pain.

The argument of the last section has now put us into a position to reply to this difficulty. For what it shows is that the qualitative feel conjunct in the analysis of 'pain' could not exist in the absence of the other. It shows, firstly, that my capacity to recognise and make judgements about my various distinctive sensations is logically dependent upon them being regularly connected with their public causes and effects. It is these connections which provide the stability necessary for me to have knowledge of my classificatory capacities, which in turn is necessary if I am to mean anything by the sensation-terms. The argument shows further, that my sensations themselves (and not just my capacities to recognise them) are logically dependent upon the existence of their distinctive causal roles. For a sensation, as we have said many times, is itself a state of awareness. I could not feel pains, for example, which I was unable to recognise as such.

Thus what makes it possible for me to think or speak about my sensations, is that each mode of classification corresponds to a regularity in causal role. But this is not to say that I necessarily classify my sensations in terms of their causal roles. On the contrary, I recognise — 'straight off' — the correctness of those classifications, without giving any explicit thought to the question of causal role; perhaps without even having any knowledge of causal role. (For example, someone might be taught to recognise their pains before they learn about the normal causes and effects of pain, and so before they can think in terms of the sort of conjunctive concept defined above. At this stage they are not, in my view, employing the concept of pain; but rather an impoverished, though related, concept.) Yet for all that it remains a necessary truth that I can only have this recognitional capacity because pains do have a distinctive causal role. And it is this fact which legitimates a conjunctive definition.

I have argued that regularities within the qualitative character of our experiences are logically tied to regularities in causal role; not in the sense that the experience is always identified via its causal role, but rather in the sense that it can only be thought about (and hence exist for us) if it does indeed occupy its causal role. This is not an easy idea to accept. For we are strongly inclined to think that similarities in qualitative feel may transcend differences in causal role. For example, although pains (in me) characteristically manifest themselves in pain-behaviour, can I not imagine a person who feels pain (that is: states with the qualitative feel of pain) but never manifests them in behaviour?

Now in one way this is indeed imaginable, even on the sort of view I am presenting. For a state may occur whose normal causal role is such-and-such, but where the circumstances are sufficiently unusual for it to fail to have either its normal causes or its normal effects or both. The simplest example may be of a person paralysed. Such a person may feel pain but be unable to show it. Yet this raises no problem for us: they are in a state whose effect would normally (but for the paralysis) be pain-behaviour. Other more exotic examples are also possible, e.g. of a person of sufficiently spartan attitude, whose desire to reveal no weakness is so strong that they successfully train themselves out of exhibiting any natural pain-reactions. Again it will still be true that they are in a state whose normal effect would be pain-behaviour (but for their spartan beliefs).

What is not really imaginable in my view, is that a person may feel pain, where this feeling is neither normally caused by injury nor causes in them any inclination to pain-behaviour. So despite the appearance to the contrary, it is not really imaginable that some might feel pains which are normally caused by stroking the skin, and which cause them to want to giggle. For in order to imagine this I have to be able to prize apart the qualitative feel of my own pains from their normal causal role, thinking 'Perhaps in another possible world this feeling might incline me to giggle.' But this is to presuppose that my capacity to think about this feeling could exist apart from its causal role, which we have shown in the last section to be false.

I admit that it certainly seems imaginable that our sensations could occur apart from their causal roles. But we have already had occasion (in sections 3.iv and 5.iv above) to be mistrustful of the deliverances of untutored imagination. In this case the phenomena only seem to be imaginable, because we think we can 'carve off' the distinctive feel of our sensations from their characteristic causal roles. I, as it were, cast an inward glance at my pain, or my experience of red, and think 'In some other possible world *this* experience may have quite other causes and effects.' But since my capacity to know that I can recognise pains or experiences of red is dependent upon those sensations occupying distinctive causal roles, there is (in the light of the argument of 6.iii) no thinking of this sort of experience apart from its causal role.

We have therefore replied successfully to the main objection to our proposed conjunctive analysis of sensation-terms. There are in fact no possible worlds in which the feelings occur apart from the functions.

(B) Certainty of Feeling

I have been urging that the analysis of terms such as 'pain' should properly include both causal role and qualitative feel. Now this might seem to threaten the supposed certainty of first-person judgements of pain, argued for in sections 1.iv and 4.iv. For if all judgements of pain concern both causal role and qualitative feel, then how can my judgements that I myself am in pain be completely certain, given that they are usually only based on a recognition of qualitative feel?

My reply to this is that there can be no challenge to the correctness of someone's description of their conscious experience which does not also challenge their understanding of the terms which they are using. So there is no possibility of a mistake. If we grant that they understand what they are saying, and are sincere, then we must grant the truth of what they say.

Let me elaborate. For someone to be mistaken about being in pain, on our account, they would either have to mis-recognise the feel of pain (judging that it occurs when it does not, or judging that it does not occur when really it does); or, correctly identifying the feel of pain, they would have to have recognised a state which in fact normally occupies some quite different causal role. Now the second alternative we can rule out straight away. For we have shown that someone can only be capable of recognising the feel of pain, if that state does normally occupy the causal role of pain.

But what of the first alternative? Could someone, while retaining their understanding of the term 'pain', mis-identify the feeling? But how could this be possible? For someone only understands the term 'pain' if they are capable of recognising the appropriate qualitative feel. So this would have to be a case in which they really *would* have judged correctly (so retaining their recognitional capacity) if they had not been misled in some respect. But in what respect? For in the case of sensations what you recognise — the qualitative feel — is itself the experience on whose basis your recognition is made. So there is no room for you to be misled into thinking that something is the feel of pain, which really is not.

Contrast with this, recognition of colour. Here there really is a distinction to be drawn between what is recognised (the colour), and that on whose basis your recognition is effected (your experience of the colour). So here mistakes are possible, because the experience may be produced in some unusual way. While retaining the capacity to recognise red, you may wrongly classify a white object as 'red'. For it may be true that you *would* have classified it correctly if: you had seen it in normal light; or if: you had known you were seeing it in red light; and so on.

Since in the case of pain-recognition there is nothing comparable to the 'mode of presentation' of a colour, there is no room for error. If you sincerely classify as 'a pain' some other feeling, then this will in itself be sufficient warrant for saying that you have — momentarily at least — lost the capacity to recognise pains. And if you lack that capacity, then you no longer understand the term 'pain'. So as I claimed above, there is no way to challenge the correctness of someone's description of their sensation without also challenging their understanding of what they say. There is then no conflict between the proposed conjunctive analysis and the kind of certainty which we have about our own experiences. Indeed what emerges here — somewhat surprisingly — is that the certainty-thesis is independent of the cartesian conception. It is possible to give up the cartesian conception, as we have done, while retaining the certainty-thesis.

(C) Other Minds Revisited

Our conjunctive analysis is an account of the content of sensation-statements: whether I am judging about myself or another person, the content of what I judge is that there is a state which occupies a particular causal role and which has a distinctive qualitative feel. Yet there will of course be two modes of knowledge of that content: in my own case I will recognise the qualitative feel, while in the case of others I will have to reason from observed causes and effects. How then does our analysis help with the problem of other minds? For although I can establish, in the case of other people, that they are in a state which occupies the normal causal role of pain (thus establishing one half of the conjunctive analysis), how am I to know what that state feels like to them?

Now in fact we have not only argued for a conjunctive analysis, but also for the existence of a necessary connection between the conjuncts. We have shown that regularities in qualitative feel are necessarily correlated with regularities in causal role. But how does this help? For in order to provide a direct solution to the problem of other minds, we should need to establish a necessary connection in the reverse direction as well: we would need to show that anything occupying the causal role of pain must necessarily have the feel of pain. And not only have we not established this yet, but it does not even appear to be true. For is it not conceivable that someone might be in a state occupying the causal role of pain without actually feeling anything at all?

Indeed I think this is conceivable. But it need not imply that we are in no position to provide a solution to the problem of other minds. For recall that the truth of the mind/brain identity-thesis puts us in a position to argue by analogy to the existence of other minds-in-general. So when I observe someone exhibiting the normal causes and effects of pain, I can know that they are experiencing some conscious sensation. But now I can also know, on the basis of the argument of the last section, that the feeling which I recognise as pain in my own case is necessarily tied to its normal causes and effects. Since there is no way for me to prize apart in thought, the particular experience from its occupancy of that particular causal role, it must follow that the other person is experiencing the very same sort of feeling as myself.

Consider the argument from the apparent possibility of colour-spectrum reversal. I know that other people can discriminate objects on the basis of their colours, just as I do myself. Then given the truth of the mind/brain identity-thesis, I am entitled to conclude that in other people, as in myself, there must be some conscious experience underlying their discriminatory ability (i.e. occupying the causal role in question). But then someone may object that for all I know, the experience which underlies their ability to discriminate red objects, may have the qualitative feel of the experience which enables me to discriminate green objects, and vice versa. Now I admit this seems imaginable. But it only seems imaginable because we think we can 'carve off' the feel of our own experiences from their causal role. But this, I have argued, is impossible. Since my very capacities to think about experiences of red and of green are dependent upon them occupying the causal roles which they do, there is no thinking of those experiences apart from their causal role.

Colour-spectrum reversal is, despite appearances, inconceivable. So the full solution to the problem of other minds is this: knowing of the existence of other minds-in-general on the basis of an argument by analogy, the necessary connections between particular conscious experiences and particular causal roles can then be deployed to give us knowledge of the particular feelings experienced by other people on specific occasions.

Conclusion

The argument which we developed in section 6.iii against the cartesian conception, has put us into a position to defend a conjunctive analysis of sensation-terms. And this defence, in turn, has enabled us finally to solve the problem of other minds. (Which of course enables us to say that the language in which we describe our own sensations is not a private one.) It is small wonder that the problem of other minds has proved so intractable. For its solution has not only required the elaboration and defence of the mind/

brain identity-thesis, but also a subtle and complex refutation of the cartesian conception.

Questions and Readings

You may like to discuss/think about/write about some of the following questions:

(1) If your sensation of pain causes you to say 'I am in pain', which in turn causes me to believe that you are in pain, then have I understood you?
(2) Could Tarzan — alone in the jungle since birth — speak a language?
(3) How do you know that you mean anything by the signs which you use?
(4) If the world were continually changing in unpredictable ways, then would it be possible for us to think or speak about it?
(5) Is pain, by definition, a particular distinctive feel which necessarily occupies a particular causal role?

In considering these questions you may like to consult a selection of the following readings (capitalised names refer to collections listed in the Bibliography):

A. J. Ayer, 'Can there be a Private Language', *Aristotelian Society Proceedings*, supp. vol. XXVIII (1954). Reprinted in JONES, AYER [2], PITCHER and MORICK [1].

Simon Blackburn, *Spreading the Word* (Oxford: Clarendon Press, 1984), Ch. 3.

John Cook, 'Wittgenstein on Privacy', *Philosophical Review*, LXXIV (1965). Reprinted in PITCHER.

Robert Fogelin, *Wittgenstein* (London: Routledge & Kegan Paul, 1976), Ch. XIII.

Peter Hacker, *Insight and Illusion* (Oxford: Oxford University Press, 1972), Chs. VIII–X.

Anthony Kenny, *Wittgenstein* (London: Penguin Press, 1973), Ch. 10.

Saul Kripke, *Wittgenstein on Rules and Private Language* (Oxford: Blackwell, 1982).

Norman Malcolm, 'Wittgenstein's Philosophical Investigations', *Philosophical Review*, LXIII (1954). Reprinted in JONES, PITCHER, MORICK [1], MORICK [2], and CHAPPELL.

Robert Nozick, *Philosophical Explanations* (Oxford: Clarendon Press, 1981), Ch. 3.

Rush Rhees, 'Can there be a Private Language', *Aristotelian Society Proceedings*, supp. vol. XXVIII (1954). Reprinted in JONES and PITCHER.

Ludwig Wittgenstein, *Philosophical Investigations*, trans. G. E. M. Anscombe (Oxford: Blackwell, 1953), sections 82–6, 138–55, 183–315, 348–472.

Crispin Wright, *Wittgenstein on the Foundations of Mathematics* (London: Duckworth, 1980), Ch. 2.

PART FOUR:
MATERIAL PERSONS

7 AFTER-LIFE FOR MATERIALISTS

i. Resurrection

It would seem that strong materialism is the truth about persons. The answer to the question 'What am I?' is 'A wholly material thing.' For in Chapter 3 we concluded that the subject of conscious thoughts and experiences must be a physical thing, namely the living human being, or brain. And in Chapter 5 we concluded that the conscious states of the subject — the thoughts and experiences themselves — are very likely physical as well.

In this chapter we shall consider the various possible criteria of identity (over time) for physical persons, and we will raise the question whether it is possible, as strong materialists, to hope for some kind of life after death. (This is one of those places where abstract philosophical argument comes into direct contact with matters of immediate practical concern.) Traditional views of the after-life come in three forms: disembodied existence, resurrection and reincarnation. Our arguments against dualism have ruled out the first of these three. The other two perhaps remain possible: in this section we shall consider resurrection, and in the sections following, reincarnation.

(A) General Points

The connection which apparently exists between questions of personal identity and after-life may be brought out as follows. We have to ask, of whatever entity is supposed to survive my death, 'Would that be *me*?' If the after-life — whatever it consists in — is supposed to be an object of hope or fear for me, in the way that I have hopes and fears for my old age (and as opposed to the way in which I have hopes and fears for my children), then it seems essential that the thing which continues to exist after my death should be myself (as opposed to merely a part of myself, such as my kidney; and as opposed to something merely resembling myself, such as my child). We have to ask 'Would the person that I now am be the very same person as the person who will continue to exist (or after an interval come to exist) after my death? Should we be numerically identical?'

There are a number of different considerations which we can use as a touchstone in discussing questions of personal identity. The first, already hinted at, is self-interest. In considering whether some future person would be identical with yourself, it will at least aid intuition if you ask whether or not you would be concerned for the welfare of that person in the way that you are concerned for your own future happiness. However, this test needs handling with care. For as we shall see, it is problematic exactly how to characterise the nature of self-interest as opposed to other-interest. (Certainly it is not a matter of strength of feeling anyway. I may care more for my children than for myself.)

Another consideration is moral and legal responsibility. It is one of the first principles of justice that no one should be blamed or punished for something which they did not do themselves. (This is my view anyway. But others apparently think differently. In some versions of Christianity, God is supposed to have punished the descendants of Adam and Eve for the original sin, which they themselves did not commit.) So in considering whether one of us could be identical with some person who continues to exist after normal biological death, ask yourself whether it would be fair to punish the later person for the misdeeds of the former.

(B) Human Identity

Turning now to the question of resurrection: if the criterion of bodily-identity is spatio-temporal continuity, as we have several times suggested that it might be, then for most of us there can be no question of resurrection. For we shall either be buried, to have our bodies decompose and be eaten by worms, or cremated. So, relatively soon after our death there will be no body. In which case it is impossible for any later body to be spatio-temporally continuous with the body of the person who died. The only class of exceptions would be those who have their bodies frozen or otherwise preserved. If God or the scientists can ever cause these bodies to be brought back to life, then there would emerge a living human being who is indeed spatio-temporally continuous with a person who had earlier died.

If the criterion of identity for the human organism is spatio-temporal continuity, then resurrection will only be possible for the rich. However, recall that in the case of at least some physical objects, their identity-over-time can reach across periods of non-existence. For as we saw in section 2.iv, the criterion of identity for

human artefacts allows them to survive across temporary disassembly. When my motorcycle is lying around in pieces in the
garage, there is no motorcycle. For a collection of unrelated motorcycle parts is not a motorcycle. Yet when I put those parts back
together again, what I do is rebuild my motorcycle, not create a
new one.

Analagously then: suppose that on the Day of Judgement God
brings together all the original bits and pieces which had made up
my body — all the cells, molecules and atoms — and puts them
back together in the way that they had originally been arranged
during my life. (Since God is omnipotent there can be no real
obstacles in the way of him doing this.) Would he then have rebuilt
me? Would the resulting human organism be the very same physical body that I am now? In order to answer these questions we need
to consider the extent to which living organisms are like artefacts.
In particular, is their criterion of identity such as to allow them to
survive temporary disassembly?

An example suggesting a negative answer is as follows: suppose
that a great oak tree dies and decomposes, all its constituent atoms
and molecules passing back into the soil from which it had grown.
Then some years later an acorn germinates on the very same spot
and begins to grow. Now suppose that by chance the acorn possesses the same genetic code as the original tree, and that by some
miracle all the atoms and molecules from the original tree get taken
up out of the soil as the seedling grows. Let the result be a tree as
similar in appearance to the original as you like, made up out of the
very same pieces arranged in the very same way. Should we say that
this was not a new tree, but rather the very same oak which had
earlier died and decayed? Have we imagined a case of tree-resurrec-
tion? — unlikely perhaps, but nonetheless logically possible? It
seems to me clear that we have not. I should want to say that we
have, in this story, *two* trees rather than one, despite the close
similarities in appearance and physical construction.

It is easy to find examples to pull us in the opposite direction.
Think, for instance, of the concepts of 'beaming up' and 'beaming
down' in the television series 'Star Trek'. In order to transport
people backwards and forwards between the star-ship *Enterprise*
and nearby planets, they use a machine which breaks the human
body up into its atoms and molecules, and then accelerates those
particles in a high-energy beam which can travel through solid
objects, arranging for them to be reconstituted exactly as they were

at some designated spot. Here we feel no difficulty with the idea that it would be the very same human organism which would emerge at the end of this process, despite the fact that — as in the example of the oak tree — there has been an interval during which no living organism exists as such. (A beam of living-organism-parts is not a living organism.)

We apparently have conflicting intuitions about whether a living organism can survive temporary periods of non-existence. How are they to be reconciled? I conjecture that the ground of our intuition in the oak tree example is the fact that living organisms undergo a characteristic process of birth, growth, degeneration and death. We are thus accustomed to counting them by counting life-cycles: to every such process of birth-to-death corresponds a single living organism. Then because, in the oak tree example, we have two such processes, we are inclined to judge that there are two distinct trees. In the 'beaming down' example, on the other hand, there is nothing recognisable as normal birth and death. Since the process of beaming down does not separate two distinct life-cycles, there is nothing to incline us to say that it divides two distinct living organisms.

Resurrection is like beaming down, and unlike the oak tree example, in that it does not involve two complete cycles of birth-to-death. For the process of resurrection itself, as we imagined it, is quite unlike any normal birth. Indeed it is very closely similar to the reconstitution out of atoms that would occur at the end of the process of beaming up or down. So I conclude — albeit tentatively — that resurrection is a logical possibility, even for those whose bodies have disintegrated.

(C) An Objection

An apparent difficulty for the whole idea of resurrection by reconstitution out of parts, is as follows. As everyone knows, most cells in the human body are replaced, perhaps many times over, during the course of a normal life-time. So come the Day of Judgement there will be enough of my original bits and pieces lying around in the world for God to resurrect *two* of me. Well suppose — in mischievous mood perhaps — he does just that. (It would certainly be a fault in God to have no sense of humour.) The resulting people cannot be identical with one another; for they are distinct living organisms, who may go on to lead quite different lives. And since there exists absolutely no reason for identifying one rather than the other of them with the original me, I cannot be identical with either. Yet each of them satisfies the criterion of reconstitution out of parts.

Similar cases can occur in connection with artefacts. For not only can artefacts survive across temporary disassembly, they can also survive through a considerable extent of replacement of parts. (Thus many of the parts of my car have been replaced by new ones over the years. Yet for all that it is the very same car which I bought all those years ago.) Consider the example of the ship of Theseus. Theseus owns a wooden ship which he is keeping in dry-dock over the winter. Each night a thief comes and steals a single part of the ship — now a plank, now a length of rope, etc. — and each morning Theseus discovers the theft and replaces the stolen part. By the spring the thief has enough parts to build a ship of his own, which he does. Who then owns the original ship of Theseus? If we go by spatio-temporal continuity over replacement of parts we shall answer 'Theseus'. But if we go by reconstruction out of original parts we shall answer 'The thief'. Yet they cannot both have the original, since they now have different ships. (Remember that identity is transitive and symmetric.)

What do examples of this sort show? In my view, not a great deal. In particular, it does not follow that resurrection of the body is impossible. All that is really shown is that we do not have a criterion of identity — either for human beings or for artefacts — which will cover every conceivable kind of circumstance. But this is no very serious matter, since many of our concepts are incompletely defined in this way. Many of our concepts are such that there exist conceivable circumstances in which we should have no idea what to say; yet this need not prevent us from making true judgements with them in ordinary circumstances. For example, suppose that we come across a particular chair, which we can see and touch and sit upon. But next moment it vanishes completely. Later it reappears again. Then it vanishes again. Now is this a real chair or not? I think that nothing in our ordinary concept of 'chair' determines what we are to say in extraordinary circumstances such as these. But this need not prevent me from judging truly that I am now sitting on a chair as I write these words.

The issues raised by examples like that of double-resurrection and the ship of Theseus, are essentially a matter of 'tidying up' our concepts. If examples like these arose often, we should have to extend and refine our criteria of identity for human beings and artefacts in order to be able to cope with them. We might, for example, say that artefacts are identical if and only if either (a) they are spatio-temporally continuous over replacement of less than a majority of parts, or (b) the one is reconstituted out of a majority of parts from the other. (This would give the original ship to the thief.) And in tidying up our concept of organism-identity we might give priority to atoms and molecules which came from the organism later in life rather than earlier (or vice versa). But so long as these examples don't (or don't often) arise, there is no particular reason why we should bother. So let us trust that God will not in fact behave mischieviously, and rest content with a simple account of resurrection in terms of reconstitution out of original parts.

(D) Is Bodily Identity Sufficient?

It would appear that resurrection of the body is logically possible. But would it be sufficient, by itself, to ensure personal survival of death? Is bodily identity a sufficient condition of personal identity? I shall argue that it is not. I shall argue that mere bodily resurrection, in the absence of any degree of psychological connectedness (see section 3.ii for details), would not constitute a form of personal after-life. On the contrary, in order for the resurrected individual to be the very same person as myself, it is at least necessary that they should be psychologically connected with myself.

Consider the following example: suppose that scientists have a way of freezing dead bodies to preserve them from decay, and are confidently predicting that in ten years time they will have developed the technology to be able to bring those bodies back to life again. But they also tell you that the freezing process must involve the complete destruction of all memory and personality-traces from the brain. So the human being who is revived, ten years hence, will remember nothing of your life, and will have none of your desires, interests or ties of affection. Their mind will be, in these respects, a blank sheet. Now would you in these circumstances be prepared to pay good money to have your corpse frozen and later revived? I certainly would not. For the process only ensures that there will live, at some time after my death, a human being who has exactly my physical appearance, and whose body is made up of the very same cells which currently make up my body. And why should I take any particular interest in that?

(Perhaps it might be rational to have one's corpse frozen, gambling that the scientists may yet discover some means of reviving them which will ensure that psychological connectedness is retained. But suppose we know that this cannot be done. Suppose we know that there is something about the freezing process itself, and the way in which memory and personality are encoded in the brain, which means that freezing must inevitably destroy all traces of them; rather in the way that once having switched off a computer, there is no way of recovering any programs which have not been 'saved' on to tape or disc.)

From a third-person perspective there would be every reason to regard the revived human being as a new person. For they would have to establish new interests, new personal relationships and a new life. Thus there would be no point in paying to have a dead loved-one frozen, in the hope of being reunited with them in ten years time. For the revived individual would not remember you, and would have none of the qualities of character which made you care for them in the first place. (If your attraction were largely physical then there might be some point in it. But of course there would be no guarantee that the revived person would take any reciprocal physical interest in you.) Moreover it would seem totally unfair — or at any rate pointless — to hold the revived person responsible for any evils committed by the original. For not only would they remember nothing whatever of those incidents, but they would have none of the desires, motives and qualities of character which had caused the original deeds to be committed.

From a first-person perspective, too, there would be no reason to regard the revived individual as yourself. For none of the motives which you now have for desiring your own survival will carry across the loss of psychological connectedness. A proper demonstration of this point must wait upon an analysis of the motives for survival, to be undertaken in the next section. But reflect here upon the fact that all of those things which make your life worth living — your personal relationships and friendships, projects and plans, interests you have developed and pleasures you have cultivated — would be lost to you with the loss of psychological connectedness.

Thus far the case may seem convincing. But a counter-consideration is this: suppose someone told you that your corpse would be frozen and later revived (without psychological connectedness), and that the revived body would then be tortured or used in painful medical experiments. Would you not feel fear? If so, does this not suggest that you would in fact regard the revived individual as identical with yourself, despite the lack of psychological connection?

However, the capacity to feel fear is not a very reliable guide on matters of personal identity, since it is possible to feel fear on someone else's behalf. Thus if I were told that someone I love were about to be tortured, I should of course feel fear for them. Now it is true that one has no particular reason to feel attached to the resurrected individual; so the fear one feels cannot be exactly analogous to the fear that one can feel on behalf of a loved one. But we can still explain how it can arise independently of any belief in our identity with the revived person.

We naturally imagine the threatened torture 'from the inside'. For this is what imagining an experience is: to imagine what it would be like to be tortured is to imagine, from the inside, what it would *feel like* to be tortured. This may by itself be sufficient to cause fear, since it is a familiar fact that imagining an experience can provoke the emotions appropriate to the real thing. (This is why fantasy can be fun.) But the effect will be compounded when I add to my image the thought 'And it will be this body which feels all that pain.' For I am used to thinking that anything which happens to this body happens to myself. But if I hold clearly before my mind the loss of psychological connectedness, then I no longer take this seriously. I then no more literally fear the torture of the revived individual than I would fear for myself on being told that the car I am just getting out of will be blown up in ten minutes time. (Though this too can send a shiver down the spine; for it is so close to me.)

Conclusion

Resurrection of the body is logically possible. But it will only count as a version of after-life — that it to say, as a way of continuing the life of the very same person who earlier had died — if the resurrected individual retains something of the memory and personality of the original. In the next section we shall consider whether memory and personality might by themselves be sufficient for personal survival, independently of bodily identity. We have concluded that bodily identity is not by itself sufficient for personal survival; we shall now ask whether it is even necessary.

ii. Reincarnation

Can a strong materialist consistently believe in the possibility of reincarnation? It might seem obvious that they cannot. For it might seem that reincarnation will only take place if a person exists, successively, *in* different bodies. And how could this be possible unless the person themself is something distinct from their body (e.g. a non-physical soul)? Now although believers in reincarnation have generally been dualists — indeed the theory is often called 'the theory of transmigration of souls' — I do not see that they had to be. One could equally well, as a strong materialist, believe in reincarnation by believing in a divergence between the criteria of identity and identification for persons.

(A) Divergent Criteria

An analogy will make clear what I have in mind. Consider the criteria of identity and identification for a particular school class, or form. At any given time, a class is identified by identifying its members. Thus if someone asks 'Who are 5.v?' your reply should either list the members of 5.v, or identify them in some other way ('The children in the classroom next door'). Moreover, truths about 5.v at any given time, are truths about (most of) its members at the time. Thus '5.v want to go and see the new production of *King Lear*' reduces to 'Most of John and Mary and Peter and Susan . . . want to go.'

The criterion of identity for a class over time is quite different. Often it will be given in terms of a fixed position within the age and ability range of the school, so that two distinct groups of children can in successive years constitute one and the same class. Thus if a teacher is asked 'Are you teaching the same English class again this year' they may reply 'Yes, I have got 5.v again', despite the fact that 5.v have undergone a total change in membership. So to summarise: the criterion of identification for a school class is the set of its members, whereas the criterion of identity allows a number of different sets of children to constitute, successively, one and the same class.

When I speak of the possibility of a materialist version of belief in reincarnation, I have in mind a similar divergence. As materialists, we believe that the subject of thoughts and experiences is a physical thing. So we have no option but to give the criterion of identification for persons in physical terms. We have to say that a person x at time t = a person y, also at time t, if and only if x and y are one and the same human being (or: one and the same human brain). But we can, quite consistently with this, give the criterion of identity (over time) for persons in terms of the notion of psychological connectedness. We can allow that so long as the later human being has quasi-memories of the life of the earlier, and has sufficiently similar desires, interests and ties of affection, then those human beings will constitute different stages in the life of one and the same person. This would make it possible for a person to exist successively *as* (rather than 'in') a number of distinct human beings, which would be a form of reincarnation.

However, to say that such a view is consistent is not the same as saying that it is true. To say that the criteria of identity and identification could diverge, is not the same as saying that they do. So we need to consider how *plausible* it would be to say that I shall survive just in case there exists a person who is sufficiently strongly psychologically connected with myself.

(B) An Example

Let us sharpen up our intuitions on an example. Suppose that scientists have built a machine which they claim will enable people to travel at the speed of light. (Our problem is whether this is really as case of personal travel.) Thus suppose you are wanting to visit your relatives who are colonists on a planet in another solar system. The scientists tell you that instead of having to travel by rocket, which would take many years, you can step into their machine here on Earth and (so they claim) step out of a similar machine on the colonised planet a few hours later. What the machine does is conduct a complete scan of the state of every single cell in your body, recording all this information on to a computer (the nature of the scan being such that the cells are all destroyed by the process). The information is then transmitted in the form of a radio signal to a machine on the colonised planet, which will build a replica of you which is exact right down to the last detail. Because the replica is so exact, the person who steps out of the machine at the other end will have all of your quasi-memories and quasi-intentions, as well as your beliefs, interests and general personality. Moreover, that person's body will resemble yours exactly. It is however a *distinct* body. For unlike the example of 'beaming down' discussed in the last section, no material is actually transmitted by the machine. So the new body is neither spatio-temporally continuous with the old, nor is it made up out of the same bits and pieces.

Our question is this: would the person who steps out of the machine on the colonised planet be yourself? Would this be an example of reincarnation without souls?

(C) Practical Considerations

From a third-person perspective there is every reason why the new body should be treated as a reincarnation of yourself. Consider your relatives for example: ought they to welcome the new body as yourself, or reject it as an impostor and be grief-stricken because you have ceased to exist? Well the new body would have all of the qualities, both physical and psychological, which they had come to know and love (or hate, as may be) in the old. There would be the same shared knowledge of family history and the same ties of affection. Given all this, why should they take any interest in the fact that the person possessing these qualities is made up of new matter? Why should they feel the slightest bit distressed at the destruction of the old body back on Earth? For they surely never were attached to that body as such.

Also from a third-person perspective, consider the question of responsibility and punishment, supposing that you had committed some evil deed prior to entering the machine on Earth. Now the question whether it would be fair and just to punish the new human being for the misdeeds of the old, perhaps has to wait on an answer to the question of personal identity. For the notion of 'just punishment' appears to imply that the person punished is identical with the person who committed the crime. But we can at least see that blame and punishment would have exactly the same point here as in the normal case. For the new human being would quasi-remember the crime (it would certainly feel to them as if they had done it); and all the motives and bad qualities of character which had led them to commit the crime in the first place would still be there in the new body.

Viewed from the first-person perspective of the person themself, after the fact, there would also be every reason to regard the example as a genuine case of reincarnation. For the person stepping out of the machine on the colonised planet will not in any way feel themselves to be a new person. On the contrary, their present existence will seem to them to be entirely continuous with the life of the human being on Earth. They will quasi-recall many of the events of that life, including getting into the machine on Earth; that event being separated from their present existence by what seems to them to have been a brief period of unconsciousness (like waking after a night's sleep). They will quasi-recall their feelings then, and the thoughts and discussions which led up to the decision to get into the machine. And they will now set about executing the plans and intentions which they quasi-recall having made earlier. Why should they themselves take any interest in the fact that their consciousness is now supported by a new body?

From the perspective of the person themself before the fact, the issue is perhaps not so clear. When I imagine myself in the position of someone about to step into such a machine, I find that I can easily induce in myself either of two contradictory attitudes. If I focus my thoughts on the result of the process, and slur over what takes place in between, then I imagine myself looking forward to the prospect of seeing loved ones again, and feeling apprehensive at the reputedly harsh conditions on the colonised planet. But if I focus my attention on what will happen most immediately — the destruction of all the cells in my body — then I find myself thinking 'So that will be the death of me', and I feel afraid. And then the thought of the person who will exist on the colonised planet seems merely to be the thought of someone who will exactly resemble myself, and I am concerned for *his* sufferings not at all.

Well how *ought* a person about to step into such a machine to regard the prospect? Should they fear it as they fear death, believing that they will cease to exist with the destruction of their body? Or should they regard it merely as a convenient form of personal travel? In order to answer these questions we need to look more closely at the nature of self-interest. We need to consider whether or not our normal desire for survival — however that should best be characterised — would be just as well served by the existence of the replica on the colonised planet. It will help us in this task if we recall the distinction between those desires and projects which are self-referring (like my desire that I myself should be rich) and those which are impersonal. (This distinction was first drawn in section 3.ii.) We can then subdivide our discussion accordingly.

(D) Impersonal Motives for Survival

Many of us have impersonal (non-self-referring) desires, which are for states of affairs which do not necessarily contain ourselves. For example, a political activist working for the revolution may know perfectly well that it will very likely not come during their lifetime. But what they want is that there should be a revolution, not that they should live to see a revolution. Similarly, someone wanting to save the whale may not particularly want that they themselves should save the whale, but simply that the whale should be saved. Someone who loves both Shakespeare and the Japanese language, and whose project is to translate the works of Shakespeare into Japanese, may not particularly desire that they themselves should do the translation. What matters to them is that Shakespeare should be translated, and if they thought that someone else could perform the task better they might gladly hand it over to them. Closer to home, when I desire the happiness of those I love, my desire is simply that they should be happy. If my love is genuine, then my desire must to some extent be disinterested: I must want them to be happy irrespective of whether or not I live to see it.

Where someone has impersonal desires, at least part of their motive for survival will derive from the fact that their own continued existence will normally be a necessary condition of (or at least may contribute to) the achievement of what they desire. Thus the political activist has a motive for survival, in so far as they think that their activity may make the revolution more likely. (Although if the activist is particularly single-minded — this desire dominating all others — then they may gladly lay down their life for the cause if it turns out that it is their death, rather than their continued existence, which will bring the revolution closer.) The translator has a reason for living in so far as they believe that the job will not get done properly unless they themselves do it. And disinterested love will also provide a motive for survival, since our continued existence will often contribute considerably to the happiness of those whom we love.

From the perspective of our impersonal desires, what matters in survival is psychological connectedness (and sometimes physical resemblance). Bodily identity will not matter at all. Thus in the case of the political activist what matters, from the point of view of their desire for revolution, is that there should continue to exist someone with the desires and qualities of character necessary to engage in revolutionary activity. That there should continue to exist a living body identical with the body of the activist, will in itself be of no help in furthering the cause. Indeed the really single-minded activist will fear brain-washing — where the effect is permanent loss of the desire for revolution — in the same way and to the same extent that they fear death. Similarly, what matters to the translator is that there should continue to exist someone with the desires, interests and literary sensibility necessary to perform the task. And in the case of the disinterested lover, what matters is that there should continue to exist someone who has that love, and who has the qualities (both psychological and physical) which may be loved in return.

I conclude that in so far as our interest in normal survival derives from impersonal desires, then it is best characterised as the desire that there should continue to exist someone psychologically connected with myself (and perhaps also physically similar to myself), rather than that there should continue to exist someone whose body is identical with mine. So from this point of view too, radio-transportation should be regarded as a means of personal travel. At any rate, to the extent that someone contemplating getting into the machine has impersonal desires, to that extent they should regard the future existence of the replica as being *just as good as* ordinary survival.

(E) Personal Motives for Survival

Of course many (perhaps the majority) of our desires are self-referring. When I want to be happy, or rich, or famous, what I want is that I myself should be happy, or rich, or famous. (Note however that some self-referring desires may be based upon impersonal ones. When I desire not to have a migraine tomorrow, at least part of the underlying motive may be that severe pain would interfere with my translation work, or would make those whom I love suffer with me.) In these cases the notion of personal identity forms part of the content of the desires themselves: to want to be rich is to desire that some future person who is identical with myself should be rich. So we have to ask just how the content of such desires should best be characterised. Should we say that they are desires for things to happen to a particular living body? Or are they best characterised in terms of psychological connectedness (and perhaps also physical resemblance)?

We can see that psychological connectedness should at least be included as a necessary ingredient in the content of self-referring desires, if we notice that such connectedness will often be just as much presupposed, for the satisfaction of those desires, as is ordinary survival. This is so for two reasons. The first derives from the causality of desire. As we noted in section 3.ii, desire is a causal notion: to conceive of something as a desire is to conceive of it as a state apt to cause the thing desired. My desire to be rich disposes me to try and become rich, and hence is apt to cause its own satisfaction. So if I want to be rich, I should realise that the loss of that desire (the loss of one aspect of psychological connectedness) will make it that much more likely that I shall never be rich. For without the desire I should not make the attempt. The second point is that without the continued existence of the desire, success will not be satisfying. If I have lost the desire for riches, then even if I were to become rich by chance this would not satisfy any desire which I would then currently have. So from both points of view, if I want to be rich, then I should also desire that I continue to possess that desire. (Of course I may also have other desires — for instance the desire to be humble — which may lead me to want to lose that desire.)

It seems that from the point of view of my self-referring desires, I should desire the existence of someone psychologically connected with myself (possessing those very same desires), in the same way that I desire my own ordinary survival. This completes the argument sketched at the end of the last section, that psychological connectedness is at least a necessary condition of personal survival. But it is still left open that bodily identity may also be necessary. For we have not shown that the self-referring desire for riches is not also the desire that some body identical with my own should be rich. I shall present two arguments intended to show just this.

The first argument is based upon the frequency of dualistic beliefs. Since many people believe in disembodied existence, or at least feel no difficulty with the idea of such existence; and since they entertain hopes and fears for what might happen to them in that existence; then it is hardly very plausible to construe all their desires for the future as desires for things to happen to a particular body. If someone hopes that the disembodied after-life will not be lonely, then this cannot be construed as involving the hope that some body identical with theirs will not be lonely, without accusing them of explicit, and obviously foolish, self-contradiction. It is more charitable to them to understand the content of what they hope purely in terms of psychological connectedness.

The second argument is this: when I reflect upon, and spell out to myself, the content of many of my self-referring desires, what I think of are particular events and experiences taking place against a background of desires and interests similar to mine; the thought of a particular individual body does not enter in at all. Thus suppose I am hungry, and find that what I particularly want is a hot fish curry. What exactly does this desire involve? Just this: that I think with longing of eating such a curry. And when I think of this, I imagine enjoying it; so it is presupposed that I retain my liking for curry (and indeed my hunger). But at no point does the thought occur to me 'And the human being who eats the curry is to be the physical body identical with my own.' Similarly with the desire to be rich: here I think of all the things which riches can bring, such as large houses and holidays in Sri Lanka; and I imagine these against a backdrop of desires and interests similar to my own. I do not especially imagine the riches being possessed by a body identical with mine.

Conclusion

Self-referring desires are best characterised as desires for things to happen to a person who is suitably psychologically connected with yourself. And then the desire for normal survival should also be characterised in psychological terms. So from all points of view — from the point of view of a third party, from a first-person perspective after the fact, and from a first-person perspective before the fact — the replica on the colonised planet should be regarded as identical with yourself. We have therefore imagined a case of reincarnation without souls.

iii. Double Difficulties

We argued in the last section that the best conception of the nature of persons allows their criteria of identity and identification to diverge; the criterion of identity-over-time being given in terms of psychological connectedness. In the present section we shall put forward a number of different objections to this idea.

(A) An Initial Counter-Example

Consider the following development of the radio-transportation example. The machine which scans your body here on Earth does not destroy it immediately; but it fatally weakens it. You would therefore step out of that machine again, knowing that you have only a few days to live, but also knowing that an exact replica of you has been created on a distant planet. Surely this would not give you much consolation! So far as you yourself would be concerned, you will soon cease to exist; and the continued existence of the replica on the distant planet will merely be the continued existence of someone else (although admittedly, someone who exactly resembles yourself).

Note however that the replica would not in fact be directly psychologically connected with yourself. Rather, you would both of you be psychologically connected with a common ancestor, namely the person before they stepped into the machine. For the replica would have no quasi-memories of your life since then; nor would you have any quasi-memories of their existence on the distant planet. And, more importantly, although both of you would have exactly *similar* desires and intentions, those states would not be directly causally linked: your current desire to write a detective novel would not be apt to cause their similar desire to be satisfied; nor would any intention which you now form cause them to perform actions once you are dead. So you could not possibly take the kind of interest in the future existence of the replica which you would take in your own normal survival.

One way of responding to the objection, therefore, would be to drop the claim that an overlapping series of psychological connections can give identity. We could insist instead that personal identity requires direct psychological connectedness. We shall return to this idea once again in section 8.i.

(B) Duplication

The second objection also involves a slight development of the original example. As before, you intend to visit a distant colonised planet. But suppose that there are two such planets, with a replica-building machine on each of them. Now due to an error on the part of the machine-operator here on Earth, the record of your cell-states is transmitted to both planets, so that two exact replicas of you are built. Each of these replicas would resemble you exactly, and would be equally strongly psychologically connected with yourself. So what are we to say? Do you survive as both of them? Do you survive as one rather than the other of them? Or do you not survive at all?

Clearly the two replicas are not identical with one another. They are different physical beings occupying different regions of space on different planets. And although they are psychologically exactly similar, complete similarity will only last for a moment. As soon as they attain consciousness they will start to have different experiences and perform different actions. The one may step out on to a harsh stony planet to be greeted ecstatically by their relatives. The other may step out into lush tropical vegetation, to be met by a barrage of questions from surprised strangers. The one may live happily ever after in the bosom of the family, while the other becomes totally embittered and turns to a life of crime. It would obviously be absurd to punish the one for the crimes of the other, claiming that they are one and the same person.

Now if the two replicas are not identical with one another, then they cannot possibly both be identical with yourself. For the transitivity and symmetry of identity together imply the following general principle: if x = y and x = z, then y = z. So if you *were* identical with both of them, they would have to be identical with one another; but they are not.

Morover, since each of the two replicas has precisely the same claim to be identical with yourself — both of them resembling you exactly — it cannot be the case that you survive as one rather than the other of them. For if you were identical with one but not the other, then there would surely have to be some relevant difference between them; but there is not: they are exactly alike.

If you are not identical with both of the replicas, and are not identical with only one of them, then the only remaining alternative is that you are not identical with either. Then, supposing that the original body back on Earth was destroyed by the scanning process, it must follow that you yourself do not survive. So when the machine-operator made the error which resulted in the existence of two exact replicas, they brought it about that you yourself ceased to exist.

This conclusion can now be turned into a strong argument against the claim that psychological connectedness is a sufficient condition of personal identity. For what emerges is that if we employ a psychological criterion of identity, then the question of the identity of x and y may depend not just upon facts about them, but also upon events taking place in some quite different part of the universe. Thus the identity of yourself with the replica on the planet containing your relatives, may depend upon what happens on a planet many millions of miles away. For if the machine-operator had not made their error, then you would, on our account, have survived after all. And even given that error, if the machine on the other planet had malfunctioned, so that the replica there had never attained consciousness, then too you would have continued to exist. For either way, it would have been true that the replica on the planet with your relatives is more strongly psychologically connected with yourself than is any other person.

We surely believe, in contrast, that the question of the identity of x and y must depend only on facts about those two individuals, and the relations between them. For identity is certainly not an explicitly comparative notion. One cannot, for example, speak of an object x being more, or less, identical with an object y than is some other object z. But then neither does it depend upon any implicit comparison, in the way that the concept of 'leadership' may depend upon such a comparison. (In order to decide whether or not someone is the leader of a particular group, you may have to compare their role with that of others.) Rather, we surely think that the question of the identity of an object x with an object y is an all-or-nothing, non-comparative, one.

It seems intuitively obvious that identity is not a comparative relation. For what more intimate relation could there be between any 'two' objects than the relation of identity? Since if x and y are identical there is only one object involved rather than two, how could the fact of their identity depend upon facts about other individuals? Then since the proposed account of personal identity in terms of psychological connectedness is comparative (requiring that x should be more strongly psychologically connected with y than is any other person, if x and y are to be identical) we appear to have sufficiently refuted that account.

(C) The Depth of the Problem

It is important to see that we cannot avoid the difficulties raised by the possibility of duplication through some kind of 'tidying up' of the suggested criterion of personal identity. For the similarities with the problems of duplication raised in our discussion of resurrection in the last section are only superficial. Those problems arose because we were allowing the criteria for bodily identity — like the criteria for artefact identity — to be multiple. We suggested that identity of body could be given *either* by spatio-temporal continuity over complete replacement of parts, *or* by reconstruction out of original parts. This then opened up the possibility of duplication, identity with one object being given by one criterion, and identity with some quite different object being given by the other. The problem was then merely to provide a precise formula to bring about the correct balance between the two criteria, in such a way as to yield an unique judgement in all cases.

Our difficulties in the present connection are much more fundamental. They arise out of the very nature of the relation we have chosen to use in constructing our account of personal identity. For since psychological connectedness is a 'many-many' relation, whereas identity itself is a 'one-one' relation, there are bound to be problems if we use the one to define the other.

By a 'many-many' relation, I mean a relation which can hold between more than one thing and more than one thing. For example, 'is a sister of' is the name of a many-many relation, since someone can have more than one sister, as well as be sister to more than one other person. By a 'one-one' relation, on the other hand, I mean a relation which can only hold between one thing and one thing at a time. For example, in monogamous societies 'is a spouse of' is the name of a one-one relation, since someone can only have one spouse at a time.

It is obvious that psychological connectedness is a many-many relation. For instance, it is possible for more than one person to quasi-remember events from the life of any given individual, and for one person to quasi-remember events from the lives of more than one. Yet it is equally obvious that identity is one-one. This follows from the transitivity and symmetry of identity: if x = y and x = z, then y = z. Given this disparity, the only possible way in which we can make use the relation of psychological connectedness in giving an account of personal identity, is by making the definition quantitive and comparative: relying upon the phrase 'the greatest quantity of psychological connections' to secure the uniqueness of identity, and insisting that if two different people are equally closely connected with a single original, then *neither* of them is in fact identical with that original.

We have refuted the proposal made at the outset of section 7.ii, that personal identity should be defined in terms of psychological connectedness. For any such definition must be comparative, whereas identity itself is *not* comparative. This then appears to refute the claimed possibility of reincarnation. Despite the various practical considerations raised in section 7.ii, relating to the kind of interest which we take in the survival of ourselves and others, it seems the concept of identity is such as to force us to require some element of bodily identity as a necessary condition of personal survival.

(D) Bodily Duplication

It is worth noting that similar difficulties to those raised here against the possibility of reincarnation, can also be raised against what is, arguably, the most plausible bodily necessary-condition of personal survival. I shall approach this in two stages: first arguing for what seems to be the most plausible bodily necessary-condition, and then showing how it gives rise to similar problems of duplication, which would require the account of personal identity to become comparative.

If we are to insist upon some form of bodily identity as a necessary condition of personal survival, then the very most we should require is identity of brain. For consider what your attitude would be to the idea of a brain-transplant. In the same way that doctors can now transplant a heart from one body to another, so they may one day be able to transplant a human brain. Then imagine that such a day has arrived. Imagine also that you have contracted some rapidly advancing terminal disease, which however leaves your brain undamaged. The doctors tell you that there has just arrived in the hospital a person whose brain has been destroyed in an accident, but whose body is otherwise in good working order. They propose that you should have your brain transplanted into that body. They guarantee that if the operation is a success (your brain is not rejected by the new body, etc.), then it will leave the resulting person with all of your quasi-memories, desires and intentions, as well as your general personality and ties of affection. You would surely have no real hesitation in accepting their proposal. For does it not hold out the prospect of surviving your otherwise imminent death? In which case you must think that your identity would carry over with your brain, rather than lapsing with the death of the rest of your body. (Note, by the way, that this example is sufficient to show that bodily *similarity* should not be included as a necessary condition of personal identity.)

In fact half a brain might do just as well, from the point of view of personal survival, as a whole brain. For as we have noted before, a great deal of the information stored in the human brain is duplicated on both sides of it. Moreover, there have been cases where people have survived, and recovered most of their mental functions and faculties, after the destruction of very nearly half of their brain. So imagine only a slight development of what has already occurred: that doctors discover a way of enabling an exact half of a brain to survive independently, and find a way of stimulating its activity so that the complete range of memories, faculties and personality can be preserved.

Now suppose, as in our previous example, that you have a

terminal disease; only this time one which has irreparably damaged half of your brain. As before, the doctors offer you a brain-transplant; only this time a half-brain-transplant. Why should you worry? Since the resulting person will have all of your quasi-memories, desires, etc., why should the fact that they will have only half of your present brain prevent you from surviving your otherwise imminent death? From a practical point of view, if we are to insist upon some degree of bodily identity as a necessary condition of personal survival, then the most we ought to require is half-brain-identity.

But now the possibility of duplication opens up once again. Suppose as before that you have a terminal illness which leaves your brain totally undamaged. But now the doctors are worried about the high chances of rejection by the new body. To combat this they suggest transplanting half of your brain into one body and half into another, hence (they claim) doubling your chances of survival. But then what if the unexpected happens, and both half-brains are accepted by their new bodies? There would then be two people who are not identical with one another, each of whom has an equal claim to be identical with a single original. So we should be forced to conclude that neither of them is yourself: a double success would have been a failure.

The upshot is, that if we give our account of personal identity in terms of half-brain-identity, then we shall be forced to make that account comparative: we shall have to say that x is identical with y if they are suitably psychologically connected and x has at least half of y's brain, but only so long as there exists no other person with an equal or better claim to be identical with y. And then the question whether x and y are identical will depend not just upon facts about them, but also upon facts about other individuals elsewhere in the universe. But here, as before, we should insist that identity is not in fact a comparative notion. This forces us to define personal identity in terms of whole-brain (or at least more than half-brain) identity.

Conclusion

What emerges from our discussion of brain-transplants, is yet another respect in which the concept of identity forces us to place tighter restrictions on the possibilities for personal survival than we should otherwise be inclined to do. Not only does the non-comparative nature of identity force us to accept some degree of bodily identity as a necessary condition of personal survival, whereas the kind of interest which we take in our survival would incline us to think that bodily identity is of no importance; but it also forces us to accept whole-brain identity as a necessary condition of personal survival, whereas from a practical point of view we should be just as happy with half a brain. It thus appears that the kind of interest which we take in the survival of ourselves and others, and the nature of the concept of personal identity, must to a certain extent be in tension with one another. I should be just as interested in the possibilities of radio-transportation and half-brain transplants as I am in my own ordinary survival, were it not that the concept of identity apparently forces me to think otherwise. In the next section we shall consider a radical response to this difficulty: that we should stop thinking of personal survival in terms of the concept of identity at all.

iv. Survival without Identity

In section 7.ii we argued for a conception of personal identity which would make reincarnation possible; but then in section 7.iii we raised a serious objection to that conception. Let us begin by reviewing our options.

Firstly, we can accept whole-brain identity as a necessary condition of personal survival; indeed this is forced on us if we are to work with a conception of personal identity which is non-comparative. But this option conflicts with all the arguments of section 7.ii, to the effect that bodily identity is of no particular importance to us. If we take this option, then we should have to say that we will often in fact be satisfied with something rather less than strict survival.

Secondly, we can give our account of personal identity solely in terms of psychological connectedness, as urged in section 7.ii. But if we do this, then we have to accept that questions of identity can be comparative. And in any case there might still be a conflict with the practical interest which we take in survival, since in cases of duplication we should have to say that the original person ceases to exist altogether. But would we in fact regard duplication as being just as bad as normal death? For example, in the case where you are offered a double half-brain transplant, would you really regard the unlikely possibility of both half-brains being accepted by their bodies as being just as bad as allowing the disease to take its course?

Thirdly, we can stop thinking of personal survival as involving identity. We can give our account of the notion of survival purely in terms of psychological connectedness, which fits well with the arguments of 7.ii. But if we no longer have to try and guarantee the uniqueness of identity, we can avoid making that account a majoritarian one. We might simply say this: a person x is a survivor of a person y if and only if they are sufficiently strongly psychologically connected. We thus allow that in cases of duplication the original person survives as two distinct persons (without of course being identical with either of them).

In this section I shall argue that we ought to take the third option. I shall begin by arguing that this is the option which is most in line with the kind of interest which we take in personal survival, whether our own or other people's.

(A) Practical Considerations

How ought we to regard cases of duplication from a third-person perspective? In a case of radio-transportation, for example, how should your relatives respond to the knowledge that there now exist two exact replicas of you? It is impossible to believe that they should be stricken with grief. Yet on any conception of survival as involving identity, you yourself ceased to exist when your original body back on Earth was destroyed. Of course the existence of two replicas would be disturbing and disorientating. (Imagine meeting both of them together for the first time!) But once they get used to the idea, your relatives should surely be equally interested in and concerned about both of them.

An analogy may help here. Suppose that you have spent a good deal of time with someone over a period of months, and have grown to care for them very much. But then you discover that you have in fact been in the company, on alternative occasions, of a pair of identical twins who are physically and psychologically extremely similar. Although the discovery would be devastating, you ought surely to realise, as you adjust to the idea, that you in fact care for them both. The similarity with the example of duplication should be clear: in this case you believed that you loved one person where in fact there were two; and in the other, your relatives did in the past love one person, where now there are two.

From the point of view of blame and punishment as well, we

should surely respond as though both replicas were survivors of the original. For suppose that the person back on Earth turns out to have been a vicious criminal. Are we really going to allow the two replicas to wander around free, on the grounds that the person who committed the crimes no longer exists? Surely not: for both will have the same desires, beliefs and vicious qualities as the original. Indeed both will be chuckling gleefully at the thought that the error made by the machine-operator has given them a lucky escape from prosecution. Here we would obviously be mad to let considerations of identity stand in the way of an early arrest. (And if this involves changing our conception of 'just punishment', then so be it.)

From the point of view of the replicas themselves after the fact, they too would surely regard themselves as survivors of the original. Obviously they will not feel as though they have just come into existence. On the contrary, their lives will seem to them to be continuous with that of the original: each will quasi-remember many events from life on Earth, and will quasi-remember getting into the radio-transportation machine; moreover each will find themselves with the same familiar desires, interests and affective ties as the original.

Of course their situation would bring its own problems with it. For each would presumably try to claim the same job as the original, and would try to move in with the same spouse. So some sort of compromise would have to be worked out, which might cause unhappiness. Indeed the mere existence of someone who is (initially at least) exactly similar to yourself, may be difficult to adjust to psychologically. But none of this is likely to change their view of themselves as having once lived on Earth, and as having survived the process of radio-transportation.

But how ought you to regard the prospect of duplication prior to the fact? If you know that the radio-transportation machine is faulty, so that there is no way to visit your relatives on the planet without a duplicate being created on the other; or if you are offered a double half-brain transplant and are contemplating the possibility of both half-brains being accepted by their new bodies; then what should you think? Would the outcome be one in which you have ceased to exist, to be feared as you fear death? Or would it be almost as good as normal survival? It will help here if we once again consider separately the situation as it should be regarded from the point of view of your impersonal and self-regarding desires.

From the point of view of most impersonal desires the situation is straightforward: two heads are better than one. For example, the dedicated political activist should regard the prospect of there being two persons who possess their political skills and desire for revolution, as being actually better than normal survival. Similarly with the person whose major desire is to see Shakespeare properly translated into Japanese: they should realise that there would be more chance of the task being carried out successfully if there were two persons who shared their desire, their linguistic skills and literary sensibility, who could divide the labour between them.

In the case of an impersonal desire for the welfare of a loved one the situation is marginally more complicated. In some respects the existence of two lovers would be an advantage: for example, think how much more successfully they could nurse the loved one through a serious illness. But it may also be a source of distress to the loved one, if there were to exist two different (but exactly similar) lovers, between whom they would have to divide attention. So in this respect duplication may be less welcome than ordinary survival. But it would still be a great deal better than ordinary death. For if the worst came to the worst, the two duplicates could always draw lots for one of them to absent themselves from the scene, leaving the other to care for the loved one alone.

From the point of view of our self-referring desires the issue is difficult. For such desires will normally be expressed using the personal pronoun 'I', which seems to require identity and hence uniqueness. If I want a holiday in Sri Lanka, then I want that I myself should have a holiday in Sri Lanka; and this seems to be the same as wanting that the future person who will be identical with myself should holiday in Sri Lanka. However, I doubt whether uniqueness is really an essential component of my desire. When I think of what I should really want from such a holiday, I imagine — from the inside — lying under coconut palms on white beaches and eating crab-curry in the local restaurants; all against a background of desires and interests similar to my own. At no point do I think 'And there should be no other person who is similarly psychologically connected with myself, who is also enjoying such experiences.' So why should I regard my desire as having been frustrated if duplication were somehow to occur along the way (as I should have to do, if self-identity were an essential ingredient in it)? In fact when I spell out to myself what I should really want from a holiday in Sri Lanka, I find that I am indifferent to the thought of duplication occurring in the interim.

I conclude, that from the point of view of the various kinds of practical interest which we take in survival, whether of ourselves or others, we should regard duplication as being nearly as good as normal survival. Now against this must be set the fact that we do undoubtedly think of survival in terms of identity. It is deeply embedded in our habits of thought and speech, that one person can only be a survivor of another if they are uniquely related (i.e. identical). Thus we say 'If Mary has survived then she is lucky', and take this to imply 'If Mary has survived then the living person who is identical with Mary is lucky.' But if, as we have seen, identity itself does not matter, then what we ought to do is stop thinking and speaking in this way. We should stop thinking of survival in terms of identity, and use instead a notion of survival which will allow one person to survive as two.

(B) Conceptual Pragmatism

I claim that we are mistaken in thinking of our survival as requiring identity. But this is not a mistake of fact. Rather we have got into the way of using the wrong concept. It is easy to understand how this should have happened. For since cases of duplication have never in fact occurred, we have never had occasion to distinguish between personal survival over time and personal identity over time. They have always gone along together in the past, and in some respects it is simpler to talk in terms of identity. But as we approach the time when duplication may become technically feasible, the situation will change. And even now, reflecting on imagined cases of duplication, we can see that we are strictly employing the wrong concept of personal survival; although this hardly matters for everyday purposes.

The general thesis underlying my position here, I call 'Conceptual Pragmatism'. It consists of two parts: (a) there are always more concepts available to us in a given area of discourse than we need; and (b) our selection of concepts from the range of alternatives should be governed by the purposes for which we wish to employ them.

A concept is a mode of classifying things: our different concepts represent different ways of dividing up the world. So thesis (a) tells us that there are always more ways of classifying things than we actually use, or need to use. This is obviously true. For example, think of the many different ways in which we might divide up the colour-spectrum, and hence the many different ways in which we might classify things in terms of their colours. Of course some of these modes of classification will come very much more naturally to us than others, given the causal structures underlying human perception. But it remains true that there are many alternatives available. For instance, we might classify together the shades of colour between mid-blue and mid-green (perhaps called 'bleen'), if it suited our purposes to do so. (Suppose we lived in an area where the only edible plants had leaves whose colours fell within that range.)

There is no such thing as the *right* way to divide up the colour-spectrum, unless this means 'the way which is most in accord with the purposes for which we classify things in terms of their colours'. For that spectrum certainly does not come to us already divided up, in such a way that we are constrained in our choice of concepts to respect the divisions which already exist within it. The same goes for items of furniture and foodstuffs: since there is no such thing as the correct set of concepts to use in classifying these things, we have to make a choice.

Wherever there are alternatives available, the only sense in which a choice can be correct or incorrect is that it can accord or fail to accord withour purposes. Now sometimes, but not always, our purposes will be scientific. And in that case there will be a sense in which we shall want our modes of classification to correspond to the natural divisions in reality. That is to say: to the divisions which would figure in the various causal laws of a completed science. But more often our purposes will be social, as when we choose concepts for classifying colours, foodstuffs and items of furniture. Here our modes of classification may cut right across those which a scientist would wish to employ. So as thesis (b) above claims: the concepts which we are actually to employ, from the wider range of possibilities, should be determined in accordance with our purposes.

(Note that some use has already been made of conceptual pragmatist arguments at various points in this book, without them having been named as such. For example, in section 4.iv we argued against the thesis that we might be radically in error about our own states of mind, by claiming that our classifications of mental phenomena are not intended as primitive science, but for quite other (social) purposes. The point can now be put like this: given that the main purposes subserved by our modes of classifying conscious states have to do with various different forms of social interaction, then we ought not, in general, to allow them to be replaced by others through the advancement of science. We need to defend our concepts of the mind against the threat of 'scientific imperialism'.)

Once we realise that there will always exist alternatives to the modes of classification which we presently employ; and once we realise that our selection from the range of alternatives should be governed by our purposes; then the possibility opens up that we may find ourselves, upon reflection, to have been employing the wrong concepts. For in fact we will often just have fallen into a way of classifying things, without anyone ever having consciously selected that concept in the light of our purposes. A practice will somehow have grown up, and selections may have been made for all sorts of irrelevant historical reasons. This is especially likely to have happened wherever the alternative concepts differ only in the judgements which they would deliver in various imaginable, but non-actual, circumstances.

This is exactly the situation in which we find ourselves with respect to the concepts of personal survival and personal existence-over-time. The concepts which as a matter of fact we presently employ, both of them imply identity: 'x is a survivor of y' implies 'x is identical with y', and 'x continues to exist' implies 'There is still (at some later time) a person who is identical with x'. But the concepts which would best subserve the sorts of interest which we take in the survival of ourselves and others, do not imply identity. We ought therefore to change our modes of classification. We ought to understand the term 'survive' in such a way that two distinct persons can both be survivors of a single original. And we ought to allow that a person continues to exist, at any particular time, just so long as there exists at that time some survivor of them (perhaps more than one). Since our interest in persons is certainly not a scientific one, it is irrelevant whether or not the concept of a person, so construed, would correspond to any natural division within reality (that is to say: to any division which would be recognised by a completed science).

Conclusion

The argument of this section may be summarised as follows:

(1) There are at least three alternative concepts available to us, each of which has some claim to be our concept of personal

survival; two of them implying identity and one not.

(2) Our selection of any given concept from a range of alternatives should depend upon the purposes for which we wish to employ that concept.

(3) It is the concept which does *not* imply identity which is best in line with the various forms of practical interest which we take in personal survival.

(C) So we ought to think in terms which will allow a person to survive as two distinct people; and the fact that we presently employ a concept of survival which implies identity, is an error.

This argument is valid. The truth of premiss (1) emerged from our discussion of reincarnation, and the difficulties with it, in sections 7.ii and 7.iii. Premiss (2) is sufficiently established by the argument given above for the truth of conceptual pragmatism. Premiss (3) was established by the arguments given earlier in this section, where we considered how examples of duplication would stand in relation to the sorts of practical interest which we take in survival. So the argument as a whole may reasonably be taken as a proof.

I conclude that there is a sense in which reincarnation is possible. For the best conception of personal survival is one which is defined purely in terms of psychological connectedness. This would allow one physical human being to be a personal survivor of another, provided that they are sufficiently strongly psychologically connected. (Just what should count as 'sufficient' here, will form part of the topic of the next section.) Since this preferred conception does not imply that a survivor of a person must also be identical with them, the possibility of duplication does not constitute a genuine objection to the idea of reincarnation (so understood).

Questions and Readings

Try discussing/writing about/thinking about some of the following questions:

(1) Can the human body survive across periods of non-existence?

(2) Suppose you knew your brain was about to be 'wiped clean' of all traces of memory and personality: should you have hopes or fears for what will happen to your body afterwards?

(3) What kinds of reasons do you have for wanting to survive? Are

they in any way tied to a particular body?
(4) Could you survive as each of two different people?
(5) Might we be employing the wrong concept of personal survival? What would the right concept be?

You may like to consult some of the following readings (capitalised names refer to collections of papers, listed in the Bibliography):

Daniel Dennett, 'Where am I?', in DENNETT. Reprinted in HOFTSTADTER.
David Lewis, 'Survival and Identity', in RORTY. Reprinted in LEWIS.
Thomas Nagel, 'Death', *Nous*, IV (1970). Reprinted in NAGEL.
Robert Nozick, *Philosophical Explanations* (Oxford: Clarendon Press, 1981), Ch. 1, part 1.
Derek Parfit, 'Personal Identity', *Philosophical Review*, 80 (1971). Reprinted in PERRY and GLOVER.
———, *Reasons and Persons* (Oxford: Clarendon Press, 1984), Part 3.
Terence Penelhum, *Survival and Disembodied Existence* (London: Routledge & Kegan Paul, 1970), Chs. 7, 8 and 9.
John Perry, 'The Importance of Being Identical', in RORTY.
Sidney Shoemaker, 'A Materialist's Account', in S. Shoemaker and R. Swinburne, *Personal Identity* (Oxford: Blackwell, 1984).
David Wiggins, *Sameness and Substance* (Oxford: Blackwell, 1980), Ch. 6.
Bernard Williams, 'Personal Identity and Individuation', *Proceedings of the Aristotelian Society*, LVII (1956–7). Reprinted in GUSTAFSON and WILLIAMS.
———, 'The Self and the Future', *Philosophical Review*, 79 (1970). Reprinted in PERRY, GLOVER and WILLIAMS.

8 BOUNDARIES OF PERSONS

i. Limits of the Individual

In the last chapter we argued that the best account of personal survival (strictly: the concept of personal survival in terms of which we ought to think) involves only the notion of psychological connectedness, containing no reference to bodily identity. We shall begin this section by exploring this idea in greater detail. The discussion will fall into three parts, the first two dealing with aspects of the idea of survival over time, and the third returning to the question of personal identification at a time.

(A) Does Each Person Survive Unto Death?

We have argued for the use of a concept of personal survival, which would leave room for the possibility that we might, through reincarnation, survive normal bodily death. This is a welcome result, since it means we can hope that either God or the scientists might bring it about that death will not be the end of our existence. But we come now to a somewhat less welcome consequence. Namely: that some of us might not even survive to reach bodily death.

The simplest sort of example would be this. Imagine that military scientists have developed a technique of radical brain washing — to be called 'brain wiping' — which not only destroys all quasi-memories, but also all developed desires, interests and traces of individual personality. Then a person after brain wiping will not, on our account, be a survivor of the earlier person. For the two of them will not be directly psychologically connected, nor will they be linked by a series of overlapping connections. On the contrary, the brain wiping represents a clean break. (Note, however, that a person *would* normally survive amnesia; for this only involves the loss of personal memory, leaving many other psychological connections intact.) But it is no real objection to our account that a person would therefore not survive brain wiping. For this is also a consequence of the thesis argued for in section 7.i, that bodily identity is not sufficient for personal survival. For the only connection between the persons before and after brain wiping would be the body.

220

The issues raised by cases of severe senility are more interesting. For an extremely senile individual may be able to recall nothing of their earlier life, and share none of their earlier desires and interests. There may thus exist no direct psychological connections between Mary in middle age and Mary as a senile old lady. The two will, however, be linked together by a series of overlapping connections. For the senile Mary will be able to recall events from moment to moment and day to day; and these will stretch back in a chain of connections which will eventually reach Mary in middle age. Then has Mary survived into senility or not? (Similar questions arise in connection with babies. For I can recall nothing of my earliest years; nor do I share any desires or interests with that individual. Yet we are presumably linked together by a chain of overlapping psychological connections.)

What is at issue here is this: ought we to choose to think in terms of a concept of survival involving only direct psychological connectedness? Thus:

Person x at t(1) survives as person y at t(2) if and only if x and y are sufficiently strongly psychologically connected.

Or should we choose to think in terms of a concept which is modelled more closely on the account of personal identity sketched in section 3.ii, allowing a person to survive across a series of overlapping psychological connections? Thus:

Person x at t(1) survives as person y at t(2) if and only if either (i) x and y are sufficiently strongly psychologically connected, or (ii) y is, by repeated applications of clause (i), a survivor of someone who is, again by clause (i), a survivor of x.

We need to decide which of these two concepts would best subserve the kind of interest which we take in survival. (Note that on this question will depend the adequacy of our reply to the first difficulty raised in section 7.iii, concerning the person who briefly remains alive after an exact replica of them has been created on another planet.)

From a third-person perspective there is no reason to regard one person as a survivor of another, if there exist only indirect psychological connections between them. Thus suppose that you have been friends with a person x at time t(1), but then do not see them again until the much later time, t(3). During the interim x has altered out of all recognition, changing first into person y at t(2), and then into z at t(3). y still retains many psychological connections with x, as z does with y; but z has lost all trace of psychological connectedness with x. Now when you meet z, what motive have you for regarding them as being (a survivor of) your friend at t(1)? I suggest none. For z will recall nothing of your previous friendship, and will have lost all of the interests and personal qualities which formed the basis of your friendship with x. Moreover, supposing x to have committed some evil deed, it would seem pointless to blame or punish z. For they will remember nothing of it, and will have lost all the desires and vices which led x to commit that act.

From a first-person perspective after the fact, why should z on looking back regard the things done by x as forming part of their own life? For they will in fact remember nothing of them, having to be told about those events by other people. Now of course this information will hold a certain fascination, since it may furnish explanations of features of z's own character. (As when I find an explanation of my nervous twitch in the fact that I was battered as a baby.) But this interest seems all-of-a-piece with the kind of interest which we take in the lives of our parents and ancestors: we know that things which happened to them may have had indirect effects upon ourselves.

From a first-person perspective before the fact there seems little reason to regard someone as a survivor of oneself, with whom one is only indirectly psychologically connected. This is certainly true from the point of view of our impersonal desires. For those desires themselves, and the personal qualities which might have made fulfilment of them more likely, will all have been lost in that future person. And so far as my self-referring desires go, why should I take an interest in someone merely because someone in whom I do take an interest takes an interest in them? Thus x will take a personal interest in the existence of y, and y will take a similar interest in z; but why should that provide x with any reason to think of z as being a survivor of themself? In fact when I look forward to the senile individual whom I (my body) will one day become, I find it impossible to take any personal interest in them. (If x desires that all of y's desires should be satisfied, and one of those desires is the desire that all of z's desires should be satisfied, then x will, after all, have to take an interest in z. But which of us desires that literally all of our future desires should be satisfied? — for we know that many of them may be for things we should now abhor.)

I conclude that we should think of our existence as persons in terms of a concept of survival which requires some degree of direct psychological connectedness. Then the existence of many of us, as persons, will be rather briefer than our existence as human beings; and the life of a single human being may constitute the lives of a number of different persons.

(B) Is Survival a Matter of Degree?

Psychological connectedness is of course a matter of degree. In the case of a very young child it will gradually increase in extent from day to day and month to month; and in the case of the very old it will gradually fade away. Moreover, people's personalities — interests, desires and memories — will often alter a great deal during the course of a lifetime, sometimes quite radically. We therefore face a choice. We can either select a concept which allows that survival too is a matter of degree; saying that x will survive as y *to the extent that* they are psychologically connected. Or we can insist that survival (like identity) should be an all-or-nothing matter; in which case we shall need to choose the precise degree of psychological connectedness necessary for survival. We shall then say that x will survive as y if and only if they are psychologically connected to such-and-such an extent.

There is in fact no reason to choose a concept which would make survival an all-or-nothing matter. For the interest which we take in survival is not all-or-nothing. Rather, our desires for the future are generally multifarious, as is the nature of our attachment to other people. So when I imagine a whole series of progressively more extensive brain wipings, causing greater and greater loss of psychological connectedness, I am conscious of a *gradual* loss of interest in the welfare of that future person, and (in my own case) of steadily increasing fear at the prospect of my own (partial) loss of existence. There certainly does not come any particular point at which, having been happy to regard the person as surviving till then, I suddenly think 'But that would be the end of them'.

When it comes to choosing a measure of the precise extent of personal survival, to be constructed somehow out of the extent of psychological connectedness, we might be tempted to go for fragmentation into a number of different concepts. For here the different kinds of interest which we take in survival can pull in different directions. From the point of view of the interest which a person will take in their own survival, we should perhaps choose a concept which relies upon the subject's own evaluations. We most of us have a rough hierarchy of desires and interests. Some of our projects, memories and ties of affection are more important to us than others, and should accordingly be given greater weight in determining the degree of survival. But some of them we may wish we did not have all, as when I want to be rid of my desire for wealth, and these should accordingly be given no weight. From the point of view of blame and responsibility on the other hand, the subject's own evaluations are of little relevance. What matters is the extent of the changes which may have taken place in their moral character: the virtues and vices which they may have lost or acquired, and the changes in those of their desires which have moral significance. It is these things which should accordingly be given greater weight in determining the degree to which the person has survived.

But in fact we do not have to let our concept of the degree of survival fragment in this way. We can allow for the different points of view from which we may wish to employ the concept, by writing a reference to them into the concept itself. Thus: x's degree of survival as y is given by the extent to which they have the sorts of psychological connections which are important for the purposes in hand. Then if the purposes in hand are those of x themself, we may judge one thing; but if the purposes in hand are those of determining an appropriate punishment, we may judge another.

(There would be nothing unique in our employment of a concept of this sort. Concepts which can vary in application according to our purposes are very handy things to have, and it is arguable that we already possess quite a few of them. For instance, if a tank-commander asks for a flat field on which to practise manoeuvres, you may point to one and say truthfully 'That one is flat'; but if the local bowls club come asking for a flat field, you may point to the very same one and truthfully say 'That one is not flat'. The word 'flat' seems to mean something like 'is close enough to being absolutely flat for the purposes in hand'.)

Once we start thinking of our survival as persons as a matter of degree, then we shall not only find application for the idea in imaginary examples, but also in real life. We shall say that the person I am now is only a partial survivor of the person I was as an adolescent; and that the person I shall be at retirement will only be a partial survivor of the person I am now. This is not an unnatural way of thinking of our lives. (There are many examples in literature where people's lives are described in precisely these terms.) And as a matter of fact I felt entirely distanced from the person I was as an adolescent, even before starting to think systematically about these issues. I should have said 'Looking back, it feels like the life of a stranger.' Indeed we can now see that those Christians who talk about 'being born again' may be speaking more literally than they know. For given that there is a considerable change of beliefs and values at the point of conversion, the person after that time will very likely be only a partial survivor of the earlier. They will be partially (and literally) a new person.

(C) Can One Human Being be Two People?

Up till now we have been concerned with the survival of persons over time. We have been taking it for granted since the arguments of Chapter 3 that the criterion of identification for persons at a time is identity of body (or perhaps brain). We have been assuming that the subject of thoughts and experiences at any given time is the living human body (or brain). But we can now raise the question whether the boundaries of the individual should not perhaps be drawn rather more narrowly than this. For might it not be possible for one human body (or brain) to support two distinct persons?

One range of cases where we might be tempted to say this sort of thing is provided by examples of brain bisection. There have been clinical experiments in which the network of nerves linking the two hemispheres of the human brain were cut. (For a while this was used in the treatment of epilepsy.) The two hemispheres then continued to function normally, but without the direct causal interaction and exchange of information which would usually take place between them.

Now the human nervous system is structured in such a way that information which is received in the left-half of a person's visual field is transmitted direct to the right hemisphere, while information received in the right-half of the visual field is transmitted to the left hemisphere. In a normal subject this information would then be integrated via the network of connections joining the two hemispheres. But when those nerves have been cut, the following kind of phenomenon can occur. When a picture of a book is flashed on a screen so as to be visible only within the subject's left visual field, and they are then asked to pick out from an array of objects what they have been shown, they will *say* that they have seen nothing (speech normally being controlled from the left hemisphere), while at the same time they pick up a book with their left hand (this hand normally being controlled by the right hemisphere). So we might wonder whether there are really two distinct persons here, one of whom sees the picture of a book and decides to pick up what they have seen, and the other of whom sees nothing and is sincere in reporting that they have seen nothing.

There have been many experimental findings of this general sort. But their proper interpretation is a complicated and difficult issue. (For example, one reason for insisting that the split-brain should in fact be regarded as a single person, is that most of the time they behave perfectly normally. Social interaction with them is exactly like interaction with any normal person. It requires carefully controlled experiments to elicit the contradictory responses.) For this reason I do not here propose to pursue the factual question, of whether split-brain humans are indeed two distinct persons.

However, we can at least see that there is no objection in principle to the idea of one human being constituting two distinct persons at a given time. We merely have to think of each half-brain supporting a separate centre of consciousness, each of which has its own beliefs, desires and interests. Of course the two half-brains would have to co-operate closely (communicating with one another in the ways that any other persons do, by speaking and writing) in deciding what physical movements to perform at any given moment. (Suppose that one half-brain controlled the arms and one the legs.) But this is no objection to regarding them as two separate persons. For Siamese twins, too, are in precisely this position.

Quite a different range of possible cases is provided by examples of split personality. Here a single human being will alternate from one personality to another and back again. Personality x will have one set of desires and interests, and may be unable to recall events from the times when personality y was in control. Whereas personality y will have quite a different set of desires and interests, and may be unable to recall events from the times when x was in control. Then in cases where the two personalities have absolutely no psychological connections with one another, we must (on the general principles argued for in Chapter 7) regard them as two distinct persons.

Now it does not immediately follow from this that one human being can constitute two distinct persons at one time. For since the two personalities never make their appearance together, but always successively, there remains the possibility that person x ceases to exist while person y is in control and vice versa. That is: we could treat the two persons as having only intermittent existence.

However, if we do take the more natural course — saying that the two persons continue to exist together, but merely take it in turns to be conscious — then we are forced to change our account of the criterion of identification for persons at a time. For if person x were identified with a particular brain, and person y were also identified with that brain, then it would follow (by the transitivity and symmetry of identity) that person x is identical with person y. We shall have to say, on the contrary, that a person is to be identified with a particular functional organisation of cells within the brain. Person x will have to be identified with the particular network of cellular connections which explains their behaviour, and person y will have to be identified with the (different) network underlying their behaviour. These networks need not actually be embodied in distinct regions of the brain, but may both be dispersed in an overlapping way throughout it.

Conclusion

Persons only survive so long as there exists direct psychological connectedness, and their survival is a matter of degree. Moreover, persons themselves (the subjects of thoughts and experiences, identified at particular times) may not actually be identical with the human brain, but rather with some narrower functional organisation within it. So in both senses — both 'over time' and 'at a time' — it is possible for a single human being to embody a number of distinct persons.

ii. Limits of the Class: Humans that are not Persons

We turn now to the question which will concern us throughout the remainder of this chapter: what sorts of physical things are, or could be, persons? In this section we shall consider the question whether all living humans are persons. Or are there perhaps some — such as the very young or the very senile — who are not? Then in section iii we shall raise the question whether anything other than a human being — such as a non-human animal — might be a person. Finally in section iv we shall consider whether there could be any artificial persons. For example, could a computer be a person?

(A) General Points

Most philosophers would see the task before us as one of conceptual *analysis*. They would say that by reflecting upon our understanding of the term 'person' we are to analyse and give an account
of the corresponding concept. However, in section 7.iv we saw that
there is some reason to doubt the value of this approach. For it may
be that the concept which we do in fact employ is not the concept
which we *ought* to employ, given the nature of the interest which
we take in the person/non-person classification. Our most basic
task is therefore not one of conceptual analysis, but of pragmatically-based conceptual *selection*.

I see the matter as follows. Those of us debating these issues
together are like the members of a long-established club or society,
in so far as we all belong to the class of persons. And the issue
before us is: what other beings should be admitted to the club?
Now one sort of answer would involve looking at the rules for
membership which we actually employ. We might ask: what,
according to the existing rules of the club, must someone do or be
in order to become a member? (This is the analogue of conceptual
analysis, in that we reflect upon the criteria for membership of the
class of persons — namely the concept 'person' — which we
already employ.) But then of course the existing rules may not be
very good ones. They may have evolved through the *ad hoc*
decisions of many generations of club members, in such a way that
they no longer reflect the essential aims and purposes of the club.
So a more fundamental enquiry would be to consider what we take
to be important about the club, and what we take its essential
activities to be, in order that we may settle upon appropriate
criteria for membership. This is the analogue of conceptual pragmatism. We are to think hard about what we take to be the fundamentally important features of ourselves, in order that we may
select a concept of personhood which is appropriate to that
interest.

It is important to see that our task does not fall directly within
the area of moral philosophy. The question whether or not something should be counted as a person is not the same as the question
whether it has moral rights or duties, or whether it is a moral agent,
subject to moral assessment. For the interest which we take in the
person/non-person classification is not, fundamentally, a moral
one. When we ask ourselves 'Since we are all persons, what is it that
we most importantly have in common with one another?' we do not

immediately think of such things as the right to life. Rather we think of common humanity, or rationality, or the distinctive human emotions and affections.

The concept of personhood may be *foundational* to morality without being itself a moral concept. It certainly seems likely that it will turn out to be of moral significance. (For example, amongst those who think in terms of rights, it is generally accepted that all persons have rights. However, I very much doubt, myself, whether *only* persons have rights.) But what we should do first is clarify exactly what we value (non-morally) about ourselves, before going on to raise the question of rights and duties. (I assume that non-moral values are logically prior to moral ones: if we did not already care about other things, then there could be no such thing as morality.) It is from this perspective that the concept of person-hood should be selected.

(B) Does Personhood Require Consciousness?

Let us begin by enquiring whether an irreversibly unconscious human should be counted as a person (as 'one of us'). We might try approaching this question by appealing to the sorts of considera-tions which we used in our treatment of personal survival. Thus we might ask whether, if your doctor offers you a choice between imminent death and imminent lapse into irreversible coma, you would feel there to be anything to choose between the two. Your answer to this would obviously be negative: you might just as well be dead as irreversibly unconscious. (Of course you might opt for the coma in the hope that a cure will one day be found. But this is to hope that the coma is reversible.) We might then be tempted to take this as showing that consciousness is a necessary condition of personhood.

Unfortunately this sort of approach is no longer serviceable. For clearly the comatose individual will be to no degree psychologically connected with yourself. Since they are unconscious they can possess no conscious desires, interests or memories to link them with yourself. Then by the account offered in section 7.iv, they are not a survivor of yourself. In which case the explanation of your indifference between coma and death may be your perception that in either case you will not survive. And it is compatible with this that the comatose individual should be a person, only a different person from yourself.

One consideration which does suggest that some degree of

consciousness should be set as a necessary condition of person-hood, is as follows. It is hardly credible that the kind of interest which we take in our own survival as individual persons, should diverge radically from the kind of interest which we take in membership of the class of persons. Then since what matters to our own existence as individuals is some degree of connectedness in our own conscious desires, interests and memories, we should expect that the most important aspect of membership of the class would be the capacity to possess such states. And of course only a being which is capable of consciousness (which the irreversibly comatose individual no longer is) can have such a capacity.

Another consideration is this. Many of us think it valuable and important that there should be such things as persons, quite apart from our attachments to particular persons. For instance, many people are horrified at the thought of a nuclear war extinguishing all human life. And the object of their horror is not simply the number of individual deaths which would be involved (though this is horrible enough), but also the idea that from that point onwards there would be no more persons. Now set against this the following imaginary example. The Martians have conquered Earth, and have some reason for wishing to render us all unconscious. But they declare that they are not murderers: they plan to inject each one of us with a substance which will render us permanently unconscious. They will then keep us alive by intravenous feeding, and will breed new humans in test-tubes to replace those of us who die of natural causes; but these will never be allowed to attain consciousness. Now is there anything to choose between the two prospects? Is there anything to choose between the extinction of the human race, and the continued, but unconscious, existence of that race? It seems to me obvious that there is not. (Again we might opt for unconscious existence on the grounds that the Martians may one day change their minds. But this is to hope for some third alternative.)

(C) Does Personhood Require Self-consciousness?

We should insist upon some degree of consciousness as a necessary condition of personhood. But then of course many creatures besides humans are conscious. We know that domestic cats, for example, possess mental states which at least occupy similar causal roles to those possessed by humans. I know that my cat 'enjoys' being stroked, 'feels pain' if you pull out his whiskers, and often 'wants' to be fed while 'believing' that food is being placed in his dish, and so on. But I assume that he is not self-consciously aware of these states: I assume that his mental states do not normally involve self-conscious awareness of their own existence. Rather, they are analogous to those mental states which we have been speaking of since section 1.ii as *un*conscious. (If you are inclined to disagree about this, then settle upon some lower form of life for yourself, both here and in the examples which follow. The issue will be discussed in its own right in section 8.iii.) So should we allow that simple ('animal') consciousness is not only necessary, but also sufficient for personhood? Or should we insist upon some more stringent requirement?

One argument in support of a more stringent condition, is again the thought that our interest in membership of the class of persons is unlikely to deviate radically from our interest in the survival of individual persons. Then since our interest in survival stems largely from our desires and projects for the future, it is plausible that our interest in the limits of personhood should concern those creatures which have the capacity to make plans and formulate intentions. In which case (I assume) most species of animal should not be counted as persons. Nor should babies, nor the extremely senile.

Other arguments for the same conclusion are again based upon our disinterested desire that there should continue to be persons. For example, suppose that there were a choice between the use of two different kinds of weapon. Weapon X would wipe out the whole human race, somehow leaving all other species of animal untouched. Weapon Y would reduce all human beings permanently to the mental level of a domestic cat: so that they eat when hungry and sleep when tired, but have no long-term plans, and no conception of themselves as having a past and a future. I think we should feel that the use of either weapon would be almost equally disastrous. (Of course weapon Y would leave one more species of animal in existence than weapon X, and many might think this important. But it is implausible that this sense of importance should derive from a belief that all conscious animals are persons, coupled with a desire that persons should continue to exist. For I think we would certainly regard the extinction of the human race as a much greater catastrophe than the extinction of a species of antelope.) In which case our desire that there should continue to be persons cannot be a desire for the continued existence of humans with mere consciousness.

Another example pulling in the same direction is as follows. Suppose that you have been left in guardianship of a very young child which unfortunately has a painful handicap, of a sort which must inevitably lead to a life of hardship and suffering. The only other alternative is a brain-operation to remove the handicap, which would inevitably leave the child with the mental capacity of a domestic cat. Suppose also, that as guardian you administer a considerable estate, so that if the child undergoes the operation you can guarantee that all its future needs will be met: it will lead a simple happy existence. Now it is obvious that there is no real choice here: it is unthinkable that you should do anything other than allow the child to develop into a normally intelligent, if unhappy, adult. This too suggests that what we value in persons is much more than mere consciousness. (To parody a remark by a famous philosopher: it is better to be a person in pain than a contented cat.)

It begins to seem as though by 'person' we should mean 'rational self-consious agent'. Persons are rational agents, in that they have plans and projects, and try to reason out the best ways for themselves to live and act. (This does not mean that they always act rationally. Rational agents are the sort of agents who sometimes try to reason out what to do; it does not follow that they will always succeed in reasoning very well.) Persons are self-conscious, as opposed to merely conscious, in that they have awareness of many of their own mental states, and have a conception of their own past and future. (This does not mean 'self-conscious right now'. Since sleeping persons are obviously still persons, it means 'with the capacity for self-consciousness'. But note that this does not imply that babies are persons after all. For a baby is only *potentially* self-conscious, in that if it develops normally it will grow into a fully self-conscious adult. It is no more yet *capable* of self-consciousness than it is yet capable of riding a bicycle.)

(D) Does Personhood Require Distinctive Human Feelings?

Perhaps the concept of personhood which we ought to select, should include more than rational agency and self-consciousness. For our emotional lives are just as distinctive, and just as important to us, as is our capacity for planning and reasoning. Thus human love is quite unlike the simple affection of a friendly cat: it involves a conception of what is good for the person loved, which implies some knowledge of their desires and interests and their status as rational agents. And the complex emotions which a person might experience on listening to a Schubert sonata will have no analogue in the feelings of an antelope. Moreover, this side of our nature forms an important part of what we value in the existence of ourselves and others. Faced with a choice between two different forms of brain washing (whether for myself or for someone else), one of which would remove the capacity for rational agency while leaving intact the person's feelings and emotional attachments, and the other of which would remove the capacity for distinctive human emotions while leaving intact the person's projects and plans, I should be very uncertain which to choose.

So we should think of a person as a rational self-conscious agent with the capacity for distinctive human emotions and affective ties. This fits well with our use of the term 'human' as an adjective, as when we say that something is 'inhuman', or call someone 'a very human individual'. Note also that it follows that a psychopath — an 'inhuman monster' — is quite literally less of a person than the rest of us.

(E) Is Personhood a Matter of Degree?

Since all the different strands within the concept of personhood admit of degrees, and since someone might possess some of them without the others, we should allow the dividing line between those who are persons and those who are not to be a vague one; and the question whether or not something is a person should be a question of degree. At one extreme there will be those — such as a day-old baby — who are not persons at all; and at the other extreme there will be those — such as a normally intelligent adult — who very definitely are. But in between there will be a whole range of individuals who are *more or less* persons. For example, the normal development of a human child will see a gradual increase in the range and sophistication of its desires and interests, and it will gradually attain a conception of its own past and future. I can see no reason why we should wish to fix upon any particular point in this process as being the one at which the baby first becomes a person. Rather we should say that the gradual process of development corresponds to a gradual emergence into personhood.

Note, however, that it does not immediately follow that a day-old baby has no right to life, nor that a young child has less rights than the rest of us. And it certainly does not follow that they can be killed with impunity. Since 'person' obviously does not (and should not) mean 'creature with rights', it is at least going to require some powerful independent argument to show that only persons possess moral rights. And I very much doubt, myself, whether any such argument can be constructed.

Conclusion

A human being is a person to the extent that they are a rational self-conscious agent with the capacity for the distinctive human emotions and affective ties. So there are some humans who are not persons. Our next question is whether there are some persons who are not humans.

iii. Limits of the Class: Animal Persons

In the last section we argued that not all human beings should be counted as persons. Neither the very young nor the extremely senile are persons; and those less young and less senile are only persons to a certain degree. Now in this section we shall consider whether any non-human animals might be persons.

(A) Matters of Fact and of Principle

There is no difficulty in principle about animals being persons. For the concept of personhood is certainly not in fact tied to any particular species. Thus angels and gods (if any exist) have always been allowed to be persons. Moreover it is hard to see any reason why we ought to replace our concept of personhood by one which is closely tied to the human species. For our interest in the person/non-person classification is certainly not a scientific one: we are not intending to group together things in the way in which a completed science would classify them. So provided that an animal were to display the requisite personal characteristics, then it too should be counted as a person.

Imagine, then, that an ape were brought up in a human family and successfully mastered the English language. It goes to school, and later to university. It forms a number of close friendships with human beings, and is particularly fond of the music of Mozart. All of this is easily conceivable. And were it to happen, there is no question but that we should count the ape as a person (as 'one of us'). Since it would be a rational self-conscious agent with characteristic human feelings and emotions, there can be no sensible reason why we should let the mere difference of species and physical appearance stand in the way of classifying it as a person like ourselves.

The issue before us is therefore a factual one. Our question is whether any non-human animals do in fact possess the mental qualities necessary to count as persons to any degree. I do not, however, propose to consider the empirical evidence for this in any detail. The following story will illustrate why. There was once a horse who was widely believed to be able to count. If placed in front of a group of objects and asked how many there were, it would stamp its hoof the appropriate number of times. There was no question of cheating, since it would perform equally well in the absence of its trainer. But then it was discovered that if there was no one present who knew how to count, the horse would just go on stamping. What emerged was that it had been responding to subtle changes in the behaviour of the humans present (such as a slight intake of breath) which occurred when they knew that the horse had reached the correct number. If they were not themselves capable of knowing this, then the horse did not know when to stop.

The moral of the story is that the proper interpretation and evaluation of experiments involving animals is a complicated business. But it is not that I particularly wish to *reject* the evidence people claim to have found of rationality in apes and dolphins. The story above is merely meant to illustrate the difficulty of the issues, and hence to show why it would be inappropriate to enter into detailed discussion of them in a book of this sort; especially since I myself have no training in behavioural science. I shall confine myself to considering the general sorts of things which the experiments would have to show, if they were to show that some animals are persons. The main point of the discussion will be to investigate in greater detail exactly what is involved in the concept of a person.

(B) Rationality

Let us begin with the concept of rationality. It might be said that all sorts of creatures display rational behaviour. Are not squirrels rational in laying up nuts for the winter? And are not those birds intelligent, who weave intricate nests out of a variety of materials to provide a warm safe home for their young? But not every action which performs a useful function is intentional. What we need to know is whether the squirrel intends the nuts to provide food through the winter, and whether the bird intends to build a home for its young. Or do they merely perform these actions thoughtlessly, out of instinct or acquired habit? For of course there is much more to the characteristic rationality of persons than the mere performance of useful action. It will in addition generally involve conscious representations of the states to be attained, and conscious selections between alternative courses of action to arrive at those states. In a phrase: *persons are planners*.

It might be demanded what better evidence we could have of planning on the part of squirrels and birds, than behaviour which is conducive to fulfilling the creature's long-term needs. Indeed what better evidence have we, ultimately, of planning on the part of other human beings besides ourselves? Now in a way this is right: the best evidence of rationality is rational behaviour. But it is also wrong, in so far as it suggests that a single repeated strand of rational behaviour might be sufficient evidence of rationality in general. For consider: if the squirrel really did have the capacity to represent to itself the rigours of the coming winter, as well as the capacity to calculate that the best way of meeting the threat would be to store some nuts in a dry hole somewhere, then it would be unintelligible how it could lack such abilities in other areas of its life. If it really had the capacity to know, on the basis of past experience, that after every warm spell (summer) there comes a cold spell (winter) in which food is scarce, then it ought equally to be able to know that after every warm spell the hunters come out. And if it can really calculate how best to meet the threat of winter, then it ought also to be able to calculate how best to meet the threat of being shot. Yet we do not find squirrels rigging up camouflage or decoys, or hiding in the depths of the woods with the onset of autumn.

If a creature is capable of planning at all, then it must be capable of doing so in a wide range of circumstances. For the capacities involved in planning — to think about and form beliefs about future states of affairs, and to calculate different ways of achieving or avoiding those states — are quite general ones. So the very fact that a squirrel does not exhibit *very much* rational behaviour, is itself evidence that it is not (to any degree) a rational agent. We should instead explain its behaviour in terms of instinct or habit.

Examples of rational behaviour are apt to seem more impressive, as evidence of rationality, when they are isolated or unique. For then there is no alternative explanation in terms of instinct or habit available. For example: a chimp in the wild sees some bananas in a tree that the rest of the troop have overlooked; but there is a large male asleep at the foot of the tree. The chimp goes away and waits out of sight until the male moves off, then immediately returns and gets the bananas. Has it not here realised that it cannot get at the food without waking the male, and that if the male sees it going for the bananas it will take them for himself? And has it not calculated that it must wait out of sight till the male wakes, so as not to draw the attention of the rest of the troop? But of course a more neutral description is available, namely: the chimp saw the bananas, saw the male, went away, and later came back and got them. And unless examples of this sort of behaviour became sufficiently common, it is the more neutral description which ought to be preferred. For again, if the chimp really did have the capacity to invent a plan of this complexity, we should expect it to use that capacity on many occasions throughout its life.

It might be objected that animals could in fact have the capacity to plan, but choose not to exercise it very often. It might be said that planning is a peculiarly human obsession: animals — sensible creatures — prefer to take things as they come. Their approach to life may simply be rather more relaxed than our own. However, whatever the merits of being 'easy going' within affluent societies such as ours, it can hardly be very rational to take such an attitude where there is imminent danger of death or injury, as is the situation of most animals in the wild. For planning may make all the difference in avoiding these evils. So again, the very fact that animals obviously do not plan very much suggests that they are not really planners at all.

(C) Language

Human planning is generally conducted in language. We use language when we represent to ourselves our long-term goals, and in working out how best to attain them. So evidence of language-use on the part of animals might itself be evidence of the capacity to plan and reason, even if they show little sign of exercising those capacities in action.

Many animals make noises which serve functions. Birds sing to attract mates and warn off intruders. Dogs growl and bark in threat. But none of this is yet sufficient to qualify as language. For language involves the intentional use of signs to represent things, and to represent them in one way rather than another. (The context introduced by the phrase 'the sign "X" says that . . .' is an intentional one.) And there is no reason to say that the robin's song genuinely represents that it is in need of a mate, or that the dog's growl literally says that it will bite if you come closer. You might just as well say that the cat's protruding ribs represent that it is in need of food, or that its twitching tail says that it is about to pounce.

The best evidence of genuine language-use on the part of non-human animals comes from cases where chimps and gorillas have been taught a rudimentary form of sign-language. I shall not review this evidence here, but will merely make some general observations.

Firstly, in order for a sign to represent a thing, it is not enough that it should always be used in the presence of that thing, or in the presence of a current desire for that thing. For one can train a dog to salivate whenever a bell rings, but the salivation does not represent, or describe, the ringing. And one can train a rat to press a bar whenever it is hungry, but that act does not literally say 'Food'. So neither the capacity to employ the correct signs on being presented with the things which they name, nor the capacity to employ signs as behavioural expressions of desires for the things which they name, can by themselves constitute a capacity to use those signs to genuinely represent those things. Then in order for an ape to be capable of using the word 'fruit' as a meaningful name, it is not enough that it should often say 'Fruit' when there is fruit in the vicinity, nor that it should often say 'Fruit' when it wants some fruit. It must also possess some sign for negation ('No fruit'), or some signs for different spatial and temporal locations ('Fruit in cupboard' or 'Fruit yesterday').

Secondly, if language-use is to be sufficient to show the speaker to be a rational agent, then the language used must be fairly rich. It must, for example, contain some way of indicating future time. For rational planning must involve a representation of the future state of affairs to be attained. It must also contain some way of indicating generality and conditionality, since any attempt to work out how best to achieve some desired state of affairs must involve general and conditional truths (e.g., 'Sleeping males are always easily wakened' and 'If the male wakes, then he will take the fruit'). This in turn requires some way of representing what has been learned from past experience, which is to say a past-tense operator.

So the language of a rational agent must, it seems, contain tense and place operators, as well as signs for negation, generality and conditionality. I am doubtful whether any non-human animal currently uses a language possessing this degree of richness.

(D) Second-order Mental States

There is more to rational agency than mere calculation of means to ends. It is rare that we find ourselves in possession of a single desire, and merely have to work out the best way to satisfy it. More often we find ourselves having to weigh up a number of different conflicting ends in order to arrive at some sort of preference-ordering between them. In fact rational agents not only have beliefs and desires, they also have second-order beliefs and desires. (A second-order belief is a belief about another belief or desire, as when I believe that my belief in X is probably more reliable than my belief in Y. A second-order desire is a desire about a given belief or desire, as when I wish that I believed in God, or wish that I were more generous.)

This is one way in which rational agency connects up with self-consciousness. Any rational agent will characteristically have a complicated array of different desires for the future, many of which will be fairly long-term, and only some of which will currently be *felt* as desires. (I want to be able to eat tomorrow, though just at the moment the thought of tomorrow's food leaves me cold.) So they will need to decide questions of priority where desires conflict. And they will need to be able to estimate the varying importance of those different desires, in order to decide how best to distribute their efforts. This will require that they have self-conscious awareness of their own desires, representing them to themselves by means of second-order beliefs. It will also require second-order desires about the array of first-order desires, as when I desire that desire B should be satisfied at the expense of desire D, even though desire D currently feels stronger.

A rational agent will therefore be a self-conscious agent, and will possess second-order desires as well as second-order beliefs. But now it is hard to see what a languageless creature could do to convince us that it had second-order desires. What could it do to show that it not only has desire B and desire D, but also prefers that desire B should be satisfied rather than D? (Note that it is not enough that the creature tries to satisfy one before trying to satisfy the other. For this would only show that the one desire was currently stronger, not that there was a conscious preference for it as against the other.) So once again we are thrown back onto language-use as a crucial test of personhood. But note that the language in question must now be even richer than we argued above, since it must also include terms for referring to beliefs and desires.

I suppose it might be replied that a languageless creature could at least give evidence of having second-order beliefs about the beliefs of other creatures; in which case it would surely be safe to assume that it must also have self-conscious awareness of its own beliefs and desires. For example, my dog is in the habit of bringing me her lead whenever she wants to go for a walk. She also likes to lie in my armchair. Now suppose I am sitting in the armchair, the dog lying uncomfortably on the floor. She then brings me her lead, I get up, whereupon she immediately jumps into the newly-vacated chair. Does this not show that she believed that I would believe she wanted to go for a walk (a second-order belief), and would thus get out of the chair she wanted to occupy? Indeed does it not display downright cunning? But in fact a more neutral description is available: that the dog wanted to walk and wanted to lie in the chair; that she set about satisfying the first desire, but when the opportunity to satisfy the second presented itself she tried to satisfy that instead. It would obviously require a great deal more behaviour of this general sort before we should start attributing second-order beliefs.

Conclusion

Although there is no difficulty in principle with the idea of animal persons, I am myself doubtful whether any non-human animals are in fact persons to any degree; though I have made no attempt to survey the details of the evidence. More importantly perhaps, we have seen that a rational agent must have capacities to represent the past and future, and general and conditional truths; as well as being able to have second-order beliefs and desires. It also seems likely that a languageless creature could not possess such capacities; though I have made no real attempt to argue rigorously for this.

iv. Limits of the Class: Artificial Persons

It seems unlikely that there are, as yet, any artificial persons. I doubt whether any computer yet built is sophisticated enough to count as a rational, self-conscious, affective agent. But is it logically possible that there might one day be computers who are persons? Could a thing made out of metal and silicon, which has been created by human beings, ever be a person? I shall discuss a number of different aspects of this idea, including an objection based on the claim that a person, in order to count as such, must be free. As in the previous section, much of the point of the discussion will be to throw further light on what a person is.

Note that if computers can be persons, then there is yet another possible form of after-life. For then if personal survival consists in psychological connectedness, as we argued in Chapter 7, I myself might survive as a computer. It might one day be possible for all my beliefs, desires, interests and ties of affection to be programmed into a computer, enabling me to survive normal biological death. It would also follow, if it is true that all persons have the right to life, that the destruction of such a computer would be murder. So the issues before us in this section may turn out to have considerable practical as well as theoretical importance.

(A) Language

Already there are computers with which one can hold a limited conversation, e.g. relating to airline timetables. Now it is sometimes said that the ultimate test of genuine intelligence in a computer, would be if it were indistinguishable in its conversational abilities from a normal person. So imagine that they have managed to build a computer which you can talk to down a phone-line for as long as you like without ever knowing that you are talking to a machine. Would this show that the computer possesses conscious intelligence, and is thus to some degree a person? In my view no, since there would be no reason to think that the computer understands what you say to it, nor that it means anything by its own replies.

A conversation-making computer would only need to be provided with a system of rules for constructing appropriate spoken replies to any given verbal stimulus. Of course this system of rules would have to be immensely subtle and complicated. But the important thing to notice is that it would only have to deal with linguistic signs (sounds) and not with their meanings. Thus one simple rule might take the form: if you hear the sounds 'How are things with you?' respond with the sounds 'Not so bad thanks; and yourself?' A rule of this sort could be given to someone who understands no English, so long as they have the capacity to recognise and mimic the sounds of English sentences. To possess a set of rules for responding appropriately to any given verbal stimulus is not necessarily to understand what is being said.

The most basic aspect of linguistic understanding is the capacity to apply linguistic signs to things in the world. A competent speaker must be able to recognise and identify the various types of thing for which the terms of their language stand. So in order to count as a genuine language-user, a computer would have to be capable of much more than engaging in agreeable conversation. At the very least it would have to be provided with sensors of various kinds to inform it about its surrounding environment. It could then make simple recognition-statements, such as 'This is a dagger that I see before me.'

However, even this would not be enough. For in order to mean something by utterance it is not sufficient that you emit sounds which other speakers can understand, and which generally represent accurately (if so interpreted) some feature of the world. Otherwise we should have to say that a chiming clock speaks a (simple) language, and that by chiming eight times it says that the hour is eight o'clock. You must also *intend* that the sounds you utter should represent accurately some aspect of the world. So a genuine language-using computer would need to be capable of having intentions, and would thus somehow have to be provided with desires.

(B) Desire

A similar conclusion can also be reached from another direction. If computers are ever to be persons to any degree, then they must be given desires, irrespective of whether or not they are programmed to use language. For a rational agent is a being which does things for reasons. And to do things for reasons means doing them either because you want to, or because you believe that they may secure something which you want. So a rational agent is also a desiring agent.

Now there is no logical difficulty about programming a computer to do things, in the sense of causing certain changes to take place in the world. But can it be programmed to want those changes to take place? Of course it can be programmed with states which cause it to move in certain directions, but these will only count as desires if there is such a thing as 'the good' for that machine. Only entities which have a good can have desires: there must be things which are literally good for it (in a non-derivative sense). And it may be said that only biological entities can have a good: things which are said to be 'good for' a computer (such as dust-free conditions) are in reality only good for the person who makes or uses it.

It is hard to believe that this objection is really insurmountable. To make the case as strong as possible, suppose we have created an android. This is a computer housed in a physical structure similar to the human body, with similar possibilities of movement. It has sensors of various kinds, corresponding to eyes, ears, etc., to inform it about the states of the surrounding environment. It also has various internal sensors to inform it about some of its own states, especially those related to the continued functioning of the whole machine. For example, it requires a source of electricity in order to work, and has a sensor to inform it when its batteries are running low. It also has a sensor to measure the lubrication in its joints. And so on. Moreover, it has been programmed to respond appropriately to this internal information: seeking new batteries when the old are running low, looking for a shot of oil when its joints are not sufficiently lubricated.

I see no reason why we should not say that the android sometimes desires new batteries, or more oil. For it needs these things to function properly, and is itself often aware of these needs. Moreover, it is now capable of acting autonomously (without human direction) on the basis of information received from its internal and external sensors; indeed it has a 'life' of its own. So full batteries are good for it, not just in the derivative sense that they are good for us who made it, but also in the sense that they are necessary for it to continue its own autonomous pattern of activity.

Someone might concede that a computer could have desires of the sort which a cat or a mouse does. That is to say: it could have behaviour-directing states which are related in some way to its own continued functioning. But could it have the sort of self-conscious desires which are characteristic of persons? I can see no reason why not. Suppose that besides having representations of both external and internal states, our android also has representations of some of its own internal representations. So it can represent, in one part of its program, the various informational and behaviour-directing states which currently exist in other parts. These can then be compared with various programmed hierarchies of importance, to yield decisions as to which of the current behaviour-directing states should, in this instance, be acted upon.

For example: the sensors report that both batteries and

lubrication-oil are running low. These reports are themselves reported elsewhere, where they are compared with a hierarchy giving greater importance to a source of power than to the requirements of smooth motion. But there is also a report that there is a source of oil close at hand, and the android calculates that it would be more efficient to replenish that first. So it moves off in the direction of the oil, deferring the satisfaction of its more important desire until later. I can see no essential difference between this, and some of the kinds of reasoning about practical matters which a person might go through.

Now of course nothing in this example corresponds to 'normal human desires and affections'. But if we are prepared to allow that computers could have desires at all, then it is hard to see how there can be any objection in principle to the creation of a computer having a similar range of desires to a human being. If we can create a computer with a conscious preference for electricity over oil, then why should we not one day be able to create one which prefers Schubert to Chopin?

(C) Personal Freedom

It might be objected that one crucial element in the rationality of persons is missing from the above example: genuine freedom. It may be said that a computer can only do what its programmer has instructed it to do. So it does not really act autonomously ('for itself'), but merely carries out the instructions written into its program. Then if a person, on the other hand, really is a free agent, with the capacity to act for itself, it will follow that no computer can be a person. This is the argument from freedom.

Now we might wonder whether there can really be any fundamental difference between a computer and a human being. For are not humans merely biological computers? Do we not have a basic 'program' laid down in our genes, which is modified and developed by up-bringing and training, and which then has the capacity to modify itself, to some degree, in the light of further experience? (Some computers, too, can be programmed to modify their own programs in the light of later inputs.) But let us try to discover what might lie behind the objection in any case. In what sense is it true that we are free agents? And is it also true that no computer can be free in that sense?

First of all consider some uninteresting senses of 'free', in which the fact that (some) persons are free raises absolutely no difficulty for the idea of artificial persons. For instance, a person can be free rather than in chains. Here 'free' means something like 'lacking any humanly imposed obstacles to action'. Or a person can do something freely rather than with a gun in their back. Here 'free' means something like 'lacking any humanly imposed threat which makes it irrational to act otherwise'. Then so long as it is possible for computers to act, and have motives, it will be possible for them to be free in both of these senses.

More interestingly, it may be said that persons are free in the sense of being unpredictable. It might be claimed that human beings (or at least those human beings who are persons) are essentially unpredictable creatures, in a way that no computer ever could be. But in fact this unpredictability may have a number of different sources, none of which raises any difficulty for the idea of computer persons.

Firstly: sheer complexity. Human beings are immensely complex creatures, the human brain alone containing many millions of different cells. But the differences between humans and computers here are merely a matter of degree. Although no computer yet built approaches anywhere near the complexity of the human brain, there is no logical objection to the idea that we may one day build one just as complicated, and so just as difficult to predict.

A second source of unpredictability in human beings has already been mentioned. It is that they are constantly being modified in various subtle ways by the impact of the environment. It will therefore be impossible to make accurate predictions unless you know exactly what that impact has been; but as a matter of empirical fact we never can possess such knowledge. However, this may be true of computers too. The state of a computer can depend not just upon its original program, but also upon the information which has been fed into it since. It may also have been programmed to modify itself in various ways in the light of later inputs. Then no computer programmer, no matter how clever, will be able to make accurate predictions unless they know all of the input which has occurred since the computer was turned on. But in the case of a free-moving android, which is constantly receiving new information about the environment through which it moves, such knowledge will in practice be impossible to obtain.

Thirdly, people can be bloody-minded. Once a human being has become aware of your prediction of their behaviour, they can straight away set about falsifying it by doing something else instead. And if you try to allow for this by predicting how the person will react to the knowledge of your original prediction, they they can set about falsifying that in turn. And so on. But I can see no reason why it is supposed to be impossible, in principle, to build a bloody-minded computer. And in any case the moral of the story merely is: if you want to make accurate predictions of the behaviour of intelligent agents, then keep your predictions to yourself.

It may be said that there is a fourth, and much more radical, sense in which the behaviour of persons is essentially unpredictable. It may be said that even given complete knowledge of all the laws of nature, together with complete knowledge of all current physical states of a human being, as well as complete knowledge of all future sensory stimulations, it would still be impossible to make accurate predictions of what the human will do. Now I have not the faintest idea how it is supposed to be possible for us to know that this is the case. We certainly have no evidence of it at the moment. But even if it were the case, nothing in principle would stand in the way of creating a computer which is unpredictable in precisely this radical sense. All we should need, would be a computer with a randomiser in its decision process: for example a radiation source. We could fix up the program in such a way that certain decisions only get made if an alpha-particle is given off by a uranium source within a specified time-period. Then since such emissions are random, the resulting behaviour of the machine would be essentially unpredictable, even given complete knowledge of prior physical facts.

Of course a free decision is not the same thing as a random one. A free decision is one which is made on the basis of reasons. So it might be said that persons are free agents in the following sense: they take decisions which are not determined by the laws of nature together with all prior physical facts, but where those decisions are taken for reasons rather than randomly. Now I agree that it is difficult, if not impossible, to see how any computer could be free in this sense. But again I ask how we are supposed to be able to know that any human beings are free in this sense either.

Indeed it is doubtful whether this sense of 'free' can even be made coherent. For to make a decision on the basis of reasons is for that decision to be explicable in the light of your beliefs and desires. ('Why did you decide to do it?' — 'Because I believed this and wanted that.') Yet if the decision is not itself *caused by* the beliefs and desires which explain it, then it is problematical — to say the least — quite what the relationship between them is supposed to be. How do reasons underly or explain the making of decisions, if not by causing them? What is it to take a decision for a reason, if that reason did not (together with the thoughts, etc., surrounding it) cause the decision? I myself can see no answers to these questions.

Perhaps the most interesting sense of 'free' arises out of our possession of second-order beliefs and desires. Since we have the capacity to act upon our second-order preferences (together with our second-order beliefs about the reliability of our other beliefs), we are not slaves to our first-order desires. On the contrary, we are normally free to choose which of our first-order desires (whether present or future) we should try to satisfy. So here 'free' means something like 'action in accordance with second-order desires and preferences'.

As we saw in the last section, our capacity to act on second-order preferences is intimately connected with our status as rational agents. For a rational agent will generally have many long-term desires and intentions, only some of which will be present to consciousness at any given time as a felt desire. A rational agent has the capacity to weigh up the competing claims of desires which they currently feel against desires which they will feel on the morrow. And they are capable of acting on their second-order preference for the satisfaction of tomorrow's desire, ignoring the claims of the desire which they feel at the moment.

This is certainly a large part of our sense of our own freedom. We know that we are not normally driven to act by the desires we happen to feel at the time. We know that we are not at the mercy of our own desires. On the contrary, we know that we have the capacity to stand back and reflect, forming preferences over the desires we feel as well as the desires we believe we will feel, and assessing the reliability of the beliefs on which our various plans are based. And we know that we are capable of acting on our considered judgement, based upon these second-order beliefs and preferences. (This is why we find such things as weakness of will — as well as more extreme phenomena like kleptomania — so disturbing. For they threaten our status as rational agents. In such cases we find ourselves acting in accordance with a presently-felt desire *against* our own considered judgement.)

Thus we are not in general slaves to our passions, but have the capacity — deriving from our possession of second-order beliefs and desires — to choose between them. (Most if not all animals, in contrast, are *wantons*. They are driven to act by whichever of their desires is currently strongest.) But I can see no objection in principle to the construction of a computer which is free in this sense. It need only be constructed so as to contain representations of its own representational states, with the part of the program which is concerned with these second-order representations being given ultimate control over the direction of the computer's behaviour.

Since all the various proposed senses of 'free' are such that either there is no reason to believe that any persons are free in that sense, or there is no objection to a computer being free in that sense, I conclude that there is no objection in principle to a computer possessing personal freedom.

Conclusion

It is logically possible that there might one day exist an artificial person. But whether it will ever prove technically feasible to construct such a thing is of course quite another matter. The degree of complexity involved may quite out-reach our capabilities, both now and in the future.

Questions and Readings

You may like to discuss/write about/think about some of the following questions:

(1) People often say 'I am not the person I once was.' Is there any literal truth in this?
(2) Should the normal development of a human child be seen as a gradual emergence into personhood?
(3) How would an animal have to behave, in order to give sufficient evidence of being to some degree a person?
(4) Is it possible for non-biological creatures to have desires?
(5) Persons are not, in general, slaves to their passions. Is there any other fundamental sense in which they are free?

In considering the above questions, you may like to consult a selection of the following readings (capitalised names refer to works in the Bibliography of collected papers):

Jonathan Bennett, *Rationality* (London: Routledge & Kegan Paul, 1964).

Paul Churchland, *Matter and Consciousness* (Mass.: MIT Press, 1984), Chs. 6–8.

Daniel Dennett, 'Conditions of Personhood', in RORTY. Reprinted in DENNETT.

Harry Frankfurt, 'Freedom of the Will and the Concept of a Person', *Journal of Philosophy*, LXVIII (1971). Reprinted in WATSON.

Thomas Nagel, 'Brain Bisection and the Unity of Consciousness', *Synthese*, 22 (1971). Reprinted in NAGEL, GLOVER and PERRY.

Derek Parfit, 'Personal Identity', *Philosophical Review*, 80 (1971). Reprinted in GLOVER and PERRY.

Hilary Putnam, 'Robots: machines or artificially created life?', *Journal of Philosophy*, LXI (1964). Reprinted in PUTNAM and HAMPSHIRE.

John Searle, 'Minds, Brains and Programs', *The Behavioural and Brain Sciences*, 3 (1980). Reprinted in HOFSTADTER.

Geoff Simons, *Are Computers Alive?* (Brighton: Harvester Press, 1983).

Peter Singer, *Practical Ethics* (Cambridge: Cambridge University Press, 1979), Ch. 3.

A. M. Turing, 'Computing Machinery and Intelligence', *Mind*, LIX (1950). Reprinted in HOFSTADTER.

Gary Watson, 'Free Agency', *Journal of Philosophy*, LXXII (1975). Reprinted in WATSON.

Bernard Williams, 'Persons, Character and Morality', in RORTY. Reprinted in Bernard Williams, *Moral Luck* (Cambridge: Cambridge University Press, 1981).

RETROSPECT

Let us conclude by looking back over some of the twists and turns which our investigation has taken. Our basic concern has been with three main questions, each of which sub-divides into a number of further questions, thus:

(1) How do we have knowledge of conscious states?
    (a) of other persons?
    (b) of ourselves?
(2) What are conscious states?
    (a) how are they to be analysed? (meaning-problem)
    (b) what is their intrinsic nature? (factual-problem)
(3) What are persons (selves, conscious subjects)?
    (a) what is an individual person at a time?
    (b) what is personal survival over time?
    (c) what are the boundaries of the class of persons?

Let me briefly remind you of the way in which our treatment of these seven questions has proceeded.

Chapter 1 was our preliminary discussion of all of the questions under (1) and (2), which are closely related to one another. We began with an argument suggesting that it is impossible to have knowledge of the conscious states of other persons (question 1a), and then showed how this argument depended upon certain very plausible answers to questions 2a and 2b. These answers were respectively that (a) the meanings of terms referring to conscious states are wholly concerned with the subjective qualities of those states (the 'cartesian conception'), and (b) that those states themselves are non-physical ('weak dualism'). We also showed how the cartesian answer to question 2a is closely connected with a plausible answer to 1b, namely: that we are immediately aware of our own conscious states, it being impossible that we should be mistaken about them.

In Chapter 2 we turned to consider question (3), beginning by developing an argument for strong dualism ('persons are souls'), premised upon the weak dualist answer to 2b. We then considered an objection to this argument, turning on the issue of whether or not thoughts must have a substantive thinker. This was not sustained. We also raised some difficulties for strong dualism, included in which were points about the causal interaction of mind and body which were later to be put to work in Chapter 5, providing an argument for the mind/brain identity-thesis. We concluded the chapter with the case for strong dualism looking convincing.

In Chapter 3 we distinguished questions 3a and 3b from one another, and considered what answers a strong dualist might give to them. It turned out that they were unable to provide any adequate answer to question 3a, relating to the identification at a time of non-physical souls. We took this to be a sufficient refutation of the strong dualist's position. But we also developed a dualistic answer to question 3b, relating to the identity over time of souls, which was later to be put to work in the context of a materialist conception of persons in Chapter 6. We concluded the chapter by examining once again the argument for strong dualism, and succeeded in unearthing a serious flaw in it.

In Chapter 4 we returned once again to questions (1) and (2). We focused primarily upon 2a, the question of the correct analysis of terms referring to conscious states. We considered various attempts to define those terms behaviourally, or by causal role; these attempts having obvious implications for the questions under (1). Had they been successful, they would have shown that there is no special problem of arriving at knowledge of other minds (question 1a). But they would also have made our knowledge of our own minds more like our knowledge of others, in that it would be possible for us to make mistakes (question 1b). Now one aspect of all this we endorsed: we accepted a functionalist account of our dispositional states such as beliefs and desires; thus accepting that it is possible for us to be mistaken about them. But we rejected behaviourist or functionalist accounts of episodic experiences, such as pains and sensations of red. So at this stage the cartesian conception remained the most plausible account of the meanings of sensation-terms, and the problem of other minds remained only partially resolved.

In Chapter 5 we focused upon question 2b, relating to the nature of conscious states themselves. Taking for granted the cartesian conception of the meanings of sensation-terms, we argued all the same that conscious sensations are very probably brain-states. In fact we argued for the contingent identity of every conscious state with some particular brain-state. We then rebutted a number of attempts to refute this thesis, mostly deriving from supposed breaches of Leibniz's Law. We were left in a position to make a further advance in our search for a solution to question 1a, in that having rejected the various strands in the supposed uniqueness of consciousness, we could then argue by analogy to the existence of other sensations-in-general. But we could still discover no right to claim knowledge of the particular sensations experienced by other persons on particular occasions.

In Chapter 6 we returned once again to question 2a, the meaning problem, and its relation to question 1a, the problem of other minds. We argued that it follows from the cartesian conception of the meanings of sensation-terms, that we each of us have our own private understanding of those terms. We then attempted to argue that since private language is impossible, the cartesian conception must be false. Although this argument was a failure, sufficiently many points emerged for us to be able to construct a slightly different refutation of the cartesian conception. We then proposed to analyse terms such as 'pain' into a conjunction of qualitative feel and causal role, the former being necessarily bound to the latter. This enabled us to complete our solution to the problem of other minds, the solution being accomplished while retaining a basically cartesian approach to question 1b. For we were still able to say that we have immediate awareness of our sensations, it being impossible that we should be mistaken about them.

In Chapter 7 we returned to question 3b, this time from a materialist perspective. Taking a materialist answer to question 3a as having been established by the arguments of Chapter 3 (so taking it that persons-at-a-time are physical things, rather than non-physical souls), we considered once again what counts as the survival over time of a person. We argued that the correct account should be constructed in terms of the notion of psychological connectedness, thus allowing it to be possible that the life (over time) of a single person might be constituted by a number of distinct bodies. In response to various objections to this idea, we further suggested that we ought to stop thinking of personal survival in terms of identity, and should think instead in a way which would allow one person to survive as a number of distinct people.

We began Chapter 8 by considering the other side of the coin of personal survival, namely the conditions under which a person will cease to exist. We argued that this will occur whenever there is complete lack of psychological connectedness, and also argued that personal survival should be thought of as a matter of degree. But the bulk of the chapter was directed towards answering question 3c, relating to the boundaries of the class of persons. Our answer was that a person is a rational self-conscious agent with characteristic human feelings and desires. Nothing in principle stands in the way of other species of animal being persons, though it seems unlikely that any are as a matter of fact persons. Nor does anything stand in the way of the idea of artificial persons. Specifically, there is no respect in which a person is free, in which a computer could not (in principle) also be.

In summary, my answers to our seven main questions are as follows:

(1a) We have knowledge of the conscious states of others partly by inference within a holistic framework (where those states are dispositional), partly by a combination of argument from analogy with a demonstrated necessary connection between qualitative feel and causal role (where those states are episodic experiences).

(1b) Our knowledge of our own conscious states is partly quasi-perceptual (where those states are dispositional), partly by immediate awareness of qualitative feel (where they are episodic sensations).

(2a) Terms referring to conscious states are to be analysed functionally, where they refer to conscious dispositions; and into a conjunction of qualitative feel with causal role, where they refer to experiential episodes.

(2b) Each particular conscious state and event is, as a matter of fact, identical with some particular brain-state or event.

(3a) Persons are physical things: the criterion for identifying a person at a time is (roughly) identification of a brain.

(3b) Personal survival over time should be thought of in terms of psychological connectedness, allowing survival to be a matter of degree, and allowing one person to enjoy multiple survival.

(3c) Persons as a class are rational self-conscious affective agents. There is no requirement that they be members of the human species, nor even that they be made of flesh and blood.

BIBLIOGRAPHY OF COLLECTED PAPERS

AYER [1] ——— A. J. Ayer, *Philosophical Essays* (London: Macmillan, 1954)
AYER [2] ——— A. J. Ayer, *The Concept of a Person* (London: Macmillan, 1963)
BLOCK ——— Ned Block (ed.), *Readings in the Philosophy of Psychology*, vol. 1 (London: Methuen, 1980)
BORST ——— C. V. Borst (ed.), *The Mind-Brain Identity Theory* (London: Macmillan, 1970)
CHAPPELL ——— V. C. Chappell (ed.), *The Philosophy of Mind* (Englewood Cliffs: Prentice Hall, 1962)
DAVIDSON ——— Donald Davidson, *Actions and Events* (Oxford: Clarendon Press, 1980)
DENNETT ——— Daniel Dennett, *Brainstorms* (Sussex: Harvester Press, 1979)
FLEW ——— Antony Flew (ed.), *Body, Mind and Death* (London: Macmillan, 1964)
GLOVER ——— Jonathan Glover (ed.), *The Philosophy of Mind* (Oxford: Oxford University Press, 1976)
GUSTAFSON ——— Donald Gustafson (ed.), *Essays on Philosophical Psychology* (London: Macmillan, 1964)
HAMPSHIRE ——— Stuart Hampshire (ed.), *Philosophy of Mind* (New York: Harper & Row, 1966)
HOFSTADTER ——— Douglas Hofstadter and Daniel Dennett (eds.), *The Mind's I* (Sussex: Harvester Press, 1981)
JONES ——— O. R. Jones (ed.), *The Private Language Argument* (London: Macmillan, 1971)
LEWIS ——— David Lewis, *Philosophical Papers*, vol. 1 (Oxford: Oxford University Press, 1983)
MORICK [1] ——— Harold Morick (ed.), *Wittgenstein and the Problem of Other Minds* (New York: McGraw-Hill, 1967)
MORICK [2] ——— Harold Morick (ed.), *Introduction to the Philosophy of Mind* (Sussex: Harvester Press, 1979)
NAGEL ——— Thomas Nagel, *Mortal Questions* (Cambridge: Cambridge University Press, 1979)
PERRY ——— John Perry (ed.), *Personal Identity* (Los Angeles: University of California Press, 1975)
PITCHER ——— George Pitcher (ed.), *Wittgenstein* (London: Macmillan, 1966)
PUTNAM ——— Hilary Putnam, *Mind, Language and Reality* (Cambridge: Cambridge University Press, 1975)
RORTY ——— Amelie Rorty (ed.), *The Identities of Persons* (Los Angeles: University of California Press, 1976)
ROSENTHAL ——— David Rosenthal (ed.), *Materialism and the Mind-Body Problem* (Englewood Cliffs: Prentice Hall, 1979)
SHOEMAKER ——— Sydney Shoemaker, *Identity, Cause and Mind* (Cambridge: Cambridge University Press, 1984)
WATSON ——— Gary Watson (ed.), *Free Will* (Oxford: Oxford University Press, 1982)
WILLIAMS ——— Bernard Williams, *Problems of the Self* (Cambridge: Cambridge University Press, 1973)

GLOSSARY

Analysis An analysis of a term is an attempt to capture its meaning. An analysis of a thing is an attempt to capture its essential properties.

Behaviourism (philosophical) The doctrine that all conscious states are in reality behavioural states, either actual or potential.

Cartesian conception The doctrine that the meanings of all terms referring to conscious states are wholly concerned with the subjective feel of those states.

Causally impossible Something is causally impossible if and only if the laws of nature prevent it. That is: if and only if there is no possible world in which that thing occurs, and about which the laws of nature are all true.

Causally necessary Something is causally necessary if and only if the laws of nature require it to happen. That is: if and only if that thing occurs in all possible worlds about which the laws of nature are all true.

Causally possible Something is causally possible if and only if the laws of nature do not prevent it. That is: if and only if there is some possible world in which it occurs, and about which the laws of nature are all true.

Certainty-thesis The doctrine that it is logically impossible to be mistaken in simple judgements of recognition about one's own conscious states (provided that one understands the terms in which the judgement is made, and uses the terms that one intends to use).

Compatible Two statements are compatible if and only if there is some possible world about which they are both true together. They are consistent.

Consistent Two statements are consistent if and only if they are compatible. They are not contradictory.

Contingent A statement is contingent if and only if it is logically possible but not logically necessary. There are some possible worlds about which it is true, and some possible worlds about which it is false.

Contradiction Two statements contradict one another if and only if there is no possible world about which they are both true together. They are inconsistent.

Criterion of identification   What serves to distinguish an individual thing, at any given time, from all other things of the same kind; implied by a statement of identity-at-a-time.

Criterion of identity   What makes two things, existing at different times, part of the life of the very same individual thing; implied by a statement of identity-over-time.

Deductive argument   An argument which purports to be valid. The arguer intends that there should be no possible world in which the premises are all true and the conclusion false.

Empirical   A statement is empirical if and only if its truth-value can be established on the basis of experience.

Entail   P entails Q if and only if the argument from P to Q is valid. There is no possible world about which P is true and Q false.

Essence   The essence of a thing are those properties which it has necessarily. There is no possible world in which a thing exists without its essential (necessary) properties.

Functionalism   The doctrine that all conscious states are necessarily functional states, the terms referring to them being analysable into descriptions of causal role.

Follows from   P follows from Q if and only if the argument from Q to P is valid. There is no possible world about which Q is true and P false.

Holistic analysis   An account of the meaning of a term which holds that it belongs to a class of terms whose meanings form an interlocking system. Terms X and Y are related holistically if the meaning of X involves the meaning of Y and vice versa.

Inductive argument   An argument which does not purport to be valid, but in which the premises are nevertheless intended to provide sufficient reason for believing the conclusion.

Intentional context   Context created by phrases such as 'Mary believes that . . .', in which what is at issue is not the things themselves for which the terms within that context would usually stand, but rather a particular way of representing or thinking about those things.

Invalid argument   Argument which is not valid. There are possible worlds about which the premises are all true and the conclusion false.

Leibniz's Law   The thesis that identical things share all of the same properties. In symbols: if $x = y$, then for all properties, F, x has F if and only if y has F.

Logically equivalent Two statements are logically equivalent if and only if they share the same truth values as one another about all the same possible worlds. Two predicates are logically equivalent if and only if they are true of exactly the same individual things as each other in all possible worlds.

Logically impossible Something is logically impossible if and only if there is no possible world in which it occurs.

Logically independent Two things are logically independent if and only if there are possible worlds where each one of them occurs without the other.

Logically necessary Something is logically necessary if and only if it occurs in all possible worlds.

Logically possible Something is logically possible if and only if it occurs in some possible world.

Meaning Throughout I assume that the meaning of a term is the condition necessary and sufficient for its correct application; and that the meaning of a sentence is the condition necessary and sufficient for its truth.

Mind The collection of all the mental states of a person, whether conscious or unconscious, and whether they be physical or non-physical.

Modal The mode in which something occurs; e.g. either necessarily or possibly. A modal statement is one containing a modal term.

Narrow-scope A modal term occurs with narrow-scope if and only if it governs less than the whole of the sentence in which it occurs.

Necessary condition There are two forms, thus:

(a) x is a causally necessary condition for y if and only if, the laws of nature being as they are, y will not occur unless x does. It is causally impossible to have y without x.

(b) x is a logically necessary condition for y if and only if there is no possible world in which y occurs and x does not. It is logically impossible to have y without x.

Necessary truth A truth about all possible worlds.

Nonsense A sentence is nonsensical if it literally has no meaning; either because it contains a word which lacks meaning (e.g. 'snark'), or because it combines together words in impermissible ways (e.g. 'The idea sleeps furiously.').

Numerical identity A thing x is numerically identical to a thing y if and only if they are the very same thing: x and y are not two things, but only one.

Person   A person is a self. A person is whatever I (we) am (are).

Possible world   Anything which can be conceived of, or consistently described.

Proof   An argument is a proof of its conclusion if and only if it is valid and all its premises are true.

Psychological connection   These are of two basic forms, thus:
(a) a person x at t(1) is psychologically connected with person y at t(2) if y can quasi-remember something about x.
(b) a person x at t(1) is psychologically connected with person y at t(2) if x and y share the same beliefs, desires or intentions, provided that x's states are causal ancestors of y's.

Qualitative identity   x and y are qualitatively identical if and only if they share exactly similar properties (for some restricted range of properties). They are similar.

Quasi-desire   Someone quasi-desires something if and only if (a) they desire that an event of that sort should take place, where (b) they naturally represent that event 'from the inside', provided that (c) this desire is apt to cause that later event to take place.

Quasi-memory   Someone quasi-remembers an event E if and only if (a) they believe that E took place, where (b) this belief comes to them with the event represented 'from the inside', provided that (c) this belief was caused by the experience of E taking place.

Rationally convincing argument   Argument which is such that it would be reasonable for anyone to believe the conclusion on the basis of a belief in the premises.

Reductive behaviourism   The doctrine that each consciousness-term may be analysed into purely behavioural terms.

Reflexive relation   One which everything bears to itself, if it bears it to anything at all. Relation R is reflexive if and only if, for all things x, if x bears R to anything, then it is true that xRx.

Second-order (belief, desire, etc.)   Conscious state which contains a representation of another (first-order) state. E.g. a desire that I should not act upon a certain desire.

Soul   Non-physical thing which is the subject of conscious states and events, believed to exist by the strong dualist.

Strong dualism   Belief in the existence of souls. The doctrine that both persons and their states are non-physical.

Strong materialism   Belief that the mind is matter. The doctrine that both persons and their states are physical.

Sufficient condition   There are two kinds, thus:
(a) x is a causally sufficient condition for y if and only if, given

that x has occurred, then it is causally necessary that y will occur. There is no possible world about which the laws of nature are true, in which x occurs but y does not.

(b) x is a logically sufficient condition for y if and only if, given that x has occurred, then it is logically necessary that y does. There is no possible world in which x occurs but y does not.

Suppressed premiss Belief being taken for granted by the arguer, which is strictly necessary if the argument is to be rationally convincing.

Symmetric relation A relation which always 'holds both ways'. A relation R is symmetric if and only if, for all things x and y, xRy if and only if yRx.

Token-identity Mental states are token-identical with physical ones if and only if every particular mental state is identical with some particular physical state. There is no requirement that all the states belonging to a single mental type (e.g. pain) should be identical with states which all belong to a single physical type.

Transitive relation A relation which 'reaches across' chains of things related by that relation. A relation R is transitive if and only if, for all things x, y and z, if xRy and yRz, then xRz.

Truth value Either truth or falsity. The truth value of a statement is the fact of its being true, or the fact of its being false.

Type-identity Mental states are type-identical with physical ones if and only if all the individual states belonging to a given mental type (e.g. all pains) are identical with individual physical states belonging to a single physical type.

Valid An argument is valid if and only if the conclusion follows from/is entailed by the premises. There is no possible world about which the premises are all true and the conclusion false.

Vicious circle A feature of explanations where X is explained in terms of Y, but then Y itself is explained in terms of X.

Weak dualism The doctrine that although persons themselves are physical things, the conscious states of persons are non-physical.

Weak materialism The same as weak dualism (q.v.). The doctrine that although conscious states of persons are non-physical, persons themselves are physical things.

Wide-scope A modal term occurs with wide-scope if and only if it governs the whole of the sentence in which it occurs.

INDEX

action
  alternative concepts of 50–1
  as a kind of event 50
  mental 49–50, 110
  without an agent 49–51
after-life 2, 40, 44–5, 69, 189–218
  passim, 241
  see also disembodied; reincarna-
    tion; resurrection; personal
    identity; personal survival
agent *see* rational agency
  see also action
analogy, argument from 12–14,
    19–21, 136–8, 157, 182–3,
    252–3
analysis 102, 104–7, 111–12, 138,
    158, 228, 250–1
animals
  language of 237–8
  mental states of 135, 230–1,
    239–40
  personhood of 234–5, 240
  rationality of 235–7
artificial person 240–8 *passim*
  desires of 242–4
  freedom of 244–8
  language of 241–2
  see also computers
attribute *see* property

behaviourism
  and other minds 101–4, 108
  arguments against 109–11, 114–15
  arguments for 103–4
  holistic 105–8
  methodological 102
  philosophical 102–3
  reductive 102, 104–5
  see also pain (definitions of)
belief
  cartesian conception of 32–3
  conscious vs unconscious 17–18,
    33, 129
  contrasted with knowledge 79–80
  explanation in terms of 15–19,
    246–7
  first-person knowledge of 32, 118,
    128–9, 251

holism of 53–4, 104–7
intentionality of 23–4
see also second-order
body
  criteria of identification for 73–4,
    75–6, 85–6
  criteria of identity for 60–1, 73,
    77, 190–4
  essence of 41–4, 59
  see also materialism; personal
    identity
brain
  and criteria of personal identity
    209–11
  mental states as identical with
    states of *see* identity-thesis
  persons identified with 97, 197
  split 225–6
  transplants 209–10
bundle theory
  argued against 51–8 *passim*
  explained 48–9
  see also conscious states

capacity conceptual/classificatory
    53–4, 164–8, 171–7
  see also knowledge; meaning (verb)
cartesian conception 27, 101, 162,
    250
  arguments against 104, 118,
    127–8, 175–7
  arguments for 27–9, 122–3,
    128–9
  logical independence of certainty-
    thesis 27, 114, 180–2
cartesian dualism *see* dualism
causal
  connection between mind and
    body *see* interaction
  explanation 65–6
  law 62–3
  notion 80, 84, 159–60, 202
  over-determination 64
  role 17–18, 33, 111–13, 116–23,
    135–8, 157–8, 177–83,
    251–3
certainty-thesis 28–34, 120–1,
    127–8, 180–2

260